Critical Theories
Indian and Western

Critical Theories
Indian and Western

M.P. Sinha
Neeraj Agnihotri

Published by

ATLANTIC

PUBLISHERS & DISTRIBUTORS (P) LTD

7/22, Ansari Road, Darya Ganj, New Delhi-110002
Phones: +91-11-40775252, 23273880, 23275880, 23280451
Fax : +91-11-23285873
Web : www.atlanticbooks.com
E-mail : orders@atlanticbooks.com

Branch Office
5, Nallathambi Street, Wallajah Road, Chennai-600002
Phones: +91-44-64611085, 32413319
E-mail : chennai@atlanticbooks.com

ISBN 978-81-269-1827-0

Printed in India at Nice Printing Press, A-33/3A, Site-IV,
Industrial Area, Sahibabad, Ghaziabad, U.P.

PREFACE

The aim of this book is to acquaint the postgraduate students of English Literature to the basic concepts of the leading critical theories of India and the West. As the paper of literary criticism is considered to be the most difficult, the theories are explained in a plain and simple language. The approach is pedagogical. Each concept has been explained separately for easy understanding by the students.

Critical Theories: Indian and Western covers the entire criticism paper of all Indian universities. Earlier, the paper began with Aristotle and ended with I.A. Richards. Later on, after the establishment of ASRC in Hyderabad, American criticism was added to M.A. English syllabus. The eighties saw Russian Formalism, French Structuralism, Marxist Criticism, Myth Criticism, Feminist Criticism and Post-Colonial Theory of Literature. UGC curriculum makers added Indian Poetics to the criticism paper.

The inclusion of Indian Poetics has posed a difficult challenge to both students and teachers. Most of the students and teachers of English do not have a good Sanskrit background. Besides, there is no book, to the best of our knowledge, that deals with both Indian and Western literary criticism. We hope this book will fill this gap and cater to the needs of students and teachers as well.

We have quoted Sanskrit originals in Devanagari script as Bharat Ratna P.V. Kane has done in his monumental *History of*

Sanskrit Poetics. We have followed S.K. De's approach in the analysis and interpretation of the concepts of eminent Sanskrit theorists and used all Sanskrit texts edited by Dr. Nagendra and Acharya Vishweshwar except Kuntaka's *Vakroktijeevitam*. Dr. Radheshyam Mishra's edition of *Vakroktijeevitam* is recent and complete; besides he has followed S.K. De's monumental edition of the text. For a better understanding and evaluation of Sanskrit theorists, I have often compared their concepts with those of modern Western critics.

We are indebted to all Sanskrit scholars, Indian and European, whose works we consulted in writing this book, and thank Dr. K.R. Gupta, Honorary Adviser, Atlantic Publishers and Distributors (P) Limited and Mr. Harjeet Singh, Publishing Co-ordinator for publishing the book in a short time.

M.P. Sinha
Neeraj Agnihotri

CONTENTS

INTRODUCTION

"What is criticism?", students generally ask in the classroom. Guided by the meaning of the root word "criticism" and the dictionary meaning "criticism, the expression of disapproval of someone", they come to the classroom with the false notion that "criticism" is finding out faults in a literary work and that "appreciation" is the expression of approval of its merits. The distinction between criticism and appreciation is quite common in everyday life but in the world of letters, criticism is a well-defined term and it means "a critical assessment of a literary or artistic work".

Literary criticism is a body of principles, which defines literature, distinguishes it from other modes of discourse, and assesses the value of a literary work after adequate analysis and interpretation. The principles are objective, systematic, and based on facts. The word "objective" means that principles are free from an individual's subjectivity and prejudice, and are formed on the basis of reason. A critic may have his mind while reading the text. He is like a pathologist who analyses the blood of patients without taking note of their caste, religion, and race. Secondly, the principles must be systematic and aspire for universality, i.e. they should have the quality of being applied in the same way to all creative writings. For example, Aristotle's principle of catharsis is applicable to all kinds of tragedy and so is Bharata's *rasa siddhanta* to all kinds of plays. The other aspect of systematicity is that the principles are coherent, not self-contradictory, wayward or illogical, and be based on facts. A good critic while forming his principles studies a number of texts, notes the common features of good texts, and makes a generalisation or hypothesis. His method is inductive, viz. he goes from particular to general. After forming the hypothesis he applies them to other texts, and if he finds the hypothesis satisfactory, he posits a theory of literature. In our time, literary criticism has become almost a science. Northrop Frye, in his famous paper "Archetypes of Literature", has compared criticism to physics. According to him, nature is apparently wayward but its study, physics, is systematic and tries to find a system in the phenomena of nature and explain how and why they happen. So is the case with literary criticism; it also tries to explain the phenomena of literature, which is apparently wayward.

The first aim of literary criticism is to define literature and distinguish it from other modes of discourse. Aristotle placed poetry in the category of productive arts and said that poetry differs from music and painting as its medium is word, whereas of the former are sound and paint respectively. As epic, drama and *dithyramb* were the only forms of literature in his time, he did not think of poetic-prose. The Indian tradition was different. The *kathas* and *akhyaikas*, though written in prose, had the intensity of poetry. Naturally, Dandin and Bhamaha defined poetry (*kavya*) from a new angle. They made a distinction between verse and poetry, and declared that even prose can be poetic if it is written in an embellished language. Bhamaha said that *vakrokti* (a statement, strange and striking) is the base of all tropes which make a work literary. Kuntaka expanded and perfected Bhamaha's concept of *vakrokti*—how the language of poetry, because of the poet's peculiar turn of expression, is different from other modes of discourse.

The Russian Formalists of the OPOYAZ group, Viktor Shklovsky and Boris Eichenbaum, almost echoed Bhamaha and Kuntaka when they said that literariness lies in the art of defamiliarization or bestrangement. A creative writer describes the everyday reality in a new way to make it strange and striking, and this he does by means of the art of making the familiar into unfamiliar.

The Western theorists defined poetry from the point of view of meaning and function. For Plato, it is imitation, and for his disciple, it is a creative imitation. Longinus laid stress on its function, transport, and the elements that make poetry sublime. Wordsworth laid stress on its emotional quality and called poetry a recollection of spontaneous overflow of powerful feelings aroused by a heart-touching experience. The best definition, according to form, was given by Dandin. Dandin defined poetry as a body made of words, organized in a special way for the expression of intended meaning. We think that the definition of Dandin is still unsurpassed.

The Sanskrit critics discussed the function of poetry from the point of view of the post and reader as well. If we look at the relationship between the writer and the reader, the following diagram appears before us.

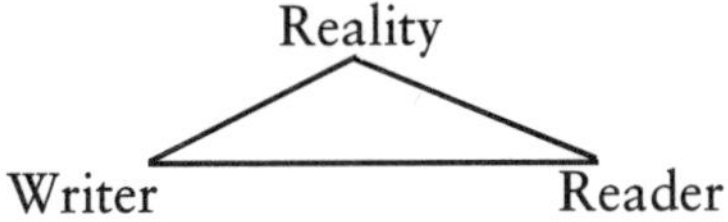

The writer perceives reality, codes it in language, and presents it to the reader to share his views. As the reader is the most important person for the writer, the material must be presented in a pleasant way and must have an aesthetic appeal. In other words, poetic diction must be embellished (*alankrit*).

The next point for discussion is the relationship between literature and criticism. It is certain that creative writing is primary and literary criticism is secondary; poetry came first and criticism followed it. Yet, criticism has its own importance and we can safely say that without criticism, poetry could not develop and poets could not learn their art better.

The poet himself is the first critic. Jon Stallworthy's books *Between the Lines* and *Vision and Revision in Yeats's Poetry*, and Curtis Bradford's *Yeats At Work* illustrate how the celebrated poet drafted and redrafted many of his great poems more than ten times. Yeats redrafted them again and again for the expression of the intended meaning. We can easily say that Yeats was the first critic of his original and the subsequent drafts.

It should also be kept in mind that there is a difference between appreciation and criticism. Appreciation is usually subjective and it varies from individual to individual, whereas criticism is objective, its methods are well-defined, and if there is a variance between two critics, it is usually on the level of interpretation but little on the merit of the evaluated writer or text. It is free from individual's whims and idiosyncrasies.

The first proponent of the theory of literature, Aristotle himself was one of the greatest philosophers. Poetics is a part of his philosophical system. Naturally, his critical theory is scientific, methodical, and objective. The critics, whether of Italy, France, or England, continued to follow his ideas and methods till the eighteenth century and even in the twentieth century, R.S. Crane, Elder Olson, and Wayne C. Booth of America followed his method.

In India too, Bharata founded his critical theory on the prevalent philosophical systems of his time. His *rasa* theory influenced the later critics and creative writers and is still influencing them in India. Discused in brief in the pages that follow is how literary criticism has developed and grown like a bunyan tree and how critical theories have analysed the same text in different ways—all valid.

M.P. Sinha
Neeraj Agnihotri

1

INDIAN POETICS

(A) BHARATA

Bharata, popularly known as Bharata Muni, lived most probably in the second century B.C. Many traditional Sanskrit scholars believe that he was born much earlier, but there is no evidence, external or internal, to prove that he existed in the time of king Ashoka even.

There may have been a few writers who wrote on the theory of drama or poetry earlier than him, but their works are not extant. We can assume on the basis of the maturity of *Natyashastra* that Bharata might have come across some works on dramaturgy that were written earlier. Besides, as Kapila Vatsayan has pointed out, he was influenced by the *Upanishadas*, especially *Kenopanishada*, *Kathopanishada*, and *Ishavasyopanishada*, which describe *Brahman* manifesting itself in all the objects of the universe and yet beyond it.

Bharata called dramaturgy *Natyaveda* and claimed that it was the fifth *Veda* and that the aim of drama was to ennoble man's consciousness to attain Supreme Bliss. He declared at the end of *Natyashastra*:

> "He who always hears the reading of that (*shastra*) which is auspicious, sportful, originating from Brahman's mouth, very holy, pure, good, destructive of sins, and who puts into practice and witnesses carefully the performance will attain the same blessed goal, which masters of Vedic knowledge and performers of *puja* attain."

It is because of this high ideal set by Bharata that all Sanskrit plays begin with a prayer for the well-being of the audience and end with a benediction.

Kapila Vatsayan in her small but scholarly book *Bharata* (Sahitya Akademy, New Delhi) has very clearly explicated the influence of Indian philosophical systems on *Natyashastra*.

Later on, religion played a great part in determining the ideology of critics of both Europe and India. If Christianity was the dominant force in Europe, Shaivism was in India, especially in Kashmir and the south.

Politics entered a little later in England. Critics of the eighteenth century England praised books written by authors of their own party and condemned those which were written by the opposing party. Sometimes they criticised those authors with whom they were on bad terms.

Happily, the situation has changed and personal enmity is a matter of by days. Besides, modern critics evaluate an author from a well-defined point of view.

With the beginning of the twentieth century sociology, psychology, anthropology, and linguistics made a great impact on the development of literary criticism. Critics began to analyse and evaluate a literary text from new angles. The result was the beginning of Marxist criticism, psycho-analytic criticism, myth criticism, structuralism and feminist criticism, which are the dominant critical theories of today. One thing, common in these theories, is that they all rely on the close or textual analysis of the works of an author and interpret them in the light of their postulates.

The pages that follow briefly explain the concepts of the leading critics of the past and of the important critical theories of our time.

The Natyashastra

The *Natyashastra* is a massive work divided into thirty six chapters. In some editions there are thirty seven chapters, but most of the scholars are of the opinion that the thirty seventh chapter is carved out of the thirty sixth chapter, that is, some editors have divided the thirty sixth chapter into two parts and the second part is called the thirty seventh chapter.

Following the tradition of the *Mahabharata*, Bharata begins his treatise with an explanation how he came to write it. The explanation is very much in the line of the *Mahabharata* where Ved Vyasa says that he was asked by the God to write the story of the great war fought between the Pandavas and the Kauravas for the benefit of mankind. Bharata says that he was commanded by Brahma to write the *Natyashastra* as the *Vedas* could not be read by the *Shudras* for social reasons. So he wrote the treatise on dramaturgy for the people of all *Varnas*. He took *recitation* from the *Rigveda*, *song* from the *Samveda*, *acting* from the *Yajurveda*, and *rasa* from the *Atharvaveda*, and blending all these together he produced the fifth *Veda*, called the *Natyaveda*.

The idea that the fifth *Veda*, *Natyaveda*, is meant for the *Shudras* too, is revolutionary because in Bharata's time, the *Shudras* were not allowed to receive education. Bharata's intention of creating this mythical explanation may be that he himself came from the Bharata clan, a clan that excelled in performing arts. As dancers and actors were not given due honour they really deserved, Bharata wanted to raise their social status by equating the performing arts with the higher forms of knowledge stored in the four *Vedas*.

Bharata's Literary Theory

Bharata is the propounder of the theory of *rasa*. *Rasa*, according to him, is the essence of poetry. The main objective of a creative writer is to arouse the dormant emotions in human beings by means of his creative writing. The emotions, called स्थायी भाव, are ever present in man. If they are expressed in their original form, they would be too crude to give pleasure. The writer transforms an emotion into *rasa* that gives aesthetic pleasure to the reader or the listener. He defines *rasa* cryptically:

> विभावानुभाव व्यभिचारि संयोगाद्रसनिष्पत्तिः
>
> (*Rasa* is the production of the sequential combination and dialectical interaction of *vibhava*, *anubhava* and *vyabhicharibhava*)

Because of this cryptic definition, the term *rasa* has never been explicitly explained nor appropriately translated. It has been translated into English as *sentiment* and, recently, as *poetic configuration*. S.K. De has translated it into *poetic effect.** We shall see later that none of the three—sentiment, poetic configuration, and poetic effect—mean what the term *rasa* actually means. It is better to retain the original Sanskrit term *rasa* as it is; western critics have tried to explain Aristotle's *Catharsis* or *Katharsis* but never translated it.

As *rasa* is the product of blending of *vibhava*, *anubhava* and *vyavicharibhava*, it is necessary to know their meaning and function. First, the *bhavas*. According to Bharata there are eight *sthayi bhavas* that are ever present in man's psyche. They are:

1. *Rati* (Sex)
2. *Hasa* (Laughter)
3. *Shoka* (Sorrow)
4. *Krodha* (Anger)
5. *Utsaha* (Vigour)
6. *Bhaya* (Fear)
7. *Jugupsa* (Hatred)
8. *Vismaya* (Wonder)

The task of the creative writer is to establish one of these emotions in his text artistically. In other words, a particular emotion should dominate the entire text. But this emotion should not be presented in its crude form; the text must have artistic excellence and for this the author should make use of *vibhava*, *anubhava* and *vyabhicharibhava*.

Vibhava comes first in the transformation of *bhava* or emotion into *rasa*. What is *vibhava*? It is the cause of the arousal of an emotion. It is a concrete object. For example, fear is an emotion which is ever present in us, but it is aroused when we face something fearful. A chance meeting with a large cobra in our path arouses the emotion of fear. The writer deliberately creates a *vibhava* to arouse a particular emotion. *Vibhava* is of

* In my opinion De's translation is most satisfying.

two kinds: *alamban* and *uddipan*. In a play *alamban* is the actor. His/her body and costumes make him/her a perfect *alamban*. *Uddipan* is the words and activities of the actor. The man/woman on the stage, his/her physique, costumes, dialogues, and actions arouse the desired emotion.

Anubhava is the feeling aroused in the other actor who watches the first actor. His/her feelings are reflected in his/her dialogues and movements. *Anubhava* is followed by *vyabhicharibhava*. Acharya Vishwanath has used the term *sancharibhava* at the place of *vyabhicharibhava*. *Vyabhicharibhava* is the fleeting feelings that come and go. In fact, they are conflicting emotions. Bharata has named thirty three *vyabhicharibhavas*. They are:

1. *Nirveda* (hopelessness)
2. *Glani* (remorse)
3. *Sariki* (anxiety)
4. *Irshya* (jealousy)
5. *Mada* (pride)
6. *Shrama* (tiredness)
7. *Alasya* (laziness)
8. *Dainya* (Weakness)
9. *Chinta* (worry)
10. *Moha* (affection)
11. *Smriti* (remembrance)
12. *Dhriti* (satisfaction)
13. *Vrida* (disgrace)
14. *Chapalata* (fickleness)
15. *Harsha* (joy)
16. *Avega* (protest)
17. *Jadata* (trance)
18. *Garva* (arrogance)
19. *Vishada* (desolation)
20. *Autasukya* (inquiritiveness)
21. *Nidra* (sleep)
22. *Apasmara* (hysteria)
23. *Supta* (dormant)
24. *Vipodha* (awakening)
25. *Amarsha* (resentment)
26. *Avahittha* (dissimulation)
27. *Ugrata* (ferocity)
28. *Mati* (assurance)
29. *Vyadhi* (sickness)
30. *Unmada* (derangement)
31. *Marana* (demise)
32. *Trisha* (fright)
33. *Vitarka* (reflection/introspection)

The *vyabhicharibhavas* are fleeting emotions; they come and go according to the changing words of characters. Secondly, they are the different forms of the eight *sthayi bhavas* and, so, they do not have an independent existence.

The playwrighter produces the desired *rasa* by arousing the intended *bhava* (emotion) and transforming it through *vibhava*, *anubhava* and *vyabhicharibhava*.

Now, what is *rasa*? First, it is different from *bhava*. *Bhava*, as said earlier, is ever present in man. *Rasa* is the total poetic effect of a literary text. The eminent critic Dr. Nagendra has explained the term *rasa* in his monumental work *Rasa Siddhanta*. He says that *rasa* has got four meanings. They are:

(a) juice of leaves and fruits,

(b) essence of herbals and chemicals,

(c) the resultant of the different emotions aroused in a literary text, and

(d) the *rasa* of devotion or liberation of the mind or soul.

However, the basic meaning is the first, the juice of herbs and fruits. Each kind of juice has a special taste and effect. *Rasa* is obtained by crushing leaves and fruits. The obtained juice is not taste in itself; it gives us taste and strength too. In *Ayurveda*, *rasa* is prepared to cure a sick man of his disease and give strength and vigour. The general meaning and the *Ayurvedic* meaning suggest that *rasa* is physically observable, that is, it is something concrete. In literature, it is abstract. It means *Kavyasaundarya* (artistic beauty) and *Kavyananda/Kavyaswad* (aesthetic pleasure). In religion or mysticism it refers to *atmananda* or *brahmananda* (supreme bliss).

The summary of this explication of the term is that it was first used in the sense of juice of herbs and fruits in the Vedic period, for example *somarasa*, and later on, it acquired its extended meaning in *ayurveda*, literary criticism and mysticism.

The most popular example given by Abhinavagupta is that of the first act of *Abhijñānaśākuntalam*. Dushyanta goes to Kanva's *ashrama* where he sees Shakuntala. Shakuntala's matchless beauty attracts him greatly. He falls in love with her and decides to marry her.

Here, the *bhava* is *rati* and the *vibhava* is the meeting with Shakuntala. Shakuntala's body and costumes are the *alamban* or *ashraya*, and her action is *uddipan* that arouses the emotion of *rati* greatly. Once, the emotion is aroused, the *anubhava* follows immediately. The *anubhava* is Dushyanta's love for Shakuntala and strong desire to get her. Shakuntala, too, has the same kind of feeling. Her friends augment her love for Dushyanta. Then follow the *vyabhicharibhavas*, the different kinds of feelings that come and go. Dushyanta has no idea that Shakuntala is the daughter of Vishwamitra, a *Kshatriya* sage and Menaka an *apsara*. He considers her to be *rishi* Kanva's daughter. As she is a *rishi kanya*, he cannot marry her. This thought goes counter to his idea of marrying Shakuntala. The two ideas are conflicting emotions in the drama. Later on, everything is revealed. Dushyanta has no hesitation in marrying Shakuntala. The viewers taste the *shringara rasa*.

The drawback of Sanskrit scholars is that they have been more concerned with scholarship than criticism in interpreting *Natyashastra*. *Natyashastra* is basically a manual of dramatic performance. Bharata's aim is to stage a play for the desired effect on the audience.

A play is written to arouse a particular emotion in the audience. The eight emotions are ever-present. The playwrighter creates characters whose actions arouse the intended emotion in an artistic manner. The characters, their features, costumes and actions transform the emotion in its corresponding *rasa* which gives the audience aesthetic pleasure. Bharata has enumerated the *bhavas* and their *rasas* as follows.

Bhavas	***Rasas***
Rati	*Shringar* (love)
Hasa	*Hasya* (mirth)
Shoka	*Karuna* (compassion)
Krodha	*Raudra* (anger)
Utsaha	*Veera* (bravery)
Bhaya	*Bhayanaka* (horror)
Jugupsa	*Vibhatsa* (disgust)
Vismaya	*Adbhuta* (wonder)

Later on, Abhinavagupta, propounder of *rasa-dhavani* theory, added the emotion, *shama* (tranquillity) of which the corresponding *rasa* is *shanta* (transcendental peace). Perhaps, he was influenced by the *shanti parva* of the *Mahabharata* and, so, added, and rightly so, the *shanta rasa* to Bharata's list.

Bharata divides the different types of characters and their characteristics. The *nayaka* (hero) is the most important character in a play. The *nayaka* must have majesty and gravity. Therefore, all the four types of heroes have *dheeratva* (self-control) as the basic element in their character. The dominance of one other element distinguishes one from the other. Thus, the heroes are divided into

1. *Dheerodatta* (Noble)
2. *Dheeroddhata* (Arrogant)
3. *Dheeralalita* (Loving)
4. *Dheeraprashanta* (Calm)

Rama of the *Ramayana* and Dushyanta of *Shakuntlam* are *dheerodatta*, Duryodhana and Bheema of the *Mahabharata* are *dheeroddhata*, Udayana of *Swapnavasavadattam* is *Dheeralalita* and Yudhisthir of the *Mahabharata* is *dheeraprasanta*.

Bharata's division of drama is formal, whereas Aristotle's is semantic. As the Indian audience demanded a happy ending, even the serious dramas do not have a tragic end. Of course, comedies are in abundance. The ten types of drama differ in size and number of characters. However, the first type *nataka* is of serious nature and has a well-built plot. The *nayaka* is of heroic quality, that is, he must be *dheerodatta*, *dheeroddhata*, *dheeralalita* or *dheeraprashanta*. The plot should be well-organized and have *arambha* (exposition), *prayatna* (complication), *praptyasha* (climax), *niyatapti* (anti-climax), and *phalagama* (conclusion).

A play is not a mime. Actors on the stage speak. Bharata knew that movement and language are equally important in the production of *rasa*. His views on the language of drama are very important. He has written on *lakshana*, *alankara*, *dosha*, and *guna* of dramatic language.

1. *Lakshana*

Bharata gives more importance to *lakshana* than *alankara*. *Lakshana* is the inner beautifying element. Abhinavagupta explains it as an innate beautifying element belonging to the body of poetry. It is also that it constitutes the body itself. *Alankara*, he says, is added from outside but *lakshana* is not a separate entity. It is inseparable. Since the concept of *lakshana* is rather vague and physically not verifiable, the later theorists merged it with *alankara*.

2. *Alankara*

For Bharata, *alankara* is added from outside. It is inferior to *lakshana*. This is why he mentioned thirty six *lakshanas* but only four *alankaras*. They are: *upama* (simile), *rupaka* (metaphor), *dipaka* (illuminator), and *yamaka* (repetition of words or syllables of the same sound).

3. *Doshas*

Surprisingly, Bharata pays more attention to the ten *doshas* (faults) in comparison to the ten *gunas* (merits). Perhaps, his view was that people look more at faults than merits. The ten faults of poetic diction are:

(a) *goodhartha* (circumlocution or periphrasis)
(b) *arthantara* (digression into another matter which is not relevant)
(c) *arthaheena* (incoherence/meaninglessness)
(d) *bhinnartha* (change of the desired sense by another sense or rusticity (*gramyata*))
(e) *ekartha* (tautology)
(f) *abhipulartha* (faulty construction of a long sentence)
(g) *nyayad apetam* (defective logic)
(h) *visham* (defective *metre*)
(i) *visandhi* (wrong *sandhi*)
(j) *shabda-heena* (use of ungrammatical words)

4. *Gunas*

The number of *gunas* is also ten. Bharat expects a good writing should have all the ten *gunas* (merits). They are:

(a)	*Shlesha*	(coalescence of words connected with one another to convey the desired meaning, simple in appearance but rich in meaning)
(b)	*prasada*	(clarity)
(c)	*samata*	(evenness and absence of compound words)
(d)	*samadhi*	(superimposition of something special in meaning)
(e)	*madhurya*	(sweetness)
(f)	*ojas*	(forcefulness)
(g)	*saukumarya*	(smoothness)
(h)	*arthavyakti*	(explicitness/clarity)
(i)	*udara*	(sublimity)
(j)	*kanti*	(gracefulness)

It is the greatness of Bharata that almost all men of letters, except Bhamaha, accepted his list as it was. All that they did was to modify the meaning and application of the terms.

As said earlier, Bharata was more concerned with the performance on the stage. This is why he has described in detail the size of the stage, the appearance of the characters, their costumes, movements, and methods of expression of different kinds of feelings and emotions.

The fact is that he is more a stage director than a critic. His detailed description of gestures, gesticulation, facial expression, and symbolical movement shows that he was both an actor and a stage director. This is why the classical dance of South India is called *Bharatanatyam* and the dancers still adhere to the directions given in *Natyashastra*. He has remained a perennial influence on Indian drama and dance.

His poetic theory is still valid. It can be favourably compared with Aristotle's poetic theory. Aristotle is primarily concerned with the arousal and purgation of the emotions of pity and fear. Bharata, too, is of the view that the aim of drama is to arouse the dormant emotions ever-present in man and transform them into *rasa*, which will give aesthetic pleasure. Aristotle's stress on "beautiful" very clearly indicates that a play, especially tragedy, should be well-proportioned to give aesthetic pleasure to the audience. In other words, both are the proponents of the affective theory of poetry and art. The difference is that Aristotle remains satisfied with telling that tragedy purgates the base emotions of pity and fear, and Bharata goes a little further and demonstrates how a play is to be performed on the stage to arouse emotions and transform them into the desired *rasa* for the aesthetic pleasure of the spectators.

His concept of *vyabhicharibhava* is very close to I.A. Richards's idea of "conflicting emotions". Richards is of the view that a good poem does not progress in a straight line. It arouses one kind of emotion in the beginning, which is soon countered by another kind of emotion, and towards the end all the conflicting emotions are harmonized. The term he uses for this kind of harmonization is synaesthesis. If we take Milton's sonnet "On His Blindness", we find that the poet is a kind of rebel who questions God's justice in the octave. This is one kind of emotion. In the sestet, patience consoles him that God does not need his services as He is great and all that He wants is man's willingness to wait for His command—"They also serve who only stand and wait." The last line harmonizes the conflicting emotions. Gray's "Elegy Written In A Country Churchyard" presents a richer variety of emotions, which are synthesised in the last section of the poem where the poet chooses the simple and honest life of the country bard. This poem can be very well analysed in terms of *rasa* theory, where the conflicting and fleeting emotions (*vyabhicharibhava*) play an important role.

Bharata is great and his *rasa* theory can be fruitfully applied in the analysis of even modern poems and plays.

(B) DANDIN

Dandin is the first critic who saw the limitations of the *rasa* theory. No doubt *Natyashastra* is an exhaustive treatise on the theory and art of drama, it excluded the other forms of poetry that existed in its times. Dandin challenged the *rasa* theory and defined poetry scientifically. His oft-quoted definition of poetry is

शरीरं तावदिष्टार्थ व्यवछिन्ना पदावली

(The body of poetry is a composite of words organized in a special way to express the desired meaning)

Dr. D.K. Gupta in his book *A Critical Study of Dandin* explains this laconic definition of poetry.

This is because in modern criticism the phrase "desired meaning" is more appropriate than "intended sense", and *padavali* does not exactly mean "a string of words", the term Robert Frost has used in his definition of poetry. The Neo-Aristotlians and French structuralists prefer the word "organize" to "characterize" as used by Dr. Gupta. For the rest of the quoted passage we have followed Dr. Gupta with due reverence to his scholarship and what follows in the next paragraph is a paraphrase of his further explication of the definition.

Dandin's emphasis is on *ishtartha*, the desired meaning, that is, he does not set an ideal for poetry. He limits it to the poet's perception of reality. He rejects Bharata's notion of *rasa* as the soul of poetry. For him poetry is a body, or if we accept the new critics from America, poetry is an organistic whole and exists by itself.

Dr. Gupta is silent on the term *vyavachhinna padavali*. The prefix *vi*—वि is used to mean special as in the term *vibhava* and *vyanjana*. Here the term *vyavachhinna* literally means "strung in a special way". The total meaning of the term *vyavachhinna padavali*, then means "the words strung in a special way". Coleridge has said that poetry is the best words in the best order. Dandin is already ahead of him and tells us that poetry is a body and its constituents are words which are organized in a special way or, if we follow S.K. De, in an agreeable way.

Kavyadarsha

Dandin is wrongly dubbed as an *alankarist*. The title of his treatise is *Kavyadarsha* not *Alankarashastra* nor *Kavyalankara*. *Adarsha* means mirror. The title, therefore, means that the treatise mirrors poetry. A soul, being abstract, cannot be imaged in a mirror but the solid body can be. Dandin's effort is to show the body of poetry in his treatise. *Kavyadarsha* is divided into three parts (*parichheda*) consisting of 660 verses. The main contents or topics of the treatise are as follows:

1. Benediction and introductory remarks, Part I, verses 1-9.
2. Definition and classification of *Kavya*, Part I, verses 10-39.
3. The *margas* and *gunas*, Part I, verses 40-102.
4. Purposes and sources of poetry, Part I, verses 103-05.
5. Poetic figures, Part II, verses 1-368.
   Verbal figures, Part I, verses 55-61.
   Anuprasa, Part III, verses 1-124.
6. Defects (*doshas*), Part III verses 125-85.
7. Concluding remarks, Part III verses 186-87.

Definition and Classification of *Kavya*

Dandin's definition of *Kavya* has already been discussed. His classification of *Kavya* follows the definition. The division of *Kavya* into (a) prose, (b) verse, and (c) *misra* (mixture of both prose and verse) is based upon the two main forms of language.

The verse or metrical composition is divided structurally into (a) *Muktaka* (a single verse), (b) *Kulaka* (a group of five verses), (c) *Kosha* (unconnected verse), and (d) *Sanghata* (short poem with a story). These forms are said to be included in the main variety, namely, the *mahakavya* (extended narrative poem), also called *sargabandha* (a composition divided into cantos). Here the main criterion is the size of a poetic composition.

He dwells at length on *mahakavya* (epic) as Sanskrit literature has a rich epic tradition. Since he had read the *Ramayana*, the *Mahabharata*, Kalidasa's *Kumarsambhavam* and *Raghuvansham*, and Bharavi's *Kirtarjuneeyam*, he knew the main characteristics of the epic. He has listed the following features of an epic.

(a) It should begin with a benediction, dedication or indication of the subject-matter.

(b) It should have an exalted subject-matter or theme.

(c) It should aim at the four principal objects of life: *dharma*, *artha*, *kama* and *moksha*.

(d) The hero should be noble and his adversary too, but the hero is superior in both thought and bravery.

(e) There should be description of cities, oceans/seas, mountains, seasons, the rise of the sun and the moon, sport in gardens and in water, drinking, love, dalliance, separation, marriage, birth of a son, meetings of councils and embassies, army campaigns, battles and the hero's victory.

(f) The language should be embellished.

(g) The length must be sizable.

(h) Cantos should be metrically-formed and well-connected and of moderate length.

Finally, he carefully adds that if some of the features are absent, a *mahakavya* is accepted provided the features present are charming.

The prose form is divided into *akhyayika* and *katha* broadly. The story in an *akhyayika* is narrated by the protagonist himself while in *katha* the narrator is a different person. The *akhyayika* may contain some verses in *vaktra* or *aparvaktra metre* which is not found in *katha*. The subject-matter of an *akhyayika* is abduction of a maiden, war among kings, separation of lovers or victory of a king. The intention of the author is clearly manifest in this kind of prose writing. There is no such a thing in *katha*.

Yet, Dandin does not favour this kind of distinction and is of the opinion that the demarcation line is not only blurred but also arbitrary. The following are his arguments as explained by Dr. Gupta in his scholarly book *A Critical Study of Dandin*.

1. The mere fact that the narrator is the hero himself or some one else cannot form the basis of any distinction. Moreover, exceptions to this are observed in *akhyayikas* where persons other than the heroes appear as narrators.
2. Verses in the said *metres*, like *arya* verses, can occur in a *katha* also.

3. It is immaterial whether the chapters are called *lambhas* or *ucchvasas*.
4. Themes like abduction of a maiden, battle, etc., are, in fact, characteristics common to all species of *kavya*, and they occur in a *mahakavya* also.
5. The peculiar mark, said to be characterising an *akhyayika*, cannot be a fault in the other form of prose also.

Perhaps, while writing *kavyadarsha* and commenting on the division of *gadya kavya* Dandin had his own works *Dashakumaracharitam* and *Avantisundari katha* in his mind. He is right in the sense that *katha* is in no way inferior to *akhyayika*, though it may be written in *apabhransha* or *prakrit*. He is right as Gunadhya's *Brihat katha* was considered equal to the *Mahabharata* and the *Ramayana* in his time and before him. Dr. Gupta rightly comments:

> "Although Dandin was not followed by later theorists in his contention, the fact remains that his viewpoint was, to a great extent, logical and sound, for it is futile to make distinctions, in the matter of literary form, on the basis of minor details with regard to the nature of the introduction, the occurrence of verses in particular metre or the naming of chapters."

The third form *mishra* (now called *champoo*) is that kind of *kavya* in which there is a mixture of both prose and verse. Dandin includes drama in this category.

This tree diagram gives a clear picture of Dandin's classification of *kavya*.

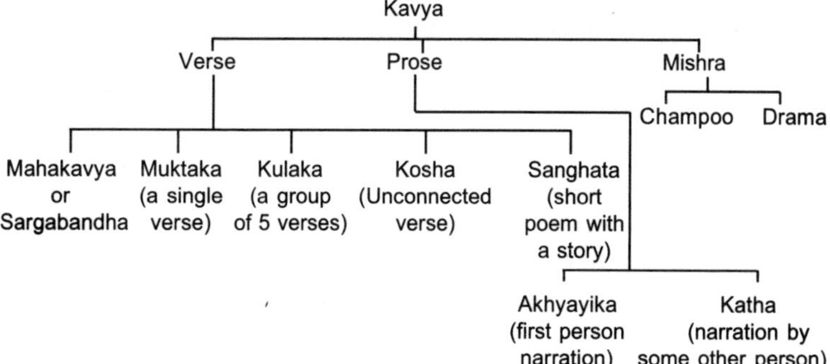

The next principle of classification is linguistic. Here Dandin's grammar is quite modern. He accepts the importance of the language of the people and their creative writing. He recognizes the importance of *Prakrit*, which was rather disparaged by Sanskrit scholars of his time. *Kavyas* in Sanskrit (*Devavani*), *Prakrit*, *Apabhransha* and *Mishra* are taken into account. The different branches of *Prakrit* are *Maharashtri*, *Shauraseni*, *Gaudi*, *Lati*, and *Paishachi*, also called *Bhootbhasha* (language of the forest people).

Dandin has also followed the traditional classification of *kavya* into *Drishya* and *Shravya*. But he has used the term *prekshya* at the place of *drishya*. Secondly, the term *prekshya* is confined to dramatic dance performances, especially erotic, such as *lasya* (modern *ras*), *chalita*, and *shalya*. He places drama in the category of *shravya*.

The *Marga* Theory

Dandin is the first Sanskrit critic who analysed poetic diction seriously. However, the pioneer is Bharata. Bharata made a passing reference to *pravritti* (trend) in his brief discussion of the *gunas* and *doshas* of poetic diction. *Pravritti*, according to him, signifies the various manners with regard to costumes, language, custom, and practice in different regions. Dandin may have also taken inspiration from Bharata's classification of the dramatic manners or language of the plays of the four main regions—Kurukshetra, Gujarat, Vidarbha, and South Baluchistan. He gave the name *vritti* for the dramatic language and classified it into *Bharati*, *Sattvati*, *Kaishiki*, and *Arabhati*.

The great grammarians Yask and Patanjali must have influenced Dandin as both had marked the linguistic features that differentiated the verbal forms and derivatives from the Kamboj country language and that of the Aryas or the Easterns.

Bana who was born earlier than Dandin casually mentioned various literary manners prevalent in different regions. He pointed out that there is abundance of *shlesha* (double intendre or pun) in the northern region, of sense over word in the western area, of *utpreksha* (frequent play of fancy) in the southern country, and of *Shabdambara* (verbosity) in the Gauda (eastern) region.

Although fully aware of Bana's classification, Dandin recognizes two only: *Vaidarbha* of *Dakshinatya* or the south and *Gauda* of the eastern region. The main reason for dividing poetic diction in two broad categories is that Dandin, though fully aware of individual characteristics, was basically interested in the special features of the poetic diction of the two large regions. This is why he did not use the term, *pravritti* or *paddhati*, which are quite narrow and vague in sense. *Marga* means a road, wide and long, travelled by many.

As Dr. Gupta has pointed out Dandin's concept of *marga* is a key to the explication of his definition of poetry. If poetry is a body made up of words organized in a special way for the expression of the desired meaning, it is necessary to know how poets employ their skill in the composition of a literary text. In his words,

> "It (the definition of poetry) drew his attention to the appropriate combination of word and sense, which has been technically termed *marga* or *riti*."

Dandin's concept of *alankara* is not mere embellishment; it comprehends both arrangement of words and poetic figures. Therefore, his notion of *marga* is the proper organization of words, both plain and figurative, for the expression of the intended meaning. It, also, then follows that meaning and structure sentence are correlative and interdependent.

The following are the main points of Dandin's concept of *marga* as explained by Dr. Gupta in *A Critical Study of Dandin* (pages 136-40).

1. The path of speech is multifold, since every poet possesses a distinct way of expressing an idea or describing an object. It is difficult to draw a clear line of distinction between the various paths or dictions which differ from poet to poet, the mutual difference among them being too subtle to be defined. In our time, we recognize easily the style of poets like Hopkins, Eliot or Cummings as they are bold experimenters. Kalidasa's

style is quite distinctive and scholars have recognized *Ritusamharam*, *Meghadutam*, *Kumarsambhavam*, *Raghuvansham*, *Malvikagnimitram*, *Vikramovarshiyam*, and *Abhijñānaśākuntalam* as his genuine works on the basis of his style, although his *marga* is *Vaidarbha*. We determine the style of a writer on the basis of her/his favourite words, phrases, syntactic structures, symbols, metaphors, and peculiar turns of expression. However we cannot expect too much from the pioneers like Dandin and Vamana.

2. He recognized the two *margas*, *Gaud* and *Vaidarbha* and ignored *Panchala* and *Avanti* recognized by Bana for the reason that they were not much different from the first and the second respectively.
3. The *margas*, the *paths* of poetry, are characterised by two kinds of elements. The general elements are common to both the *Gaud* and *Vaidarbh* poetic dictions. The particular elements are specific to one kind of *marga* or poetic diction and they are not found in the other kind of *marga*. In other words, the particular elements are those linguistic features that distinguish one *marga* from the other. We can understand the concept of *marga* better if we look at the different *gharanas* in Indian classical music. Each of the *gharanas* has its peculiar features or style of singing, though all sing *khayal*. Thus, Kirana *gharana*, Jaipur *gharana*, Gwalior *gharana*, and Patiala *gharana* are the different styles of *khayal gayaki*.

   The ten *gunas* or excellences referred to by Dandin are present in *Vaidarbha* but are largely absent in *Gauda*, and are substituted by their *viparyaya* (alternatives).
4. The *gunas* that were considered characteristic of good composition by Bharata were converted by Dandin to be the special quality of *Vaidarbha* only.

For Dandin, the *Vaidarbha marga* or poetic diction is the ideal, and the *Gauda* poetic diction is inferior. The former is marked by the refined manner of expression and tenderness of feeling. There is compactness and force in the arrangement of words and evenness of diction, with regard to it possesses majesty of movement, explicitness, sublimity, spontaneity, appropriate use of tropes and *madhurya* (sweetness). On the other hand, the *Gauda marga* or poetic diction prefers fervidity, harshness, alliteration, unevenness and *shabdadambara* (verbosity). Perhaps, Dandin had Kalidasa's poems and plays in his mind. We all know that he is the best representative of the *Vaidarbha marga*.

The Ten *Gunas*

Dandin has followed Bharata almost to the letter in classifying the *gunas* (excellences) of poetry. His modification and definition of the ten *gunas* of Bharata may be said to be an improvement upon the old master's. The ten *gunas* are:

1. *Shlesha*:[1] Compactness or the quality of being well-unit or the absence of laxity. The poet uses *alpaprana* (unaspirated) consonants, short vowels and avoids the aspirated consonants and long vowels as far as possible.
2. *Prasada*:[2] It is lucidity in the use of words. The words are free from obscurity and affectation.
3. *Samata*:[3] It means evenness in the grouping of sounds. Sounds can be divided into three kinds: soft, harsh, and middle. A good poet does not mix soft and harsh sounds together in a line or a stanza. Soft or harsh sounds should be systematically used. If there is the need of mixing them together, it should be done skilfully and adroitly to produce the desired sound effect.
4. *Madhurya*:[4] It means sweetness. It may mean melody or harmony and elegant rhythm. Here Dandin confuses *samata* with *madhurya*. He says that *madhurya* is the elegance consisting of (i) a alliteration *(shrutyanuprasa)* and (ii) absence of vulgarity. The verbal form of *madhurya* is called *vag-rasa* and the ideal is *vastu-rasa*. It is really difficult to make a clear-cut distinction between *samata* and *madhurya*. It would have been

1. श्लेष 2. प्रसाद 3. समता 4. माधुर्य

better if Dandin had combined these two *gunas* into one.

5. *Sukumarata*:[5] Most of the Sanskrit scholars have translated this term as softness but we feel that the word tenderness is better. Dandin means by this term absence of harshness or cacophony. Mahamohopadhyaya Tarkavagish comments that *sukumarata* consists in tenderness as a total effect arising from the commingling of soft and harsh sounds.
6. *Arthavyakti*:[6] It is the explicitness of sense or absence of truncated expression. We can say that while describing an effect, the writer should hint at the cause too. It also and, perhaps, more importantly, means that words must be meaningfully used and redundancy should be avoided. In other words, there should be a proper balance of sound and sense, word and meaning, and absence of vagueness.
7. *Udaratva*:[7] In our time, it means generosity. Dandin uses it in the sense of sublimity. *Udaratva* is that quality which expresses high merits in a grand manner. We can say that Milton's *Paradise Lost* has the quality of *Udaratva* or sublimity.
8. *Ojas*:[8] It means forcefulness. Poetry can be forceful if there is abundance of *samasa* in it. *Samasa* helps a poet to achieve brevity and forcefulness.
9. *Kanti*:[9] It means grace. Poetry must be graceful. *Kanti* is achieved by avoiding *atyukti* or excessive exaggeration. *Atishayokti* or hyperbole is all right as there is no repetition of the same idea. On the other hand, in *atyukti* the same idea is repeated in many ways.
10. *Samadhi*:[10] It means metaphorical expression. It is very much like I.A. Richards's concept of metaphor—transference of the quality of one object to the other—"life is a walking shadow" or "time is out of joint".

---

5. सुकुमारता 6. अर्थव्यक्ति 7. उदारत्व 8. ओजस 9. कान्ति 10. समाधि

Though Dandin considers *Vaidarbha marga* to be the ideal, he is not averse to the *gauda marga*. Therefore, he uses the word *viparyaya* for those features which go against the *gunas* enumerated by him. There are five *viparyayas* (the opposites). We must remember that the *viparyayas* are not *doshas* or defects in poetry and they are the special features of *Gauda Marga*.

1. *Shaithilya* (looseness of structure) is the opposite of *shlesha* (compactness). It consists in the employment entirely of the *alpaprana* (liquid) consonants and is desirable in *Gauda marga* if it brings about dignity of diction (*bandhagaurava*), say, in the use of alliteration, for example, *malatimala lolalikalila*. (मालतीमाला लोलालिकलिला).

2. *Vyutpanna* is the use of two words dissimilar in spelling and meaning, but derived from the same root. He gives the example of a famous line in Sanskrit, which can be translated into English as:

   The white-beamed one (the moon) has a spot to the not very white water-born ones (the lotuses). It is very much like Hopkins's famous line, "The unchilding, unfathering, widow-making deep". The use of the prefix *un-* and the verb *make* is bold and meaning giving.

3. *Vishama* is the *viparyaya* of *sama* or *samata*. Poets of *Gauda Marga* Yoke all the three kinds of words—soft, moderate, and harsh—together, a practice which is not seen in *Vaidarbha marga*.

4. *Nisthura* is the *viparyaya* of *sukumarata*. It is the use of harsh sounds which strike the ear. Besides, the sentences are difficult to pronounce. Sometimes, they look like tongue-twisters.

5. *Atyukti* is the opposite of *Kanti*. It is an exaggerated expression that crosses the limits of conventional usage. Sometimes *atyukti* causes laughter, although the writer intends to be serious. For example, a lover praises the largeness of his beloved's breasts:

"Surely the creator has made this sky too narrow, oblivious of the huge expansion of thy breasts".

The Doshas

For Bharata the *gunas* are opposite to the *doshas* (flaws). Dandin goes the other way. The *gunas* are positive and the *doshas* are negative in character. The following are the *doshas* as enumerated in *kavyaprakasha.*

1. *Shitthilata* (loose construction). Too much use of unaspirated and liquid sounds causes looseness in total composition. It is important that aspirated and plosive consonants are skilfully used.
2. *Vyutpanna* is the opposite of *prasada*. If there is the use of those words in their derivative meaning which are not yet standardized, there is every possibility of obscurity. Poets should avoid obscurantism.
3. *Vishama* is the opposite of evenness. The flaw of *vishama* (unevenness) occurs when there is indiscriminate use of soft, moderate, and harsh words in a number of lines or in the entire composition.
4. *Gramya* (vulgarity). It means the defect of using words spoken by the illiterate people living in villages. Use of those words which are frequently used in a low sense, may mar the dignity of poetic diction.
5. *Deepta* or *nishthura* is the opposite of *sukumarata* and occurs when there is much use of harsh words and tongue twisters.
6. *Neyatva* (lack of clarity). When a poet leaves a gap between two lines and the gap is so wide that the listener or reader is unable to decipher the meaning, there is the flaw of *neyatva*. A grammatically incorrect sentence may cause *neyatva*.
7. *Atyukti* (wild exaggeration). Exaggeration is *atishayokti*, which is permitted to hint at the largeness of an object, matchless beauty or gravity of situation. *Atyukti* is repetitious and makes the entire composition grotesque and ludicrous.

If we look at the *doshas* enumerated by Dandin, we find that except the fourth and sixth, all are *viparyaya* too. The question is what is the difference between the *viparyayas* and the *doshas*? It is clear that Dandin considers *Vaidarbha marga* the ideal and so its basic features are the ten *gunas*. The *doshas* are the opposites of the *gunas*. For him the problem is that *Gauda* poetic diction goes opposite to *Vaidarbha* poetic diction. As a rule the five salient features—*shithilata*, *vyut-panna*, *vishama*, *deepta or nishthura*, and *atyukti*—of *Gauda* poetic diction should be considered as the flaws. But, as the poets of the east were masters of language and deviated from the *vaidarbha* poets, Dandin could not find fault with their poetic diction and so, he used the term *viparyaya* (opposite or alternative) and not *dosha*.

Dandin's Theory of *Alankara*

Before coming to Dandin's concept of *alankara* it is necessary to know the general meaning of the word. According to professor G.C. Tripathi[11] the word *alam* is a variation of the original word *aram* found in the *Rigveda*. The original meaning of *aram* in the *Rigveda* is "fit" which, later on, developed into "sufficient". At the third stage, *aram* or *alam* began to mean "appropriateness" and "propriety". Therefore, *alankara* is the means by which the appropriateness (of form or appearance) is achieved. Dr. Tripathi's conclusion is:

> "...as Beauty is only another name for *Perfection* born of appropriateness, an *alankara* is a means to perfection or in other words to beauty."

Dandin's stress on the importance of *alankara* is due to the fact that he was interested in the aesthetic pleasure, which is produced by both *sound* and *meaning* of poetry. He defines *alankara* as the characteristic attribute, which produces charm in poetry and incorporates, in its scope, besides the specific *alankaras*, the *gunas* (excellences, the various forms of dramatic

11. G.C. Tripathi, "An Etymological Note on the Word Alankara", *Principles of Literary Criticism in Sanskrit*, ed. R.C. Dwivedi, (Varanasi: Motilal Banarasidas, 1969), 29-33.

joints and manners) and the *lakshnas*. Professor S.K. De writes in his *History of Sanskrit Poetics*, Part II:

> "It must be distinctly understood that the word *alankara* is used by Dandin in the general sense of that which causes beauty in poetry."

After quoting the famous line "*kavyashobhakaran dharmana lankaran prachakshate*"[12], he continues:

> "It appears to include in its wide scope both *gunas* and *alankaras* properly so called. Referring to his own discussion of the *gunas* in the previous chapter, in relation to the *vaidarbha marga* of which they constitute the essence, Dandin speaks of them in ii.3 as *alankaras* and goes on to mention the figures as *sadharanam alankara-jatam*. In other words, poetic figures are *alankaras* common to both the *margas* (*sadharana*) while *gunas* are *alankaras* belonging exclusively to the *vaidarbha*."[13]

It is clear that *alankara* (trope or poetic figure) is the basic element of poetry, *guna* is a special kind of *alankara* that makes a poem excellent. *Vaidarbha* poetic diction is superior to *Gauda* poetic diction only because it possesses all the ten *gunas*.

Following his definition of poetry that it is a combination of sound and sense, Dandin divides *alankaras* into two kinds: *shabdankara* and *arthalankara*. *Shabdalankara* is related to the words used in a literary text and *arthalankara* to the meaning. A perfect or proper blend of the two gives beauty to the text.

In the western criticism there is no such classification of figures of speech. Alliteration, assonance, and consonance are not given a special category. Here Dandin is quite explicit. *Anuprasa* and *yamaka* add beauty to sound. As there was no printing press in his time, and poetry was to be recited before an audience, sound effect was very much important. *Kaku*

12. "काव्य शोभाकरान् धर्मानलंकारान् प्रचक्षते", काव्यप्रकाश, II, i
13. S.K. De, *History of Sanskrit Poetics*, (Kolkata : Firma K.L. Mukhopadhy, 1989) 82-83.

(intonation) was studied seriously and it mattered much in dramatic performance and recitation of poetry.

Dandin gives greater importance to *arthalankara*, the figures of speech that add meaning to the text. *Arthalankara* is divided into *svabhavokti* and *vakrokti*. By *svabhavokti* he means the kind of expression which brings an object manifestly to our mind's eye—*nanavastham padarthanam rupam sakshad vivrinvati.*[14] He regards the expression of the natural disposition also as a characteristic element of the poetic figures. Besides, *svabhavokti* (natural expression) is the primary *arthalankara* and the rest is *vakrokti* (special mode of expression), the principle characterising all the poetic figures falling in the group of *arthalankara*. S.K. De has very clearly explained the character of *svabhavokti* and differentiated it from *vakrokti*.

> "According to Dandin's scheme (as indicated in ii. 362), the whole realm of poetic figures can be divided into two distinct groups, consisting of *svabhavokti*, on the one hand, and *vakrokti*, on the other. By the former, which he characterises as the first or primary figure (*adya alankritih*)[15], he implies a plain and direct description of things belonging to a genus (*jati*), or of an action (*kriya*), of a quality (*guna*), or of an individual (*dravya*). In this so-called natural description, there is apparently no scope for any artificial or ingenious mode of expression, and it should, therefore, be distinguished from all other poetic devices, figurative or otherwise, collectively designated as the *vakrokti*."[16]

Dandin's concept of natural expression (*svabhavokti*) is of utmost importance. A long poem can never be written in *vakrokti* throughout. Even the most artistic poems like *The Wasteland* and *Sailing to Byzantium* begin with plain statements. The first line of *Sailing to Byzantium* is: "That's not country for old men".

---

14. नानावस्थं पदार्थानां रूपं साक्षाद् विव्रण्वती।

15. आद्यालंकृतिः

16. S.K. De, *Histroy of Sanskrit Poetics*, 85-86.

Dandin's Contribution to Literary Criticism

Dandin is great and his greatness as a critic has been unanimously accepted by Sanskrit scholars. But, it is a misfortune that he is not known to the people outside India. It has also been the defect of Indian scholars not to apply his theory in the analysis of literary texts. Bharata has been rather a happier critic whose theory of *rasa* was employed in the analysis of Sanskrit plays.

Dandin is the first critic who widened the horizon of Sanskrit poetics. The *rasa* theory is applicable to drama only. Bharata, being solely interested in dramatic performance, wrote at best a manual of dramatic performance. Of course, he enumerated the *gunas* (merits) and *doshas* (defects) of dramatic language, but did not take notice of poetry as a whole. Dandin's critical theory is for all kinds of poetry.

First, his definition of poetry is quite modern. No critic of the West, even Horace and Longinus, defined poetry linguistically. Being himself a creative writer and fully trained in Sanskrit grammar, he defined poetry as a body constituting strings of words organized in a special way for the expression of (the poet's) intended meaning. His definition is far superior to that of Robert Frost who defined poetry as a string of words. He is very near to the Russian formalists who defined literature as "semiotic mediation of reality". Dandin's use of the word *shariram*, meaning a poem is a body, is very close to the American new critics who considered a poem as an organistic whole. Dandin's statement that poetry is concrete (being made of words) and that it has its own existence as a body surprises us as this kind of statement was made by the Russian Formalists and American critics in the twentieth century.

His *marga* theory anticipates modern stylistics. He rejects the earlier classification of the trends (*pravrittis*) in different regions. The Southern diction was called *Vaidarbha*, the Northern *Panchali*, and the Western *Avanti*. Dandin classified the dominant poetic dictions or styles into *Dakshinatya* and *Paurastya* on the basis of their linguistic features. The other name that he gave to the *Dakshinatya* (Southern) poetic diction was *Vaidarbha* and to the North-eastern diction *Gauda*. He also said that the two kinds of poetic diction were not solely confined to these regions. There were poets who wrote in the *Gauda* style though they belonged to the Southern region and likewise *Vaidarba* style was practised by many poets in the North-east region. Besides, he added, every poet has his own style which can be recognized by its linguistic signals.

Dandin was the first Sanskrit critic to classify the different genres of *kavya* (poetry). His classification is so scientific that we follow it even today. The broad division of *kavya* into prose, verse and mixed is still valid and so is his acceptance of the literature written in *Prakrit*, *Apabhransha* and *misra* (mixture of *Prakrit* and *Apabhransha*). This acceptance of the regional languages made him develop his theory of poetry all-comprehensive. The division of the *Prakrit* words into *tatsama*, (words of Sanskrit in their pure form), *tadbhava* (Sanskrit words modified by *Prakrit* morphology) and *desin* (local words) has not yet been revised; so scientific is his classification.

Finally, his revision of Bharata's *gunas* and *doshas*, the emphasis on *arthalankara* (the figures of speech that determine a poem's meaning) and *svabhavokti* is of utmost importance. The new critics could not explain why "Twinkle, twinkle little star/How I wonder what you are," appeals to us and how the entire poem is a wonderful piece of poetry. Once we accept Dandin's concept of *svabhavokti* and apply it to the analysis of this poem, we immediately are in a position to explain its intrinsic merit. The poem fits in Dandin's famous definition of poetry. By laying emphasis on *alankara* as the integral part of the body of poetry he has differentiated it from other modes of writing. In fact, he is the first specifier; Roman Jakobson and Viktor Shklovsky came about twelve hundred years later and yet did not attain his height so far literary criticism is concerned.

(C) BHAMAHA

Bhamaha followed Dandin largely and accepted his concept of poetry that it is a body constituting sound and sense (word and meaning) which is beautified by *alankara*. Earlier, it was believed that Bhamaha preceded Dandin and, so, S.K. De inspite of all his learning could not make a proper assessment of

Bhamaha in his *History of Sanskrit Poetics* and gave him all the credit that was due to Dandin. P.V. Kane[17] was right and he always maintained that Dandin preceded Bhamaha.

Bhamaha is great as he corrected Dandin at many places and posited a theory that was followed by Udbhata, Rudrata and, later on, by Kuntaka. The fact is that many of the eminent critics named their works after his *kavyalankara*. The title is quite specific and pin-pointed. Dandin's *kavyadarsha* considers poetry as a whole, but Bhamaha focus his attention on *alankara* and declares that it is the essence of poetry. If Dandin takes natural expression (*svabhavokti*) as an important element of *alankara*, Bhamaha excludes it and considers *vakrokti* only and declares that it is the base of all *alankaras*.

The basic problem before Bhamaha was: How does the language of poetry differ from the language of ordinary life? His answer is that poetical language aims at being striking or arresting. Strikingness consists in *vakrokti* (a twist in expression). Bhamaha's notion of *vakrokti* is very near to the Russian Formalist's concept of defamiliarization or *bestrangement*. The British stylisticians call it *deviation*, which may be at phonological, morphological, and syntactic levels. Bhamaha's concept includes meaning also. And this is very significant. In his definition of poetry, he includes word and meaning and considers both prose and verse as poetry:

Shabdarthau sahitau Kavyam gadya padyam cha tad vidha.[18]

Following Dandin he rejects Bharata's *rasa* theory and expresses the view that the two elements that complete the structure of poetry are word and meaning (in modern terms, signifier and signified) and the *alankaras*, which adorn the structure form the essential design[19] of *kavya*. All the three are inextricably woven as words themselves are poetic figures.

---

17. P.V. Kane was awarded Bharat Ratna for his scholarship.
18. शब्दार्थौ सहितौ काव्यं गद्यपद्यं च तद् विधा।
19. This idea is very near to John Crowe Ransom's idea of logical structure (the meaning) and local texture (the tropes or peotic figures).

Kavyalankara

The treatise is divided into six chapters and deals with the following topics:

1. *Kavyasharir* (Chapter I, 60 verses)
2. *Alankara* (Chapters II & III, 160 verses)
3. *Dosha* (Chapter IV, 50 verses)
4. *Nyaya* (Chapter V, 70 verses)
5. *Shabdashuddhi* (Chapter VI, 60 verses)

Chapter I

In this chapter Bhamaha makes preliminary remarks about the general characteristics of poetry and its different forms. First, he states the purposes of poetry (*kavya-prayojana*)[20] and the qualifications of a poet (*kavya-hetu*)[21] and, incidentaly, mentions the sources of poetry (*kavya-yonayah*).

Why does a poet write? This question is answered in the heading, "The Purposes of Poetry". A poet composes poems to gain wealth, social success and escape from ills, but why does a person read a poem? The reason that Bhamaha gives is that he/she reads for solace, instruction in knowledge and proficiency in the arts and ways of the world. In the West, the ancient critics were satisfied with the functions of poetry and never thought why a poet wrote poetry. Bhamaha and his predecessors looked at both the sides and understood the relationship between the reader and the writer. Secondly, Aristotle mentioned delight, morality, and aesthetic pleasure. The Sanskrit critic's horizon is wider. Apart from aesthetic pleasure they lay stress on pure knowledge and knowledge of the social world, that is, readers gain a good idea of the ways of the world through *kavya* (literature). In other words, readers understand social reality through literature; literature and society are inextricable.

Then he gives his famous definition of *kavya*:

---

20. काव्य प्रयोजन
21. काव्य हेतु; काव्ययोनय:

Shabdarthau sahitau gadyapadyam cha tadvidha[22]. Here he includes both prose and verse within the ambit of *kavya* (poetry). This inclusion is of great significance. S.K. De comments:

> "The doctrine that prose is the opposite, not of poetry but of verse, which began to be realised rather late in European critical theories, was very early admitted without question by Sanskrit authors with whom metre[23] does not play the same part as it does in European poetry; for in India from the earliest times, it was usual to put down even the driest teachings in a metrical form."[24]

It is important to note that Dandin's *Dashakumaracharitam* and Banabhatta's *Kadambari*, both written in prose, were considered *kavya* by all.

Like Dandin, he states that there is an inseparable relationship between the author and the reader. The most important requirement of a poet is besides a sound knowledge of grammar and ways of the world, *pratibha* (poetic genius) which is *naisargiki* (bestowed by nature) or *sahaja* (inborn). He is a *malakar* (maker of garland), who makes garlands of words[25]. The reader should be *sahridaya*, that is, he should possess the ability to appreciate poetry. Bhamaha's and Dandin's concepts of *sahridaya* is very close to Dr. F.R. Leavis's, "the common reader", who reads literature without bias and appreciates it.

After defining poetry that it should possess both sound and sense and be faultless and embellished by *alankaras* he classifies *kavya* from four points of view: form, language, subject-matter and convention.

1. According to form *kavya* is broadly divided into verse and prose. Besides, there is *mishra* as defined by Dandin
2. The second kind of classification, according to the language employed, is the division of *kavya* into Sanskrit, Prakrit and Apabhransha.

---

22. शब्दार्थौ सहितौ गद्यपद्यं च तद् विधा।
23. S.K. De should have used the term "rhyme", not "metre".
24. S.K. De, *History of Sanskrit Poetics*, Part II, 45.
25. मालाकारो रचयति यथा साधु विज्ञाय मालां योज्यं काव्येष्ववहितधिया तद्वदेवाभिधानम्।

3. According to the subject-matter, Bhamaha groups poetic compositions into four divisions. In the first group are the compositions dealing with human beings. In the second group are the compositions dealing with divine beings.

   The compositions of the third group are the products of a poet's imagination, that is, the incidents described are neither legendary nor historical, and the fourth group of poetic compositions deal with science and art.
4. The fourth point view is the conventional way of classification of *Kavya* into *sargabandha* or *mahakavya* (epic), *abhineyartha* (drama), *akhyayika*, *katha*, and *anibaddhakavya* (short poems and *shlokas*).

Surprisingly, Bhamaha does not pay sufficient attention to poetic diction. He follows Dandin's *Vaidarbha* and *Gauda margas* without any comment or modification but reduces his ten *gunas* to three: *madhurya*, *ojas*, and *prasada*. Besides, he considers them to be *alankaras* because, in his opinion, they are the qualities of good poetry and not qualities of any particular diction. S.K. De writes:

It is noteworthy that this brief description of the *gunas* precedes in the context of the treatment of *alankaras*, implying probably that they are analogous to each other. It is also noteworthy that Bhamaha does not employ the term *guna* at all, except in another context in connection with the *Bhavika alankara* which he, like Dandin, designates as *prabandha-guna*[26].

Chapters II and III

These two chapters comprising 147 verses are devoted to *alankara*. By *alankara* Bhamaha means those poetic figures that beautify and enrich the meaning of poetry. As he gives equal importance to sound and sense, he lays stress on both *shabdalankara*, (the *alankara* which beautifies the sound) and *arthalankara* (the alankara which enriches the meaning of poetry). He writes that a damsel must be adorned to look beautiful.

26. S.K. De, *History of Sanskrit Poetics*, Part II, 46.

For him, *vakrokti* (indirect expression) is the base of all *alankaras*. He rejects Dandin's *svabhavokti* as it lacks strikingness. The literal meaning of *vakra* is "crooked"/"not straight". The word *ukti* means "statement". Thus, the literal meaning of *vakrokti* is "an expression or statement which is not straight or plain". A poet deviates from the natural expression or commonly accepted word structure and sentence structure to draw the listener's or reader's attention. Therefore, when a poet deviates from the norms his expression must have the quality of strikingness. Kuntaka developed Dandin's and Bhamaha's concept of *vakrokti* further in his monumental and strikingly modern treatise *Vakrokti Jeevitam*.

Bhamaha recognizes thirty-nine *alankaras* and defines them precisely. The thirty-nine *alankaras* are:

1. anuprasa	2. yamaka	3. rupaka
4. dipaka	5. upama	6. prativastupama
7. akshepa	8. vyatireka	9. arthantaranyasa
10. vibhavana	11. samasokti	12. atishayokti
13. yathasankhya	14. utpreksha	15. svabhavokti
16. preyas	17. rasavat	18. urjosvi
19. pargayokta	20. samahita	21. udatta
22. slishta	23. apahnuti	24. visheshokti
25. virodha	26. tulyayogita	27. aprastuta-prashansa
28. vyajstuti	29. nidarshana	30. upama-rupaka
31. upameyopama	32. sahokti	33. parivritti
34. sasandeha	35. ananyava	36. utprekshavayava
37. sansrishti	38. bhavika	39. ashih

He denies *hetu*, *sukshma*, *lesha*, and *vartta* the status of *alankara*, though they are recognized by others.

Chapter IV discusses the *doshas* of poetic composition and almost repeats Dandin with minor differences. Amongst his six general *doshas*, *neyartha* (far fetchedness) is very much like Dandin's *neyatra* and *klishta* (obscurity), *anyartha* (absene of sense), and *avachaka* (inexpressiveness) are developed from *vyutopanna*. Of his four defects of speech, *shrutidushta* (explicitly indecent), *arthadusta* (implicitly indecent), and *kalpanadushta* (indecent in the collocation of words) are the elaborate forms of Dandin's *gramya* and the last *shrutikashta* (cacophony) corresponds to *dipta* of the older theorist.

Chapter V

In this chapter, Bhamaha discusses the logical aspects of poetry. The topics of *Nyaya-vaisheshika* like *pramana* (evidence), *prajna* (intelligence), *hetu* (cause) and *drishtanta* (analogy) are dealt with in brief.

Chapter VI deals with grammatical correctness of poetic compositions.

Bhamaha's total concentration is on *alankara*. If he has discussed the *doshas*, logicality and grammatical correctness of poetry, he has done it all in relation to *alankara*. Udbhata and Rudrata followed him almost faithfully and Kuntaka expanded his concept that *vakrokti* is the base of all *alankaras*.

(D) VAMANA

Vamana continued and developed the concept that poetry is a body constituting words organized in a special way for the expression of the desired meaning. A true successor of Dandin and Bhamaha, he focused his attention on the organization of words into sentences that make poetry. He, too, like Dandin and Bhamaha, is a specifier mainly concerned with the question: what makes poetry? To answer this question, he coined the word *reeti*, which in our time may mean style. Professor S.K. De in his *History of Poetics* says that *reeti* does not mean "style", but in his time scholars followed Pater's vague interpretation of the term. At present, style means the organization of words in a special way. Every writer has certain pet words, phrases, and syntactic structures. We know an author's style by his linguistic signals. Modern stylistics study the linguistic features of creative writers. If we follow our present time definition of stylistics, we find that Vamana is the first stylistician. Clifford Leech and H.W. Widdowson came about one thousand years later.

S.K. De begins his appraisal of Vamana as:

> "Vamana's work in comparison with Dandin's shows further progress and elaboration of the ideas discussed above[27]. Indeed what is vague and unsystematic in Dandin appears fully developed and carefully set forth

27. The ideas of Dandin and Bhamaha.

> in Vamana who may, thus, be fittingly regarded as the best representative of the *Reeti* system. To Vamana belongs the credit of being the first writer on poetics who, before the Dhvanikara and Anandavardhana, gave us a well thought-out and carefully outlined scheme of poetics, no longer, naive or tentative, which inspite of its theoretical defects, is in some respects unique and valuable."[28]

In the same way professor A.P. Mishra praises the celebrated theoretician:

> "Vamana is in fact the first rhetorician who first (sic) conceived of the soul of poetry (The). Thought about the soul of poetry was in fact the first attempt to have a vision of the essential or the intrinsic element of poetry."[29]

S.K. De has exaggerated Vamana's merit. Dandin's vision was comprehensive. He examined poetry linguistically and refuted the *rasa* theory that had been dominating the literary world for more than one thousand years. His views are strikingly modern as discussed above. What Vamana did was an improvement upon the *marga* theory. The *reeti* theory is not entirely different from the *marga* theory; it, at best, refines it and opens the way to look at the body of poetry more scientifically. As said earlier, he is an Indian stylistician and it is unfortunate that he was not followed by others except Rajanaka Kuntaka.

Dr. Mishra has misunderstood Vamana's words, "*Reetiratma Kavyasya*". He has, like many, failed to connect the two sentences that follow it. They are: "*Vishishta padarachana reetih. Vishesho gunatma*"[30]. What, in fact, Vamana means by "soul" (*atma*) is that *reeti* is the most vital part of the body of poetry. Just as after the departure of the soul, the body is dead, the *kavya sharira* will be lifeless if there is not *reeti*. And what is

---

28. S.K. De, *History of Sanskrit Poetics*, 89-90.
29. A.P. Mishra, "Contribution of *Reeti* in the Excellence of Poetic Composition", *Principles of Literary Criticism in Sanskrit*, ed., R.C. Dwivedi (Varanasi: Motilal Banarasidas, 1969), 146.
30. रीतिरात्मा काव्यस्य। विशिष्ट पदरचना रीतिः। विशेषो गुणात्मा।

reeti? The answer is that it is the organization of words in a special way. Vamana has simply made an improvement upon Dandin's *vyavachhinna padavali*.

Vamana has propounded the *reeti* theory in his magnumopus *Kavayalankarasutra*. In making chapter divisions, he has deviated rom the current practice of making *adhyaya* as the main chapter and *adhikaran* as the subdivision, and followed the old system of *sutra*-writers who made *adhikaran* as the main chapter and *adhyaya* as the subdivision.

Kavyalankarasutra is divided into five *adhikaranas*:

1. *Sharira*. Like Dandin's *Kavyadarsha* and Bhamaha's *Kavyalankara, Kavyalankarasutra* opens with the objectives of poetry and the qualifications of a poet. The stress is on the qualities, which an initiate should possess for instruction in the art of poetry. Then follows the definition of *reeti*, its subdivisions, and the subsidiary aids. Finally, poetry and its different genres are discussed.
2. *Dosha-darshana*. As the title of the *adhikarana* shows, Vamana throws light on the different kinds of flaw in poetic composition.
3. *Guna-Vivechana*. Here, the *gunas* of poetry are discussed. Vamana rejects Bhamaha's reduction of the number of ten *gunas* and follows Bharata and Dandin. Of course, he differs from them in defining the meaning of the *gunas* at some places.
4. *Alankarika*. In this *adhikarana*, Vamana discusses the figures of speech and explains them with illustrations.
5. *Prayogika*. This *adhikarana* sets forth the conventions of poetry writing and propriety of usage. Like the last chapter of Bhamaha's *Kavyalankara*, it discusses in detail grammatical correctness.

In the very beginning of his treatise *Kavyalankarasutra*, Vamana says that word and meaning are the body of poetry and *reeti* is the soul. What *reeti* is then? He defines that *reeti* is the organization of words in a special way, and this special organization rests upon the combination of the *gunas* or fixed excellences of composition.

He follows Dandin largely in the varieties or kinds of *reeti*. Dandin had recognized two kinds of style, *Vaidarbha* and *Gauda*, and called them *marga*. Vamana changed the name *marga* into *reeti* and recognized the third kind, *Panchali* (now modern western UP). The main principle of his categorization is the frequency of the *gunas* in a particular region or writing. Following Dandin, he says that *Vaidarbha* is the best as it contains all the ten *gunas*, and *Gauda* and *Panchali* are inferior as the former abounds in *Ojas* and *Kanti* and the latter in *madhurya* and *saukumarya*.

Like Banabhatta, Dandin, and Bhamaha, he names the *reetis* after the regions where they flourished. Here is the paraphrase of his statement in Sanskrit.

> "The names of different *reetis* are given according to prevalence of the *gunas* in Vidarbha, Gauda, and Panchala countries."[31]

S.K. De comments on the original passage:

> "This makes it probable that the theory of diction, peculiar to this school, originally arose from the empirical analysis of the prevailing peculiarities of poetic expression in different places and furnishes another proof of the general *a posteriori* character of the discipline itself."[32]

The *Gunas*

The *gunas* are the determining features of style. Vamana follows Bharata and Dandin and rejects Bhamaha so far their number is concerned. He accepts the idea that there are ten *gunas*. But he doubles the number by classifying *gunas* into *shabdagunas* and *arthagunas*. The ten plus ten *gunas* of Vamana are given below.

---

31. विदर्भ गौडयाऽचालेज़ु तत्रत्यैः **कविभीयथास्वरूपम्** उपलब्धत्वाद् तत्समाख्या न पुनर्देशैः किंचिद् उपक्रियते काव्यानाम्।

32. S.K. De, *History of Sanskrit Poetics*, Vol. II, 91.

Shabdaguna	*Arthaguna*
1. *Ojas* = *gudhabandhatva* (compactness of word organization)	1. *Ojas* = *arthasya pravadhih* (maturity of conception)
2. *Prasada* = *shaithilya* (easiness of structure)	2. *Prasada* = *artha-vaimalya* (clarity of meaning)
3. *Shlesha* (coalescence of words resulting in smoothness)	3. *Shlesha ghatana* (blend of many ideas)
4. *Samata* (smoothness of construction)	4. *Samata* (logical sequence of ideas)
5. *Samadhi* (symmetry)	5. *Samadhi* (grasp of the original meaning)
6. *Madhurya* (distinctness of words and avoidance of long *samasas*)	6. *Madhurya* (strikingness of expression)
7. *Saukumarya* (softness/tenderness)	7. *Saukumarya* (agreeable ideas)
8. *Udarata* (liveliness)	8. *Udarata* (the quality of being cultured)
9. *Artha-vyakti* (concrete words)	9. *Artha-vyakti* (easy grasp)
10. *Kanti* (brilliance)	10. *Kanti* (prominence of the *rasas*)

Vamana has deviated from Bharata's meaning of the ten *gunas* and also from Dandin's. His inclusion of *rasa* in the tenth *guna Kanti* is something new. However, Vamana has complicated the relationship between the word and its meaning. It would have been better if he had not classified the *gunas* into *shabdaguna* and *arthaguna*. He is rather prescriptive here and we all know now that the relationship between the *vachaka* (signifier) and the *vachya* (signified) is arbitrary and there is always the possibility of plurality of meaning in a literary text.

The *Alankaras*

Vamana does not follow Dandin and Bhamaha in his analysis of the *alankara*. For him *gunas* are primary qualities or merits of poetry and *alankaras* come next to them. This is because it is they that make poetry good poetry. The Vaidarbha *reeti* is the best as it contains all the ten *gunas* whereas the Gauda and the Panchala *reetis* possess only two *gunas* each. So far *alankaras* are concerned they are common to all the three *reetis*.

Vamana reduces the number of *alankaras* to thirty only. *Alankaras* are important as they make poetry beautiful and charming. But his treatment of *alankaras* is rather idiosyncratic and he defines them in a very different way. He tells that *Upama* (simile) is the base of all *alankaras*. On account of this postulate, he excludes such important poetic figures as *paryayokta*, *preyas*, *rasavat*, *urjasvin*, *udatta*, *bhavika*, and *sukshma*. He gives a strange definition of *vakrokti*. For him it is a metaphorical expression.

While comparing *gunas* and *alankaras*, he says that *gunas* are *nitya* (constant) and *alankaras* are *anitya* (variable) and, so, good poetry will be shorn of its splendour if its *gunas* are taken off but nothing will happen if its *alankaras* are dropped off. This view of Vamana is erroneous for us. We all know that metaphor, metonymy, paradox, symbolism, parallelism, and imagery make a piece of writing poetic.

Because of its inherent *doshas* (flaw) and contradictions Vamana's *reeti* theory was not carried on by the next generation. However, his contribution to Sanskrit poetics is of great value. The propounders of *Dhvani* theory, Dhvanikara and Anandavardhana, and the two greats, Abhinavagupta and Mammata, praised him and accepted the truth that *reeti* (style) matters much in the making of poetry. Besides, Vamana opened the way to Rajanaka Kuntaka to develop his famous concept of *Vakrokti*.

(E) ANANDAVARDHANA

Anandavardhana, a scholar from Kashmir, propounded a new theory of poetry, which is generally known as *dhvani* theory. Earlier it was believed that he was the writer of both the *Karika* and the *Vritti*[33]. Now, it is established by internal evidence that the *Karika* was written by another person whose name is still not known. For the sake of convenience he is called by the name of Dhvanikara[34]. Anandavardhana wrote *vritti* (commentary) on the text in verse (*Karika*) and developed the *dhvani* theory. So, comprehensive and authentic is the commentary that scholars accepted Anandavardhana as the propounder of *dhvani* theory.

33. Vritti = Commentary/explication

34. The other name is Sahridaya.

We shall discuss the theory in this chapter on the basis of both *Karika* and *Vritti* combined. It is also that *Dhvanyaloka* is always published with *Karika* and *Vritti* together as if written by the same person. Dhvanikara's *Karika* is in verse and needs explanation. Anandavardhana's *vritti* is in prose and explains the verses with comments and illustrations.

In the very beginning of *Dhvanyaloka*, Anandavardhana declares that *dhvani* is the soul (*atman*) of poetry. Perhaps, because he did not find a better word, he used the word *atman*, but in fact, like Dandin and Bhamaha, he differentiated poetry from other modes of discourse and set a standard for distinguishing good poetry from the ordinary. Dhavanikara and Anandavardhana deviated from Dandin, Bhamaha, and Vamana in the sense that whereas those three focused their attention on the structure of a literary text and its literal and metaphorical meanings, these two laid stress on the suggested meaning (*dhvani* or *vyangyartha*), the meaning coming out of the total work but seldom said overtly in the text.

What is *dhvani*? In general sense it means sound. The grammarians of *Sphota* theory used it in a different sense. According to them a listener understands a spoken word with *sphota* (plosion). For example, the word *sin* consists of three speech sounds, s + i + n. The listener understands the word when the speaker utters the last sound (phoneme). The first two sounds or phonemes remain meaningless till the sound *n* is reached. Once the listener hears the phoneme *n* the meaning is realized with a plosion or *sphota*. The question arises, how does he come to know that the word is *sin*? The answer is that the word is already present in his mind. If it were not so, he would not have understand it. The grammarians divide words into two groups:

(a) the *nitya* or original word, which is in the listener's mind, and
(b) the articulated or imitated word, which the listener hears.

This concept of the *nitya* word and the uttered word is very much close to Ferdinand de Saussure's concept of *langue* and *parole*. *Langue* is the system of language and *parole* is the actual speech act. Noam Chomsky's concept of *competence* and *performance* is also very close to the Sanskrit grammarians. *Competence* is the native speaker's ability to understand all the sentences of his language and *performance* is the actual use of language. The difference is that the *sphota* theory of grammar takes both words and syntactic structures in its province, whereas Saussure and Chomsky are concerned with the system of language only.

Anandavardhana has used the term *dhvani* differently. It is the suggested meaning which is realized with a plosion (*sphota*). The suggested meaning is more important than the literal meaning. Good poetry is always suggestive. In the first *Karika* of *Udyota* 1, he says that *dhvani* is the soul of poetry. He accepts the definitions of poetry by Bhamaha and Dandin and, also, Vamana's theory of style. But he continues, these critics touch only the periphery and ignore *dhvani*, which is the essence of poetry. After rejecting his predecessors, excluding Bharata, he states

> योऽर्थः सहृदयश्लाघ्यः काव्यात्मेति व्यवस्थितः।
> वाच्यप्रतीयमानाख्यौ तस्य भेदावुभौ स्मृतौ।।

(*Dhvani* is that meaning embedded in the text, which is admired by the *sahridaya* reader. *Vachya* and *Prateeyamana* are its two kinds.)

We can interpret this definition of *dhvani* in the following way: *Dhvani* is the total meaning of a literary text. *Vachya* is the overt meaning and *prateeyamana* is the implied meaning. For example, Wordsworth's "A slumber did my spirit seal" mourns Lucy's death. Wordsworth does not use "die", "death" or "dead" in the poem. We read that she has no motion of her own and that she neither hears nor sees. This is the overt meaning. But, these words suggest the meaning that she is lifeless, she is dead. This is implied meaning or *prateeyamana*. The term *prateeyamana* is explained in *Karika* 4 of *Udyota* 1.

> प्रतीयमानं पुनरन्यदेव वस्त्वस्ति वाणीषु महाकविनाम्।
> यत् तत् प्रसिद्धावयवातिरिक्तं विभाति लावण्यमिवाङ्गनासु।।

(Just as a damsel's beauty shines besides the parts of her body, *prateeyamana* glitters in the language of great poets.)

In simple words, *vachya* is the expressed meaning and the implied meaning is *prateeyamana*. Anandavardhana lays more emphasis on *prateeyamana* as the essence of good poetry. The knowledge of morphology and syntax will help a reader to know the *vachyartha* of a text but, will not help in knowing its implied meaning. For this, he has to be a *kavyamarmajna*[35]. In order to be a *kavyamarmajna*, he has to develop a literary taste by studying good poetry.

Anandavardhana uses the term *vangya* (व्यंग्य) in *Vritti* 7. This word is derived from the word *vyanjana*, which means "the thing that enhances the power of seeing". The other term he uses is *vyanjaka*. A great poet chooses those words, which mean more than their literal meaning. The artistic use of *vyanjna* and *vyanjaka*[36] makes a poem great, not the use of mere *vachya* and *vachaka*. However, the relation between *vachya* and *vyanjna* is of inter-dependence. The *vyangyartha*, the implied meaning, can be deduced from the *vachyartha* only. *Vachya* is the foundation and *vyangya* is the edifice built on it. *Vachya* is the lamp and *vyangya*, the light. It is the lamp that gives us light. Likewise, a reader goes from *vachyartha* to *vyangyartha* of a poem. And that poem is a good poem where there is the dominance of *vyanjana*, not of *abhidha* and *lakshana*.

As has been rightly pointed out by S.K. De, P.V. Kane, and as early as Abhinavagupta, the *Karikas* were written by an unknown person (Dhvanikara/Sahridaya) and the *vrittis* (commentary) by Anandavardhana. Anandavardhana, perhaps, compiled the verses called *Karika*. Perhaps, he missed a few and so, there is a sudden jump from *prateeyamana* to *vyangya* in *vritti 7* and *vritti 8* and after that *prateeyamana* is seldom mentioned. Because of this, we can assume that *prateeyamana* and *vyangya* refer to the same concept and the term *dhvani* and *vyangartha* are synonymous.

---

35. काव्यमर्मज्ञ = an appreciative reader who understands poetry to the core.

36. व्यंजक is the signifier व्यंग्यार्थ (signified) or *dhvani* is the suggested meaning.

In the second *Udyot* (chapter), the two kinds of *dhvani* are discussed. The first is *avivakshitvachya* (*lakshanamool*) and *vivakshitanyaparvachya* (*abhidhamool*) footnote. Before coming to the subdivisions of these kinds, it is important to understand the meaning of the terms *abhidha* and *lakshana*.

The term *abhidha* means a plain statement or referential use of language. All the words used in a sentence are denotative and the sentence itself is not structurally ambiguous.

The term *lakshana* is equivalent to metaphor, metonymy and synecdoche. When we say, "He is a donkey", we mean that "he is a fool". In other words, he has the characteristics of a donkey.

The other term *vyanjana* on which Anandavardhana lays great emphasis, literally means "one that gives extra power of seeing". We all know that *anjana* is a medicine to make our eye-vision clearer. The prefix *vi* means "one that wakes". Thus, *vyanjaka* is the word, word group, or sentence that leads the reader to see *vyangyartha* or *prateeyamana*. For example, there is *vyanjana* in these lines of W.B. Yeats.

> "Only an aching heart/conceives a changeless work of art."

Here the phrase "an aching heart" refers not to the physical pain, but to spiritual or mental pain and similarly "a changeless work of art" to a work of art which is permanent and not affected by time. The explained phrases in the quoted lines are *vyanjakas*.

Avivakshitvachya[37] is divided into *arthantarsankramitavachya*[38] and *atyantatiraskritavachya*[39]. *Vivakshitanyaparvachya*[40] is divided into *asanlakshyakramavyangya*[41] and *sanlakshya-kramavyangya*[42]. The first one is constituted by *rasa*, *bhava*, *rasabhasa*, and *bhavaprasham*, and they occupy the principal position. When *rasa*, *bhava*, *rasabhasa*, and *bhavaprasham* are *subordinate*, and *rasavadalankar*[43] is prominent, there is *sanlakshyakramavyangya*.

---

37. अविवक्षितवाच्य 38. अर्थान्तर संक्रमितवाच्य 39. अत्यन्त तिरस्कृतवाच्य 40. विवक्षितान्यपरवाच्य 41. असंलक्ष्यक्रमव्यंग्य 42. संलक्ष्यक्रमव्यंग्य 43. रसवदलंकार (रसवत् + अलंकार)

It is important to note that Anandavardhana does not negate the values of *alankara* and *rasa*; what he says is that both the two are subordinate to *dhvani*, which is the soul of poetry. After all a reader/listener is primarily concerned with the total meaning of poetry.

In the second *Udyota*, the division of *dhvani* was made from the point of view of *vyangyartha*; in the third *Udyota* it is from the angle of *vyanjaka*. *Vyanjaka* is of two kinds: *padaprakasha* and *vakyaprakasha*. The first, *padaprakasha*, is a group of words that give expression to the suggested meaning (*vyangya*) and the second is the whole sentence. Anandavardhana quotes from the *Mahabharata*, *Meghadutam*, and *Abhigyanshakuntalam* to explain the use of *padaprakasha vyanjaka* and a *shloka* from Prakrit with Sanskrit translation for the second one.

After discussing the *Abhidhamool* and *Lakshanamool* poetic dictions Anandavardhana declares that the poem or creative writing where the suggested meaning (*vyangyartha* or *prateeyamanartha*) is dominant is of the best kind and it is called *dhvanikavya*. The next, slightly inferior, is *gunibhoot-vyangya* where, though there is *vyangya*, the expressed sense (*avivakshitvachya*) is more appealing. The third which is really inferior is *chitrakavya*, where *vyangya* (suggested meaning) is least manifest.

The fourth and the last *Udyota* is the shortest and is devoted to *Kavipratibha*. The term *Kavipratibha* is quite comprehensive and it includes both imagination and poetic art. The poetic art lies in composing either *dhvani kavya* or *gunibhootvyangya kavya* under the inspiration of the old greats like Valmiki, Vyasa, and others. If a poet studies them and follows them meticulously, he gains novelty, though the words are old ones. This statement leads us to Matthew Arnold's touchstone method. He says that the greatness of a poem can be evaluated by comparing it to the old classics. Pope, too, advised the young poets to follow Homer and his art. Secondly, Anandavardhana has explicitly stated his inclination to experiments in diction in poetic composition.

He concludes the treatise by advising poets to focus on only one *rasa* as mixing of many *rasas* will dilute the effect of the main *rasa*. And so is the case with the use of figures of speech. The main aim of the poet should be to produce a *dhvani kavya*.

While making an assessment of Anandavardhana as a critic, it is pertinent to add that *Dhvanyaloka* was written by two persons. The *Karikas* (the original verses) were written by an unknown person, called Sahridaya or Dhvanikara and the *Vritti's* (commentary/explication) by Anandavardhana. The greatness of Anandavardhana lies in compiling and editing the *Karikas* and explaining them in prose. His contribution to Indian poetics is of immense value. In the words of Professor B.B. Paliwal:

> "The treatise itself is remarkable. It does not start with a technical definition of *kavya* and other allied topics. On the contrary, it refers to the very genesis of poetry and thereby gives a super mundane grandeur to the art of poetry. Secondly, the treatise totally avoids detailed discussion of the figures of speech, the *doshas*, the *gunas* and the like, which had so long been invariably associated with all the treatises on poetics.... On the other hand, it is he who for the first time saw these in the proper perspective. It is *Kavya* that he is dealing with and not merely the embellishment or blemishes of poetic composition."

Professor Paliwal is a bit off side in praising Anandavardhana and sidetracking Bharata, Bhamaha, Dandin, and other theorists. What we feel is that the Dhvanikara and Anandavardhana hit upon one of the most important aspects of poetry; they rightly pointed out that poetry is not a direct statement nor a series of figures of speech; it is the embedded meaning which, though very much based on the literal and metaphoric meaning, flashes before the appreciative reader (in Leavisian terms the Common Reader) with a *sphota* (plosion). Anandavardhana illustrates this embedded or suggested meaning (*vyangyartha* or *prateeyamanartha*) with quotations from the *Mahabharata*, *Meghadootam* and *Shakuntalam*. We quote the opening lines of Thomas Gray's *Elegy*.

The curfew tolls the knell of parting day,
The lowing herd wind slowly o'er the lea,
The plough man homeward plods his weary way,
And leaves the world to darkness and to me.

If we apply Anandavardhana's *dhvani* theory, we find that this stanza means more than the literal meaning of the words it contains. First, the arrival of evening is suggested by the tolling of the curfew bells, the departing day, the return of the cows from pasture, and of the tired ploughman from the field. Secondly, the word "darkness" is both physical and mental. The meaning of "darkness" is realized in its denotative sense, but the suggested meaning (*vyangyartha*) is the gloom (sad feeling) that envelopes the poet's mind. In the western criticism, it may be interpreted that the poet describes the arrival of the evening through a set of images, or according to Eliot, there is objective correlative, but Anandavardhana's theory better explains the total meaning of the stanza as it moves from *vachyartha* to *vyangyartha*, and is very near to Roland Barthes' textual analysis. Barthes writes in his famous article, "Textual Analysis: Poe's Valdemar":

> "Textual analysis does not try to find out what it is that determines the text (gathers it together as the end-term of a causal sequence), but rather how the text *explodes and disperses*."[44]

This statement of Barthes "how the text explodes" comes very near to the *sphota* theory of Sanskrit, the theory that became the base of *dhvani* theory in *Dhvanyaloka*. If Barthes had come across *Dhvanyaloka*, he must have paid a tribute to *dhvani* theory as did Ferdinand de Saussure to Panini. He, too, would have realized the greatness of Dhvanikara and Anandavardhana with a *sphota*.

(F) ABHINAVAGUPTA

Abhinavagupta was born in the latter half of the tenth century and lived for a long time. It is said that towards the end of his life, accompanied by 1200 disciples (both Hindus and Muslims), he entered the *Bhairava Gupha* and never returned

44. Italics mine.

from there. He remained a celebate throughout and lived the life of a yogi. He was a devout *Shaiva*, a profound philosopher, and eminent critic. Naturally, his theory of poetry, called *rasa-dhvani* theory, lays emphasis on tranquillity and *brahmananda* (supreme bliss). Whereas, critics before him considered *shringar rasa* supreme among the eight *rasas*, he declared that it is the *shanta rasa*, which is supreme.

Abhinavagupta removed the flaws and inconsistencies in *Dhvanyaloka* and built a well-defined poetics in *Dhvanyaloka Lochana*, popularly called *Lochana*. In the words of Professor Paliwal:

> "In Sanskrit poetics, these three (the Dhvanikara, Anandavardhana and Abhinavagupta) are like the *munitraya*[45] (Trinity) of Sanskrit poetics. If the Dhvanikara supplied the outline of a new approach to creative literature (*sic*), Anandavardhana developed it into a full-fledged theory by adding his *vritti* to it, and lastly, Abhinavagupta rendered it fool proof against all possible attacks and established the theory on the highest pedestal."

Abhinavagupta's commentaries on *Natyashastra* and *Dhvanyaloka* (both *Karika* and *Vritti*) explain not only the obscure parts of both the treatises but also perfects them. Because of the addition of original concepts and blend of the *rasa* and *dhvani* theories, he is considered as original as Bharata, Dhvanikara, and Anandavardhana. As his *Abhinava-Bharati* and *Dhvanyaloka Lochana* elucidate the *rasa* theory and *dhvani* theory respectively, it is more fruitful to enumerate the basic concepts of his poetics.

1. *Rasa-Dhvani* theory

According to Bharata, a literary text produces *rasa* to be relished by the reader or audience. This *rasa* is produced through the process of the arousal of one of the emotions dormant in man and addition of conflicting and transitory emotions to it to make it agreeable and appreciable. Since, *Natyashastra* is basically a treatise on dramaturgy, the main

---

45. मुनित्रय

focus is on dialogue and acting. Naturally, the later critics propounded new theories of poetry. Dhvanikara and Anandavardhana took poetry in its entirety for discussion and answered the most important question, What makes poetry"? In other words, what is that element that distinguishes poetry from other modes of discourse? The *dhvani* theorists answered that the basic element of poetry is *dhvani* or suggestion. In the words of Professor Bisvanath Bhattacharya.

"The words used by the poet do not convey merely the conventional expressed sense (*vachyartha*), nor the indicated (*lakshya*) one, but the suggested sense (*vyangyartha*) or *dhvani*."

Anandavardhana and his followers hold that the function of suggestion (*dhvani*) is the basic feature of poetry. Abhinavagupta fused the two opposing theories of poetry and propounded the new theory called *Rasa-dhvani* theory. He posited the view that poetry possesses two levels of meaning: direct and suggested. The direct meaning is of two types: the literal meaning of words (*vachyartha*) and of figures of speech (*lakshyartha*). The suggested meaning (*vyangyartha* or *prateeyamana*) is different from the direct meaning. It can be realized by the reader or listener with a plosion or flash. This meaning is the basic characteristic of poetry. In the writings of great poets the suggested meaning (*dhvani*) is more important than the direct meaning.

The suggested meaning (*dhvani*) is of three types. The first, *vastu dhvani*, suggests a thought or situation; the second, *alankara-dhvani*, suggests a figure of speech; the third, *rasa-dhvani*, which is of the highest kind, suggests a particular *rasa*. Professor G.T. Deshpande gives the following chart of the suggested meaning[46].

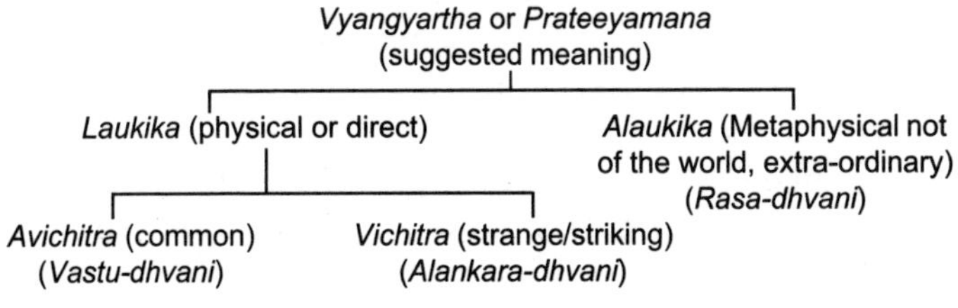

46. G.T. Deshpande, *Abhinavagupta*, (New Delhi : Sahitya Academy, 1989), 10T.

Abhinavagupta calls *rasa-dhvani alaukika* or *lokottara* (transcendental) as it gives a kind of aesthetic pleasure, which is beyond any kind of physical pleasure. The *vastu-dhavani kavya* leads the reader to the idea of an object or situation and nothing more. It never stirs the reader's imagination nor moves him deeply. The *alankara-dhvani kavya* makes the reader to marvel at the use of figures of speech like *upama* (simile), *rupaka* (metaphor), *anuprasa* (alliteration), and the like. The *rasa-dhvani kavya* produces *rasa* to be relished by the reader or the listener. The *rasa* of *rasa-dhvani kavya* is not the effect of direct statement (*vachya*) nor of figurative words (*lakshana*) but of *dhvani*, the suggested meaning.

Abhinavagupta's scholarship and literary taste are reflected in the analysis of passages in Sanskrit in the light of *rasa-dhvani* theory. So brilliant is his analysis of the passages and addition of logic to *rasa* theory and *dhvani* theory that literary critics of the past followed him faithfully, and even today, most of Sanskrit critics consider *rasa-dhvani* theory the perfect theory of poetry.

2. The Concept of Poetic Freedom

Abhinavagupta defended the character of *Pururavas* as depicted in *Vikramovarshiyam* by Kalidasa on the principle of aesthetic propriety.

He wrote in *Lochana*:

न वै दोषा दोषाः न च खलु गुणैव च गुणाः
निबद्धुः स्वातंत्र्यम् सपदि गुणदोषान् विभजते
इयम् सा वैदग्धी प्रकृतिमधुरा तस्य सुकवेः
यदत्रोनमादादपति-सुमगभावः परिणतः।

(The faults do not become faults, nor do excellences become excellences simply because of their enumeration of the *shastras*. In fact, it is the poetic freedom that distinguishes excellences from faults in a poem. It is the genius of that the scene has been made beautiful and effective by the poet through the insanity of *Pururavas*.) Unfortunately, his *Pururavovichara* (पुरूरवोविचार) is not available to us now.

In the same way, he defends poetic licence in *Ghatakarparakulakavivriti* (घटकर्पर कुलकविवृति). Critics rejected *Ghatakarpara* as a work of Kalidasa because there is the use of *yamaka*, an *alankara*, which would not be used by a great poet, it being of a very inferior quality. Abhinavagupta considers it a work of Kalidasa and defends the use of *yamaka* and shows how this *alankara* and the *vipralambha rasa* (sentiment of separation from lover) are effortlessly conjoined. He refers to Anandavardhana who wrote in *Dhvanyaloka*:

> "A figure of speech which can be used without a separate effort for it, while writing a poem containing *rasa*, such an *alankara* can be an integral part of the *Dhvanikavya*."

Abhinavagupta's deviation from the trodden path and descriptive criticism is a significant step in the development of Sanskrit poetics and his views on poetic licence or poet's freedom are valid for all time.

3. The concept of *Shanta Rasa*

Abhinavagupta added *shanta rasa* as the ninth *rasa* to Bharata's list of eight *rasas*. According to him, it is the basic *rasa* to which other *rasas* correspond. He devotes a full section on *shanta rasa* in *Abhinava Bharati*. Here is a brief summary of his views on this *rasa*.

There are four main aims of life: *dharma*, *artha*, *kama*, and *moksha*. Like the shastras, poetry (*kavya*) also presents them covertly. If it can present the first three through the eight *rasas*, it can also present the fourth aim of life, which is *moksha*. He asks the question: Why should it not be possible to present the *bhava* responsible for attaining *moksha*?

The *bhava* of *shanta rasa* is the *tattvajnana*[47]. The realization of ultimate reality or truth is the only means for liberation or *moksha* and the realization of the ultimate truth is nothing but the realization of the self (*atmajnana*)[48]. "Who I am". This

47. तत्त्वज्ञान

48. आत्मज्ञान

realization of the reality of "who I am" is pure bliss (*ananda*). Abhinavagupta says:

> "*Shanta rasa* is to be known as that which arises from the desire to secure liberation of the Self, which leads to the knowledge of truth and is connected with the property of highest bliss. Various feelings because of their particular respective causes arise from *Shanta* and when these causes disappear they melt back into *Shanta*." (G.T. Deshpande's translation)

Professor Deshpande summarises Abhinavagupta's notion of *Shanta rasa*: "The aesthetic universe should never be confused with the ordinary world of ours. This mundane world of ours is infested with pleasure and pain because of its empirical nature, while the aesthetic world has nothing of that type. It arises from Bliss (*ananda*), it manifests itself in Bliss, and it merges in Bliss from end to end."

4. The Audience and Dramatic Performance

Abhinavagupta's view of the audience's response to a dramatic performance is classic and reminds us of the German *Aesthetic-rezeption* theory developed by Woolfgang Iser and Godamar.

Abhinavagupta does not use the word "audience" or spectator (*darshaka*) but *sahridaya*, a person with a literary taste. When a *sahridaya* goes to a theatre, he goes with an aesthetic attitude like Charles Lamb. His attitude is different from the practical attitude of day-to-day life. He goes there to forget the world around him and live in an idyllic world, again like Charles Lamb, who forgot everything around him and was with Viola in the world of Illyria[49]. Here, wafted on the wings of poetry, the viewer is with the characters of the play and empathises with them. While watching the action, he forgets the limits of time and space, illusion and reality, and even the sense of right and wrong. The whole object presented cannot be called either illusion or reality of day-to-day life. It is poetic presentation of the world we live in. The characters are neither historical nor

---

49. See Charles Lamb's essay "Old China".

the people around us. What are they then? One may ask. The answer is that they are *alaukik* or *lokottara*, that is, they do not belong to our mundane world. We can compare Abhinavagupta's view with that of G. Wilson Knight who, too, says that Shakespeare's dramatic world is not worldly: but it is, on the other hand, a poetic world which needs imaginative interpretation.

The dramatist writes and presents his play in such a way as to elicit the desired responses from the audience, especially the *sahridaya*. The opening of *Abhijnana Shakuntalam* illustrates the author's art. There are small gaps between dialogues and situations till Dushyanta arrives at the stage, pursuing a terror stricken deer. The *sahridaya* fills in the small gaps through his imagination, and experiences the *bhayanaka rasa* when he hears the king's words about the deer running for its life. Although the *rasa* is *bhayanaka*, its *charvana* is aesthetically pleasant.

There is a difference between a layman and a *sahridaya*. A layman's aesthetic experience is limited to the senses of seeing and hearing. The *sahridaya* has imagination that leads him to *vyangyartha* through *vachyartha* and *lakshyartha*. The words spoken by king Dushyanta depict the pathetic and terrifying condition of the running deer. The total picture terrifies the *sahridaya* too. There is the *bhayanaka rasa* produced with the mixing of *bhava*, *vibhava*, *anubhava*, and *vyabhicharibhava*, and its *charvana* has the cathartic effect to free the self from the *sthayibhava* of *bhaya*. The total aesthetic experience is pleasant as it frees the self from fear and leads to bliss (*ananda*).

There is the process of *sadharanikarana* (universalization) in both viewing and reading processes. The *sahridaya*, whether a reader or viewer, empathises with the objects of the poetic world and shares their emotion. The relishing of *rasa* is possible only when he responds adequately to the different kinds of *bhavas* and for that his imagination plays the most important role.

(G) KUNTAKA

Rajanaka Kuntaka is the last original theorist. A junior contemporary of Abhinavagupta (mid tenth century to mid eleventh century), he was almost eclipsed by the giant personality of the elder. His book *Vakrokti-Jeevitam* was quoted occasionally and his name was also mentioned but critics like Mammata and Vishwanath did not pay any importance to his concept of *vakrokti*. The manuscript was found in the late nineteenth century and tribute must be paid to the late S.K. De for editing *Vakrokti-Jeevitam* and writing an enlightening introduction. Because of his old age and fading eyesight, he could edit the first two *Unmeshas* (chapters) only. Now all the four *Unmeshas* have been printed, excepting the last verses which are lost for ever.

Kuntaka inspite of his brilliance remained in oblivion for a very long time and when Dr. Hemlata R. Satpati read her "*Vakrokti* and Literary Criticism" in a national seminar organized by Rajasthan University in 1969, scholars did not ask her any questions.

Those who are well-acquainted with Russian Formalism, French Structuralism and American New Criticism will be struck with Kuntaka's modernity if they come across *Vakrokti-Jeevitam*. Before making a brief summary of the treatise, it is necessary to explain the concept of *vakrokti*.

The Concept of *Vakrokti*

The word *vakrokti* is made of *Vakra* (crooked, curved, not straight) and *ukti* (utterance, statement, speech). The general meaning of *Vakrokti* is a speech act which may be indirect, suggestive or ironical; it is never a straight forward or denotative. Dandin, the first great critic after Bharata, made difference between *svabhavokti* and *vakrokti*. For him, *svabhaokti* is the *adya alankritih* (आद्या अलंकृतिः), the first or primary poetic figure. In the following verse he speaks of both *svabhaokti* (स्वभावोक्ति) and *Vakrokti* (वक्रोक्ति):

> श्लेषः सर्वासु पुष्णाति प्रायो वक्रोक्तिषु श्रियम्।
> द्विधा भिन्नम् स्वभावोक्तिर्वक्रोक्तिश् चेति वाङ्.मयम्।।

Bhamaha rejected Dandin's idea that *svabhaokti* could be a figure of speech. He considered *vakrokti* as the base of all poetic figures. He wrote:

सैषा सर्वैव वक्रोक्तिरनयार्थो विभात्यते।
यत्नोऽस्याम् कविना कार्यः ओकऽलङ्.कारोऽनया विना।।

S.K. De explains this verse as:

'What is a poetic figure without *vakrokti?*', he characteristically asks; and as he lays down elsewhere that the *vakrokti* must be present in various kinds of poetic effort like the *mahakavya nataka*, *Katha*, and *akhyayika* as well as underlie a poetic figure as its essential mark, it is no wonder that he should regard *vakrokti* as primarily manifesting the sense of poetry and call upon the poet to be diligent with respect to it.[50]

Vamana followed Rudrata's notion of *vakrokti* partly. Rudrata had said that *vakrokti* is a mere poetic figure (काव्यालंकार) based upon a play upon words, and occurs in speeches of double meaning. The first meaning is the surface meaning, understood by the listening character, and the second the underlying meaning, which is usually opposite to the surface meaning. In other words, it is an ironical speech.

Vamana designated *vakrokti* a special poetic figure and gave it "a more or less general connotation to indicate a particular mode of metaphorical expression based on *lakshana* (लक्षणा).

The *arthalankara*, according to him, occurs where the indicated sense (लक्षणा) is based on the idea of similarity (सादृश्य). It is, thus, essentially a metaphorical mode of speech and is distinct from the *vakrokti* of earlier writers."[51]

Kuntaka followed the tradition of Dandin and Bhamaha, but rejected Dandin's classification of *alankara* into the broad divisions of *svabhaokti* (natural expression) and *vakrokti*. He followed Bhamaha who had posited the view that *vakrokti* is the base of all poetic figures.

Kuntaka's concept of *vakrokti* is complex, being the central point of his poetics. It is very near, but more comprehensive than Cleanth Brooks's concept of irony as propounded in his famous essay "Irony as a Principle of Structure", where he

50. S.K. De, "Indtroduction" *Vakrokti-Jeevitam,* xix.

51. *Ibid.*, xxiv-xxv.

defines irony as meaning warped by context and explains how irony is the structure of a good poem.

For Kuntaka, it is *vakrokti* that distinguishes poetry from other modes of discourse. In the very beginning of his treatise, he writes that his aim is to establish the concept of *vaichitrya* (strangeness, strikingness), which provides extraordinary charm to poetry.

लोकोत्तर चमत्कारि वैचित्र्य सिद्धये

In his *vritti* (prose commentary), he explains the term *Lokottara* (लोकोत्तर) that it is *extraordinary* (असामान्य) and the term *Vaichitraya* (वैचित्र्य) that it is strange. The term चमत्कारि means thrilling.

This pithy sentence means that Kuntaka is going to prove how poetry thrills the reader or listener with a kind of joy or wonder, which is extraordinary and strange (not experienced earlier). Kuntaka's concept of strangeness of expression is very much like Boris Eichenbaum's "bestrangement". While analysing Tolstoy's *Sevastopol Sketches*, Eichenbaum coined the term "bestrangement", which is derived from the root word "strange" with the addition of the prefix, *be* and the suffix, *ment*.

Viktor Shklovsky, leader of Russian Formalism in the twentieth century explained how Tolstoy made familiar objects unfamiliar or strange:

> "Tolstoy makes the familiar seem strange by not naming the familiar object. He describes an object as if he were seeing it for the first time, an event as if it were happening for the first time."

In other words, Tolstoy describes an object or event in an indirect way or in an unconventional way. And this is what Kuntaka says about *vakratva* or *vaichitraya* in the following quotes:

i. शास्त्रादि प्रसिद्ध शब्दार्थोयनिबंध व्यतिरेकि।
ii. प्रसिद्ध प्रस्थान व्यतिरेकि।
iii. अतिक्रान्त प्रसिद्ध व्यवहार सरणि।

S.K. De comments on the meaning and nature of *vakrokti*.

"...[It] consists of strikingness of expression, which is different from the established or current mode of speech, such as we find in the *shastras* and the like. It is, thus, a deviation from the matter-of-fact manner of treatment established in the sciences and the scripture; or, more widely from established usage in general."[52]

He refers to the great Sanskrit critic Mahimabhatta and his explanation of the term *Vakrokti*:

> "Mahimabhatta explains this standpoint clearly when he says that when contrary to established usage, an idea is expressed with a view to attain strikingness, we have what is called *vakrokti*."
>
> प्रसिद्धं मार्गं उत्सृज्य यत्र वैचित्र्य सिद्धये।

It follows then that *vakrokti* includes all kinds of deviation from the established convention. W.B. Yeats's line "Man has created death", Donne's "Death thou shalt die", and Keats', "Heard melodies are sweet/ But those unheard are sweeter" are some of the examples of *vakrokti*.

Vakrokti is not limited to a word, phrase, a line or a stanza; it is the very structure of a literary text.

Vakrokti-Jeevitam

The treatise is divided into four *unmeshas* (chapters) and *vakrata* is the basic concept that is dealt with in all its details in the text.

The first chapter is primarily concerned with the definition of poetry and the role of *vakrata* in making it different from other modes of discourse and endowing it with its special quality of thrilling the reader's/listener's heart. After defining poetry and explaining the concept of *vakrata,* Kuntaka analyses the previous theories of poetic diction, especially those of Dandin, Bhamaha, and Vamana. Then, he discusses Kshemendra's principle of

52. S.K. De almost echoes Viktor Shklovsky here without knowing him. The fact is: Kuntaka's and Shklovsky's ideas are almost identical, though the difference of time is about one thousand years.

auchitya (propriety) and his own concept of poetic diction and the three *margas*.

The second *unmesha* discusses the kinds of *vakrata* and *vaichitrya*, and explains how *vakrata* operates at different levels, from the *varna* (phoneme) to the entire text.

The third *unmesha* limits the number of *alankaras* to twenty only and does it rightly as many of the *alankaras* enumerated by the previous *alankarists* are superfluous.

The fourth *unmesha* is of great significance to modern readers as it discusses *prakaranvakrata*[53] (*vakrata* at the level of an episode) and *prabandhavakrata*[54] (*vakrata* underlying a text). Unfortunately, the last two or three pages of the fourth *unmesha* are lost.

Now, a detailed analysis of the treatise follows.

The word *unmesha* means the opening of eyes. Rajanaka Kuntaka very intelligently connects chapter division of *Vakroktijeevitam* with the key terms *vakra*, *vaichitrya*, and *bhangi*, the terms related to the eye.

The first *unmesha* (chapter) discusses the nature of literature, the features that distinguish it from other modes of discourse, the concepts of *vakrata*, *vaichitrya*, *ahlad*, *bhangi*, and the three kinds of *marga* (stylc) practised by poets. The great quality of Kuntaka is that he states his ideas in the *karikas*, which are in verse and explains them in the *vrittis* in prose and what is more significant is that he, like Anandavardhana, quotes profusely from established poets, both Sanskrit and Prakrit, for illustration and analysis.

He begins the treatise in the traditional way with a prayer to Shiva, the life giver. After that he prays to Shakti, the goddess who executes Shiva's will and gives life to all in the universe and whose dance is the source of all great poetry.

After the prayer and the declaration that poetry has its source in Shakti's dance, Kuntaka announces that he is going to write a treatise on *alankara*, which will explain how strangeness

53. प्रकरणवक्रता

54. प्रबन्धवक्रता

or strikingness forms the base of poetry, which gives an unearthly pleasure to man. This pleasure is miraculous in effect and is superior to the sweet taste people realize through the four fruits — अर्थ, धर्म, काम, मोक्ष — of life. The *shastras* are bitter medicines that cure people of their mental sickness, but poetry is heavenly nectar that enlightens the ignorant.

After declaring that poetry is superior to the *shastras* in both taste and effect, Kuntaka leads us straight to the concept of *literariness*, the basic quality that distinguishes literature or poetry from other modes of writing.

शब्दार्थौ सहितौ[55] वक्रकविव्यापारशालिनि।
बन्धे व्यवस्थितौ काव्यं तद्विदाह्लादकारिणि।।

Accepting Dandin's and Bhamaha's definitions of poetry that literature is a composite of sound and sense and that the words (the signifiers) are organized in a special way for the expression of the intended meaning, Kuntaka adds two more points. The first is the poet's creativity (प्रतिभा) in deviating from the convention for strangeness or strikingness, and the second is that he does so to make his poetry thrillingly joyful (आह्लादकारिणि). He lays great stress on कवि प्रतिभा or *kavi karma* (*vyapara/ Kaushal*). As the signifier (*vachaka*) and the signified (*vachya*) are inseparable the poet must choose them discreetly for *vaichitrya* (strangeness) and *ahlad* (great pleasure).

Kuntaka accepts Anandavardhana's and Dhvanikara's concept of *dhvani*, *vyanjana*, and *vivakshita*, and says that the poet has a number of words in his hands to express the intended meaning but uses the most appropriate word that signifies the intended meaning, the meaning, which transcends the literal meaning, and which gives a lively and aesthetic pleasure to the sympathetic reader or listener. However, selection of appropriate words and deviation from the conventional use is not sufficient. What is most significant is *vaichitrya* (strangeness, strikingness or wonderfulness) in the expression that gives a great pleasure.

---

55. Kuntaka uses the words शब्द and अर्थ in the *Karika* but the more technical terms *vachaka* (signifier) and *vachya* (signified) in the *vritti* (explanation in prose).

It is certain that poetic language differs from the natural expression. Dandin is wrong in making the division of *alankara* into *svabhaokti* (natural expression or plain statement) and *vakrokti* (indirect statement[56]) as a plain statement is neither a deviation from convention nor does it contain *vaichitrya*. Kuntaka supports Bhamaha's idea that *vakrokti* underlies all *alankaras*. In the famous *shloka* 10, he defines his concept of *vakrokti* and explains the concept in the *vritti* that follows it.

उभावेतावलंकार्यौ तयोः पुनरलंकृतिः।
वक्रोक्ति वैदग्ध्यभङ्गीभणि तिरुच्यते।।

(Both the signifier and the signified are the objects of embellishment (अलंकार्य) and the basic *alankara* of the two is the poet's peculiar turn or mode of expression.)

He explains the term in the *vritti*; as the signifier and the signified are a composite and do not exist in separation like तिल and तैल (sesame and its oil) both are अलंकार्य (objects of embellishment). Here Kuntaka has followed the Sanskrit grammarians who proved that form and meaning are inseparable, and that they are the same in the mind or what Chomsky has termed the deep structure. If the signifier and the signified (वाचक and वाच्य) are अलंकार्य, then what is their *alankara*? Kuntaka answers that *vakrokti* is *the alankara*, which embellishes both the two and distinguishes them from the rest[57]. Then, he puts the question: what is *vakrokti*? He himself answers:

> "*Vakrokti* is deviation from the standard convention of expression and is marked by its strangeness or wonderfulness. It is the poet's peculiar turn of expression. The term वैदग्ध्य means the poet's art of composition and भङ्गी is विच्छित्ति (turn) and भणिति is expression. In short, *vakrokti*, because of its peculiar turn, from the standard or popular way of expression bears the quality of strikingness and the signifier and the signified gain

56. I.A. Richards's "pseudo-statement" is very near to Bhamaha's *vakrokti*.
57. तयोर्द्वित्वसंख्या विशिष्टपोरव्यलंकृति।

exquisite beauty in conjunction. Therefore, *vakrokti* is the base of all *alankaras*.[58]

In verse 11, Kuntaka rejects Dandin's idea that natural expression is a kind of *alankara*. Kuntaka says that *alankara* embellishes an object. As *svabhaokti* is a plain statement and describes the nature of the given object objectively, it needs to be embellished to become poetic. It follows then that *vakrokti* is the hallmark of literariness and literature differs from other modes of discourse for its strangeness or strikingness of expression. Kuntaka is very near to the Russian formalists, but goes beyond them. He defines literature:

साहित्यमनयोः शोभाशालितां प्रति काव्यसौ।।
अन्यूनानतिरिक्तत्वमनोहारिण्यवस्थितिः।।

(Literature is the fusion of word and meaning (sound and sense), which, though vying with each other, stay in proper balance to create a special beauty that thrills the heart of the appreciative reader.)

Kuntaka explains this verse in his commentary.

"Literature (साहित्य) consists of word and meaning. The cause of delighting the appreciative reader is the competition between word and meaning, and the striking turn of expression. As word and meaning, though in stiff competition, remain in perfect balance, literature delights the reader immensely."

Vakya vinyasa (literary composition) delights us as it follows a special style, consists of the *gunas* (merits), has an embellished language, produces *rasa*, and is स्पन्दित (throbbing) with beauty.[59]

Certainly, Kuntaka goes beyond the narrow limits of "defamiliarization" of Shklovsky and "bestrangement" of Eichenbaum. Towards the end of the *vritti* he acknowledges the importance of कविव्यापार or the poet's creative art and says that it is this element that gives life to a literary composition. He writes:

58. Paraphrase ours. We owe to S.K. De for his translation of वैदग्ध्यमङ्गीभणितिः (the poet's peculiar turn of expression).

59. This is summary of the long *vritti* that follows verse 17 of the *Karika*.

शरीरं जीवितेनेव स्फुरितेनेव जीवितम्
विना निर्जीवता येन वाक्यं याति विपश्चिताम्।

Just body is lifeless without प्राण and is inactive without स्पन्द, a poetic composition becomes lifeless without the meticulous art of the poet, वक्र कविव्यापार शालिनि। In other words, it is *vakrokti*, which makes poetry, poetry.

After defining literature and *vakrokti*, Kuntaka enumerates and discusses the six kinds of *vakrokti*. They are:

1. वर्णविन्यासवक्रता: *vakrokti* at phonological level.
2. पदपूर्वार्द्ध वक्रता: *vakrokti* at the beginning of a word.
3. प्रत्ययाश्रय वक्रता: *vakrokti* at the end of a word.
4. वाक्यवक्रता: *vakrokti* at the sentence level.
5. प्रकरणवक्रता: *vakrokti* at episodic level.
6. प्रबन्धवक्रता: *vakrokti* at the level of the text.

He introduces each kind or division of *vakrokti* in the first *Unmesha* and discusses them in detail in the subsequent *Unmeshas*.

1. वर्णविन्यासवक्रता

It is the arrangement of *varnas* (phonemes) in such a way as to please the ears. However, it is important that the sound should not be dominant enough to mar the meaning. Shelley's "The cloud" is a good example of *varnavinyasa vakrata*

I bring fresh showers for the thirsting flowers,
When they are in their noonday dreams.

Anuprasa in Sanskrit and alliteration in English are the figures of speech which have their base in *varnavinyasa vakrata*.

2. पदपूर्वार्द्धवक्रता

In this kind of *vakrata* the first word's meaning is shifted from its general meaning to metaphorical or metonymic meaning.

रामोऽस्मि सर्वं सहे I am Rama. I can bear everything. Here, Rama's general meaning is shifted to the metaphorical meaning that he is a person who can bear every kind of grief.

3. प्रत्ययाश्रयवक्रता

In this kind of *vakrata* the poet chooses an unusual word for strikingness. Kuntaka quotes the phrase.

मैथिली तस्य दारा: Maithilee (Sita) is his wife.

The poet could use the word भार्या at the place of दारा, but he has chosen the masculine gender word दारा for strikingness, not भार्या, which belongs to the feminine gender. Similarly, Eliot uses an unusual word at the end of this line: "I should be glad of another death." ("Journey of the Magi")

4. वाक्यवक्रता

Vakyavakrata operates at the levels of sentence and paragraph. In fact, all the previously stated divisions or kinds of *vakrata* are parts of *vakyavakrata*. The special organization of words may give birth to plurality of meaning. Irony and paradox, and all kinds of tropes are parts of *vakyavakrata*. The opening lines of "Love Song of J. Alfred Prufrock" are a fine example of *Vakyavakrata*.

"Let us go then you and I,
When the evening is spread out against the sky,
Like a patient etherised upon a table;"

Similarly, the second stanza of "Preludes" begins in unusual or strange way. The description of the morning is विच्छित्ति of the convention.

"The morning comes to consciousness,
Of faint stale smells of beer,
From the sawdust-trampled street,
With all its muddy feet that press,
To early coffee-stands."

5. प्रकरणवक्रता

Uptill *vakyavakrata* Kuntaka is concerned primarily with poetic diction and literariness. In the next two kinds of *vakrata* he widens the horizon to the artistic success of a text as whole and the function of its parts for its exquisiteness.

Deviation is here, but it is, what Chomsky says, at the deep level, the level where word and meaning converge together, and it is meaning, which determines the surface structure. The creative writer adds an episode of his own to enhance the artistic beauty of his work. Kuntaka quotes the episode of Durvasa's curse in Kalidasa's *Abhijñānaśākuntalam*. Durvasa's curse changes the course of Shakuntala's life and Dushyanta's too.

Kuntaka says that *prakaranavakrata*, when employed artistically, illuminates the beauty of the created work and delights the reader/listener with an earthly pleasure. It is of great credit to Kuntaka that he has discussed at length more than ten episodes to explain his concept of *prakaranavakrata*. His example of the dialogue between the Purusha and Rakshasa is classic. The dialogue apparently simple in language is a prefect example of *vakrata*. We easily understand the subtle policy of Chanakya and the generosity of Chandragupta. We also understand how subtly the man (*purusha*) tries to trap the wise prime-minister of Dhanananda and bring him to Chanakya's fold. The scene is a fine example of *prakaranvakrata*, brilliantly employed by Vishakhadatta.

We can see *prakaranvakrata* in Shakespeare's *Hamlet*. The play within the play (popularly called the mouse-trap scene) is a digression from the main story. Shakespeare could have avoided the scene that replicates king Hamlet's poisoning. But, this scene has a great effect in the development of the plot. In fact, this *vakrata* is the turning point in the play. Similarly, the Porter scene and the Dagger scene are not the essential parts of the story, but once they are inserted, they make the plot artistically beautiful and the audience is thrilled with joy when it witnesses the action on the stage.

6. प्रबन्धवक्रता

Prabandhavakrata is that kind of *vakrata* in which the writer deviates from history or a previously written text to produce a different kind of poetic effect. The new text may run parallel to the older one or may take a particular episode or act, and modify or enlarge it to produce a different kind of *rasa*.

Kalidasa's *Raghuvansham* has its source in Valmiki's *Ramayana*, but produces a different kind of poetic effect or *rasa*. Bhasa's *Venisamharam* is based on a particular episode of the *Mahabharata*, but its main *rasa* is *veera rasa* whereas *shanta rasa* is the main *rasa* of the *Mahabharata*. And so is the case with *Uttararamacharitam* where the dominant *rasa* is *karuna* and in its source the *Ramayana*, *shanta* is the main *rasa*. Similarly, Aeschylus' *Oresteia* is the source of Eliot's *The Family Reunion and O'Neill's Mourning Becomes Electra*. All the three plays have different effects. *Prabandhavakrata* may be said to be the highest form of *vakrata* where all the other kinds of *vakrata* merge and here a poet's ingenuity, skill, flight of imagination, and poetic art are all at their best.

Alankara

As described earlier the basic *alankara* is *vakrokti* and all the *alankaras* are its subsidiaries. Kuntaka rejects Dandin's division of *alankaras* into *svabhaokti* and *Vakrokti* on the ground that a plain statement describes the nature or property of an object in its natural form. What is natural cannot be an ornament. It is an *alankarya*, an object to be ornamented. He follows Bhamaha who says that *vakrokti* (pseudo-statement) is the basic *alankara*.

Kuntaka simplifies the intricate enumeration of *alankaras* and reduces them to 20 only. They are:

> *Rupaka, Aprastutprashansa, Paryayokta, Vyajstuti, Utpreksha, Atishayokti, Upama, Shlesha, Vyatireka, Drishtanta, Arthantaranyasa, Akshepa, Vibhavana, Sasandeha, Apnahuti, Sansrishti, Sankara, Rasavata, Deepaka, Sahokti.*[60]

Credit should go to Kuntaka for simplifying the method of classification of *alankaras* and reducing them to the ideal number of 20. It is really unfortunate that his manuscript was not maintained well and scholars could not decipher some parts

---

60. रूपक. अप्रस्तुतप्रशंसा. पर्यायोक्ता, व्याजस्तुति, उत्प्रेक्षा, अतिशयोक्ति, उपमा, श्लेष, व्यतिरेक, दृष्टान्त, अर्थान्तरन्यास, आक्षेप, विभावना, ससन्देह, अप्नहुति, संसृष्टि, संकर, रसवत, दीपक, सहोक्ति।

of the text, especially on *alankaras*. It is also unfortunate that his other works (he must have written a few) are not available.

The *Margas*

Kuntaka's classification of the *margas* is more scientific in comparison to his predecessors. Banbhatta, Dandin, Bhamaha, Vamana, and Rajshekhara classified the *margas* region-wise and maintained that the *vaidarbha marga* was the best as it contained all the ten *gunas*. Kuntaka rejected their principle of classification on the following grounds.

(a) If *margas* are named after their regions, there will be too many *margas*. This is not proper.

(b) Secondly, customs of a country are traditionally maintained by old people, but poetic creation cannot be bound by tradition or custom. A brilliant poet need not adhere to the *marga* of his region; he must make experiment.

(c) Thirdly, it is not proper to call one style *uttama*, the other *madhyama*, and the third *adhama*. The aim of a poet is to reach perfection in style, and so, no style is *madhyama* or *adhama*. It is possible that one poet's style may not be so good as that of the other, but it does not mean that people would not listen to him.

After rejecting all the previous authorities Kuntaka posits his own views on style (*marga*).

According to him, a poet's *marga* is determined by his natural disposition, creative power, and inspiration, and perfected by his practice. A poet of *sukumara* nature composes *sukumara* poetry and of *vichitra* nature *vichitra* poetry and of *ubhaya* nature *ubhayatmaka*[61] poetry. As every poet has his own disposition there will be as many styles as many poets. Since, it is not possible to enumerate each and everyone, it is more convenient to divide them into three main *margas* on the basis of their linguistic features. The three main *margas* are:

---

61. A *marga* where both *sukumara* and *vichitra* are present.

1. *Sukumara marga*
2. *Vichitra marga*
3. *Ubhayatmaka marga*. (a combination of both *sukumara* and *vichitra margas*)

These margas differ from one another in the choice of words, *alankara* and rhythm. *Sukumara marga* employs soft sounds, pleasant words, fewer *alankaras* and small *samasas*. Kalidasa is the leading poet of this *marga*. *Vichitra marga* is marked by the abundance of *alankaras* and the art of defamiliarization. Banbhatta, Bhavabhuti, and Rajashekhar are the poets who have broadened this path. The *ubhayatmaka* path is a combination of the two. Matrigupta, Mayuraja, and Manjeer are the illustrious names who have adopted this path.

The *gunas* of the *margas*

There are four permanent *gunas* of the *margas*. They are: *madhurya*, *prasada*, *lavanya*, and *abhijatya*[62]. Though, they are common to all the three *margas*, they differ in quantity in the case of each *marga*.

1. *Sukumara Marga*

(a) *Madhurya* (sweetness): *Madhurya* is produced by the discreet use of *Samas*[63] (cluster of words in their first form). *Samasas* are there, but they are not too many and so the words appeal directly to the appreciative listener/reader and gives him a great pleasure. Sound, sense, and organization of words contribute to the uniqueness of the poem that follows the *sukumara marga*.

(b) *Prasada* (clarity of expression): Clarity of expression is the second characteristic of the *Sukumara marga*. By this *guna* Kuntaka means that it makes the listener/reader relish the *rasa* and the intention of the poem as suggested by *vakrokti* effortlessly. The meaning of the poem is realized effortlessly.

(c) *Lavanya* (loveliness): By *lavanya* Kuntaka means the exquisite beauty of organization of words where sound and sense

---

62. माधुर्य, प्रसाद, लावण्य, अभिजात्य

63. समास

are in perfect balance, though both compete with each other. He writes: बन्धो वाक्यविन्यासः तस्य सौन्दर्य रामण्यकं लावण्यम् अभिधीयते (*Lavanya* is the beauty of the syntactic structure of a poem).

(d) *Abhijatya*: It is difficult to translate this term. Kuntaka says that this *guna* is that quality of poetry which is charming to ears. It is just like a pleasant touch that we feel at heart.

2. *Vichitra Marga*

It, too, has these four qualities or merits.

First, Kuntaka contrasts *vichitra marga* with *Sukumarga marga*. *Sukumara marga* is a path which passes through gardens and orchards. The whole atmosphere is fragrant with the blossoming flowers and resonant with the humming of bees; everything is pleasant and joyful and appealing to the five senses. *Vichitra marga* is, on the other hand, strenuous and painful and the traveller has to face a lot of hardship. As his movement is like walking on the edge of a sword, he has always to be alert, energetic, and untiring. The poet of the *vichitra marga* uses a cluster of *alankaras* with one nucleus. The result is that the *prateeyamana* (*vyangya* or *dhvani*), the suggested meaning, lurks behind the general meaning (*vachyartha*):

(a) *Madhurya* (sweetness): *Madhurya*, defined earlier as a *guna* of *Sukumara marga*, is present in the poetry of *vichitra marga*. It runs through the skilfully organized words and quickens the movement of the aroused emotion. It is because of *madhurya* that there is no looseness in the inter-relationship of the words. Kuntaka quotes verses to illustrate how *madhurya* functions in the poetry of *vichitra marga*.

(b) *Prasada* (clarity of expression): The poets of *vichitra marga* employ *samasarahit*[64] words as do the poets of *Sukumara marga*, but the difference is that the poetry of *vichitra marga* is *ojas*, slightly charged with energy.

(c) *Lavanya* (loveliness): In *vichitra marga* the complex and compound words end with a *visarga* (:), which is preceded by a short vowel. This kind of ending adds beauty to the entire stanza and its rhythm.

---

64. समासरहित (words without *samasa*)

(d) *Abhijatya*: As there are no extremes of softness and hardness, this *guna* makes the poetry of *vichitra marga* pleasant to the ears and thrills the heart of the listener.

The Subsidiary *gunas*

Apart from the four permanent *gunas*, there are two subsidiary *gunas*, called *auchitya* and *saubhagya*.

(a) *Auchitya*

This *guna* is the poet's ability to describe an object, action or event clearly and exactly. It is clarity and exactness that enlivens all kinds of poetry. *Auchitya* is discernible when two dissimilar objects are compared and are made similar by the poet's peculiar turn of expression. W.B. Yeats's poem "A Coat" is a prefect example of Kuntaka's *auchitya*. The opening line is:

"I made my song a coat."

(b) *Saubhagya*

Saubhagya is a *guna* chiefly related to the poet's deftness in selection of appropriate words that can be pleasant in sound and rich in meaning. This *guna* is gained by learning and practising the art of poetry.

Kuntaka's Contribution to Poetics

Kuntaka is the last and concluding theorist. When Bharata wrote the *Natyashastra*, he was chiefly concerned with drama on the stage. His *Rasa* theory, though applicable to all forms of literature, is confined to the emotional effect of poetry on the audience or the reader.

Dandin widened the horizon of poetics. His main focus was on the body of poetry. As the body of poetry consists of word and meaning, he discussed at length the language of poetry. Bhamaha followed him closely and corrected him judiciously, especially the idea of *svabhaokti* and *vakrokti* and rightly pointed out that *vakrokti* is the base of all *alankaras*.

Dhavanikara and Anandavardhana followed the tradition of Dandin and Bhamaha, but opened a new vista in the development of literary criticism. They wanted to know what makes a literary work great. Their approach was of course, linguistic. They propounded *Dhvani* theory and by *Dhvani* they meant, "suggested meaning", the meaning independent of the literal and metaphorical meanings, but is derived from them. Abhinavagupta followed both Bharata and Anandavardhana and propounded *Rasa-Dhvani* theory. He corrected and revised the *rasa* and *dhvani* theories so brilliantly that what we know by *rasa* theory or/and *dhvani* theory today is actually *Rasa-Dhvani* theory.

Kuntaka came a little later. We can say that he was a junior contemporary of Abhinavagupta. He accepted Bhamaha's idea of *vakrokti* that *vakrokti* is the base of all *alankaras*. But, he did not remain a true copy of his predecessor and developed the concept of *vakrokti* to such a great height that we wonder even today at his great achievement and modernity.

The basic problem, like Dandin and Bhamaha, he said, was what makes a literary text literary and distinguishes it from other modes of discourse. His answer was *vaichitrya*, which can be translated into "strangeness", "strikingness" or "wonderfulness". A poet creates *vaichitrya* through *vakrokti*, which consists of the words *vakra* (not straight) and *ukti* (statement/speech act). As *vakrokti* is a technical term he defined it as "a poet's peculiar turn of expression" (S.K. De's translation). In other words, a poet makes a reader wonder at his sharp turn of expression and he does so by deviating from the conventional or standard forms of expression. This deviation is there not only at the phonological, morphological and syntactic levels, but at the content level also. Kuntaka is more advanced than the Russian Formalists and French Structuralists who are of the opinion that meaning follows structure and a change in structure causes change in meaning. Deviations at *prakarana* level and *prabandha* level are related to meaning and the structure of a text changes, because there is a change in the content, that is, meaning. Kuntaka, thus, is nearer to Chomsky who says that meaning and structure exist together at the deep level or in man's mind. *Vakrokti*, therefore, is related to both form and meaning, *vachaka* and *vachya* (signifier and the signified)[65].

65. M. Monier Williams, *A Sanskrit English Dictionary*, p. 937, column 3.

It is not that he has propounded a theory only. He has analysed a large number of texts to illustrate how *vakrata* operates at different levels and produces *vaichitrya* to thrill the reader's/listener's heart.

His second contribution is his theory of the *margas* that a *marga* is not specific to a region. What is vital in the classification of *margas* is the style of the text. He is quite justified in saying that a poet takes a *marga* according to his natural disposition. He may take *Sukumara* or *Vichitra* or *Ubhayatmaka marga* according to his disposition and training.

His third contribution is that he rejected the traditional belief that a particular *marga* is excellent and the other is *adhama* (despicable). According to him, all *margas* are good and a literary text is to be judged, not by its style, but by the excellence of its diction and feeling, its success in giving us aesthetic pleasure, its ability to vibrate us with life.

Finally, Kuntaka has been considerate to his predecessors. He has accepted *Rasa* and *Dhvani* theories, and the concepts of *prateeyamana* and *vivakshita*.

Since, he was much ahead of his time, scholars neglected him. His manuscript was found in the second decade of the twentieth century and that, too, in a dilapidated condition. We all Indian should be grateful to S.K. De for editing and publishing the text in 1921.

2

GREEK AND LATIN POETICS

(A) ARISTOTLE

Aristotle is the first recognized critic. He joined Plato's academy in the year 367 B.C. After fourteen years of Plato's death in 349 B.C., he founded his own academy in 335 B.C. and named it Lyceum. Basically a philosopher, he took all knowledge in his province. His *Poetics*, as Elder Olson says, should be read along with his other works, especially the *Rhetoric*, the *Politics*, and the *Ethics*, as it is a part of his philosophical system.

When Aristotle was writing the *Poetics*, literature was not so rich and varied as it is in our time. In those days epic, tragedy, comedy, lyric, and dithyramb were the only forms of literature, and they all came under the generic name of poetry. Later on, monody and threnody were added. Naturally, Aristotle's poetic theory is based upon epic, tragedy, comedy, and dithyramb only. Yet, his theory is so profound and universal that it is still applicable in the analysis and interpretation of other genres of literature. The New Aristotelians—R.S. Crane, Elder Olson, and Wayne C. Booth—have followed him faithfully; of course, with a few modifications and innovations.

Although Aristotle was a disciple of Plato, he did not agree with his teacher's views on poets and poetry. Plato denounced poets on the ground that they were oblivious of the real world and that poetry was thrice (actually twice) removed away from reality. In the dialogue between Socrates and Ion, a rhapsode, Socrates leads the rhapsode to the conclusion that poetry is imitation of the real objects created after the idea, and so, it is unreal. Plato concludes in his *Dialogues*:

> "...the poet is a light and winged and holy thing, and there is no invention in him until he has been inspired and is out of his senses, and the mind is no longer in him: when he has not attained to this state, he is powerless and unable to utter his oracles."[1]

In *Republic*, Plato denounces poetry and says that poetry is not only an illusion but also a danger to the well-being of the state.

> "Speaking in confidence, for I should not like to have my words repeated to the tragedians and the rest of the imitative tribe—but I do not mind saying to you, that all poetical imitations are ruinous to the understanding of the hearers, and that the knowledge of their true nature is the only antidote to them."[2]

His final words are that philosophy and poetry are incompatible and that there is an ancient quarrel between them.

Aristotle did not agree with Plato on this point and said that poetry, music, and painting are all imitative arts, but they, being productive sciences, create new and real objects. For example, a sculptor takes a piece of marble, imitates a human being, and imposes the form on the stone. What he produces is a statue, which is neither a piece of marble nor a human being, but something new and original, a work of art. Aristotle's rebuttal of Plato's argument against poetry is not simplistic; it is, on the other, built on a sound theory of poetry.

Aristotle's Theory of Poetry

In Plato's philosophical system, the first is the idea. Taken individually, there is an idea of every object, say a bed. The carpenter makes a bed by imitating it, but this bed is not the same as the original. A painter or a poet who paints or describes, it is away from the actual bed. Thus, a painting or poetic composition is twice removed away from the idea of the bed.

Aristotle refuted Plato's arguments in *Poetics*. His *Poetics* is a work, which R.S. Crane and Elder Olson have called

---

1. Quoted by W.K. Wimsatt and Cleanth Brooks, *Literary Criticism: A Short History* (Calcutta: Oxford Book Company, 1965), p. 6.
2. *Ibid.*, p. 11.

"acroamatic", that is, a work to be interpreted with the help of others of his works, such as *Rhetoric*, *Politics*, and *Metaphysics*.[3]

Chapters I to IV of the *Poetics* are devoted to the definition and origin of poetry. In the very beginning Aristotle writes that art is imitation and a little later, he writes:

> "Epic poetry and tragedy, comedy also, and dithyramb poetry and the music of the flute and of the lyre in most of their forms, are all in their general conception modes of imitation".

It appears that he has followed his teacher, but soon we realize that he has refuted him in his own words. What Aristotle says in the *Poetics* is clarified by his statements in the *Meteorology* and the *Physics* on the relationship between nature and art. He writes in the *Meteorology*: "Art imitates nature", and in the *Physics*: "Art finishes the job when nature fails, or imitates the missing parts."

It follows then that art has its own existence, and hence, autonomous. It works by a plan or an idea, and parallels nature. Nature makes a tree, and artist a bed. A tree produces another tree but a bed cannot, and this is because it is a product of art, not of nature. Therefore, Plato's argument that art being imitative is not only non-productive and useless but also false and harmful is totally wrong. Art complements nature. This idea of Aristotle that art makes an improvement on the products of nature was fully developed by Alexander Pope in *Essay of Criticism*—"Nature still but Nature methodised."

He classifies sciences, according to their subject-matter, the problems they deal with, and their methodology, into three broad divisions: (a) theoretical (knowing), (b) practical (doing), and (c) productive (making). Metaphysics, mathematics, and physics are theoretical sciences and knowledge is their end. The practical sciences are ethics and politics. Here knowledge or knowing is not enough; action is more important. In the third group are painting, music, and poetry, which are more importantly concerned with

---

3. See Elder Olson, "Aristotle's Poetic Method. Its Powers and Limitations", Handy and West brook, ed., *Twentieth Century Criticism: Major Statements*, (New Delhi: Life and Light Publishers, 1979).

making; their end is neither knowledge nor action, but making of the intended object.

The practical sciences are less exact than the theoretical sciences, and derive proposition from them. Similarly, the productive sciences are less exact than the theoretical and practical sciences, and derive proposition from the both. The important difference between the practical and productive sciences is that the latter is specifically concerned with the making and quality of the product, and that they have their origin in the maker.

Music, painting, and poetry are not accidental nor are they made by nature; they are made by the conscious efforts of man. While writing a poem, the poet has a form in his mind. He takes the matter. He is not the maker of the matter nor of the form. What he does is the imposition of the form on the matter or medium to produce the artistic composite. For example, the characters of the *Iliad* or *Odyssey* were not made by Homer. All that Homer knew was about their bravery. The words (medium or matter) too were not made by him. He simply imposed the form (the characters in action) on the existing words, and produced the two epics, the works of art. Aristotle's example is the making of a marble statue. The piece of marble was not made by the sculptor nor the human form. The statue is the *synolon*, the *concretum*, of the form and the matter, and has its existence as a work of art.

Art is imitation of form by means of medium. In the words of Olson, "to imitate implies a matter or medium (means) in which one imitates, some form (object) which one imitates, and a certain way (manner) in which one imitates." While discussing and defining the arts, all these three principles of classification—medium, object, and manner—are to be applied simultaneously. Music, painting, and poetry differ in respect of medium. The first uses sound, the second colour, and the third words. The same principles of classification can be successfully applied in distinguishing one genre of poetry from the other. The given table illustrates this clearly.

Genre	Medium/Means	Object	Manner
Epic	Words	Characters above average action: noble	Narrative
Comedy	Words	Characters below average action: ignoble	Dramatic
Tragedy	Words	Characters above average action: noble	Dramatic

Epic differs from comedy in object and manner, and comedy from tragedy in object.

There remains one more aspect of the different forms of poetry. It may be asked, why is tragedy a tragedy? At a larger scale the question is: why is a thing what it is? Aristotle's answer is that a work of art has a particular form because it has a particular function. He gives the example of an axe. The function of an axe is to cut wood. In order to make it function efficiently, its maker gives it a particular form or shape. The axe will not remain an axe if its form is changed. Similarly, tragedy is tragedy because it has a particular function, the function of the catharsis of the emotions of pity and fear. All its six elements are organized in a special way, so as to lead the play end in tragedy, and shake the emotions of pity and fear violently for their purgation.

In short, poetry imitates men in action. The possible objects of imitation are not ordinary men in real life, but men either better or worse than average people, and not only things as they are, but things as they ought to be.

Origin of Poetry

Poetry is a mode of imitation and has its source in imitation. Aristotle writes:

> "Poetry in general seems to have sprung from two causes, each of them lying deep in our nature. First, the instinct of imitation is implanted in man from childhood, one difference between him and other being is that he is the most imitative of living creatures, and through it learns his earliest lessons; and no less universal is the pleasure felt in things imitated."

He explains this statement by referring to a man's experiences. People learn by imitation. They get pleasure by doing so. Related to it is the pleasure derived from the object imitated. It is natural for human beings to relive their pleasant experiences of the past. A painter paints the scene of the beautiful sun-rise or sun-set. He also desires that other people see the painting and share the pleasure he has experienced. It is also that even painful experiences painted on canvas give pleasure to the viewers. A dead animal or a sick person is a painful sight, but when painted, they become a work of art and give us pleasure. Aristotle says:

> "Objects which in themselves we view with pain, we delight to contemplate when reproduced with minute fidelity."

The second cause is the instinct for harmony and rhythm. Some persons are gifted with this instinct by nature. When they imitate some action in words, they speak poetically. In the past some people especially gifted with rhyme and rhythm made improvisations from which poetry sprang.

Pleasure was the chief characteristic of poetry in the beginning. But later on it diverged into two main currents, the serious and the comic. The serious writers "imitated noble actions, and the actions of noble men. The more trivial sort imitated the actions of meaner persons, at first composing satires, as the former did hymns to the gods and praises of famous men." Satire did not come in the beginning. It was only after Homer that lampooning began. His *Margites* was the first work of satire or lampoon. He also introduced the appropriate metre, "which is still called the iambic or lampooning measure". The *Margites* may be said to have laid down the main lines of comedy. Aristotle explains that Homer was able to write comic passages because he had the ability to "combine dramatic form with excellence of imitation." He was the originator of both tragedy and comedy. Comedy originated from the *Margites* and tragedy from the *Iliad* and the *Odyssey*. The lampooners became the writers of comedy, and the epic poets were succeeded by tragedians.

Thus, poetry has its origin in a man's instinct of imitation. As he derived pleasure in imitating the objects around and the events observed, he continued to write poetry. Thus, poetry in the beginning or the first of development was meant for pleasure. In the second stage, the comic and serious writers added morality. At this stage, the function of poetry was to delight and instruct; the mean and below average actions were satirised by lampooners and the noble, and virtuous deeds were praised by serious writers. Poetry developed further and reached perfection in the third stage when artistic virtues were added as the third element. Epic and tragedy were written in this stage, the latter came later.

Tragedy: Definition, Elements, and Function

For Aristotle tragedy is the highest form of poetry. He writes in the *Poetics*:

> "Tragedy advanced by slow degrees; each new element that showed itself was in turn developed. Having passed through many changes, it found its natural form, and there it stopped."

The reason for saying so is that tragedy is the finest flowering of the tree of poetry, and all the three components of perfect poetry—delight, morality or instruction, and beauty—are perfectly blended. Wimsatt and Brooks remark:

> "The Aristotelian poetics is the poetics of the drama and especially of tragedy."

They have remarked so, as the major part of the *Poetics* is devoted to tragedy. The celebrated definition of tragedy occurs in chapter VI of the *Poetics*:

> "Tragedy is an imitation of an action that is serious, complete, and of a certain magnitude, in language embellished with each kind of artistic ornament, the several kinds found in separate parts of the play; in the form of action, not of narration; through pity and fear effecting the proper purgation (Katharsis) of these emotions."

Explaining the terms action, magnitude, complete, embellished language, artistic ornament, pity, and fear, Aristotle enumerates the six elements of tragedy. They are *plot*, *character*, *thought*, *diction*, *song*, and *spectacle*.

(i) *Plot*

Plot is the first and most important element of tragedy. By plot Aristotle means the presentation of human action in a dramatic way. Since tragedy is an imitation, not of men, but of action and of life, and life consists in action and its end is a mode of action, not of quality, plot is the soul of tragedy. According to R.S. Crane, it is the structure of tragedy of which character, dialogue, and events are components. It is true that Aristotle does not make distinction between story and plot, and the term he uses for plot is *muthos*. Perhaps, he means by *muthos*, a story artistically organized to delight and instruct.

Since tragedy is an imitation of an action that is complete and whole, and of a certain magnitude, the plot should also be a whole and of proper size. A whole is that, which has a beginning, a middle, and an end. In order to be a beautiful whole, the plot should be not only a logical arrangement of events, it should be of a certain magnitude in relation to the play of which it is a part. This is because beauty depends on magnitude and order.

The next important feature of a good plot is unity. Aristotle lays stress on the unity of action. He writes:

> "...the imitation is one when the object imitated is one, so the plot being an imitation of an action, must imitate one action and that a whole, the structural union of the parts being such that, if anyone of them is displaced or removed, the whole will be disjointed and removed."

It is from this statement of Aristotle's, the classical concept of the three unities of time, place, and action became popular, and the dramatists of Italy, France, and England adhered rigidly to it.

As the function of tragedy is the catharsis of the emotions of pity and fear, the plot should be so constructed as to produce tragic effect. In the words of Aristotle himself:

> "Such an effect is best produced when the events come on by surprise, and it is heightened when, at the same time, they follow as cause and event."

Here the stress is, of course, on both logical and emotional connection between different kinds of actions and events, and the ending of a play.

Aristotle has divided plots into *simple* and *complex*. An action which is one and continues without complication is simple. There is no reversal of situation nor recognition of an error. In the complex plot, there are both reversal and recognition. The change from prosperity to catastrophe is not accidental; it is rather systematic and plausible. Everything is implanted artistically in the structure of the plot so as to establish cause and effect relationship, which is necessary and natural.

Hamartia (error), *peripeteia* (reversal of situation), and *anagnorisis* (recognition) are the essential components of a complex plot. *Hamartia* literally means an error in marking (with an arrow) the aimed target. When the hero makes a fatal error (he is not aware of), he is said to have committed *hamartia*. Oedipus' killing of his own father and marrying his mother is an act of *hamartia*. *Hamartia* is followed by the reversal of situation (*peripeteia*). The blight and famine that ravage Oedipus' kingdom is the reversal of the situation. When Oedipus wants to know the cause of the famine, he is stunned to know the reality from the shepherd who had reared him. What follows then is the tragedy: Jocasta's suicide and Oedipus' taking off his eyes, renunciation of the throne, and departure from the kingdom for penance.

Finally, a well-constructed plot should be single in its issue rather than double. The change of fortune should be not from bad to good, but from good to bad, and should come about as the result not of vice, but some great error of frailty. A well-constructed plot makes a tragedy artistically perfect and emotionally effective.

(ii) *Character*

The second element is character. In respect of character, Aristotle writes, "there are four things to be aimed at". These four qualities are: goodness, propriety, truthfulness, and consistency.

Goodness is the prime quality of the main characters. A speech or action manifests the purpose of the character. The character is good if the purpose is good and guided by morality. Oedipus and Jocasta are good as they are guided by morality. Both repent for their error and do penance for their sin, which they have committed unknowingly.

The second quality is propriety. By propriety is meant the true property of the character. A wrong propriety should not be ascribed to him or her. For example, man has valour but a woman is delicate. Therefore, it will be inappropriate to present a woman as valiant or unscrupulously clever.

Thirdly, characters must be true to life. This quality is quite different from goodness and propriety. So, a poet should always aim at the necessary or the probable in the portrayal of his characters. A character should speak and act in a given way. The given way is the rule of necessity and probability. The seventeenth century classicists coined the term *verisimilitude* basing it on Aristotle's notion of probability or necessity.

The fourth aspect is consistency. It means characterization should not be wayward. If a character is inconsistent, it should remain inconsistent throughout, and if some change comes to it, the change should not be altered without some reason. A fool cannot act wisely many times. Within the action there must not be anything irrational. If the irrational cannot be excluded, it should be outside the scope of tragedy.

(iii) *Thought*

Thought is the third element of tragedy, and it means the faculty of saying what is possible and pertinent in given circumstances. Aristotle's stress is on the proper correlation between idea or emotion, and the language of expressing it. He writes:

> "Under thought is included every effect, which has to be produced by speech, the subdivisions being proof and refutation; the excitation of feelings, such as pity, fear, anger, and the like, the suggestion of importance or its opposite."

If follows then that there should be a correlation between thought or emotion, and action and speech. If an action is of anger, it is proper to produce an angry speech, and if it is of pity, the speech should arouse or express pity.

(iv) *Diction*

By diction is meant the language of tragedy. Aristotle discusses the grammar of the Greek language at first, and then comes to the poetic use of words and sentences. He allows deviation from the norm as it gives novelty to style. Secondly, the coining of new words enhances the beauty of diction. The use of archaic and strange words is another device to produce the desired effect. He is of the opinion that metaphor is the most important feature of poetic diction:

> "...the greatest thing by far is to have a command on metaphor. This alone cannot be imparted by another; it is the mark of genius, for to make good metaphors implies an eye for resemblances."

(v) *Song*

The first important function of song is to add beauty and charm to tragedy. Besides, it has an emotional appeal. The Choric song runs as a commentary on the action of the play. It introduces the story and characters in the beginning, comments on the characters, their actions and the importants in the middle of the play, and makes a conclusive remark on the entire action of the play at the end. In addition, it describes some of the actions that cannot be shown on the stage.

(vi) *Spectacle*

Aristotle considers this element of tragedy the least artistic and the last in importance. Its significance lies in highlighting the emotional effect. Wimsatt and Brooks explain the reason why he is indifferent to spectacular events:

> "He seems to concur in Plato's disapproval of animal mimicry and artificial thunder claps, and is thus the second critic of antiquity to take up the long fight by men of good sense against the usurpation of the stage by vandville, operatic diversions, and slapstick—"Cato's long wig" and "Flowered gown", Pinkie and the chicken swallowed whole. It is better, says Aristotle, to depend

> on an artistic handling of the story. We ought to get the effect from simply hearing (or reading). This may be an armchair view and rather extreme—but it has the advantage of stressing the verbal and poetic element of drama, which is most stable and permanently eligible for criticism."[4]

Function of Tragedy: Catharsis

According to Aristotle, form and function are two aspects of the same coin. A thing is made with a certain purpose. The maker wants the product to work in a certain way. Therefore, he designs the product in a particular way. Tragedy is tragedy because it functions in a particular way. The purpose of writing tragedy is to purgate the base emotions of pity and fear. The definition of tragedy ends with the function of tragedy: "thought of pity and fear effecting the proper purgation (catharsis) of these emotions."

It is clear that the function of tragedy is catharsis, the purgation of emotions. However, the term catharsis has created controversy among scholars in regard to its meaning. Perhaps, Aristotle may have explained it in the second part of the *Poetics*, which is not extant.

The first view is that tragedy drives out the selfish emotions of pity and fear by arousing them violently in the audience. Just as poison is driven away from the body by an antidote, which is also the same kind of poison, the base emotions of pity and fear latent in man are driven away by the same kind of antidote. Commenting on this kind of interpretation, Wimsatt and Brooks write:

> "The first or hygienic view, though crude, appears to be what Aristotle meant—if we may judge from what he says of music in the *Politics* and from the usual syntax of the noun *Katharsis* with an objective, genitive of the harmful thing purged away."[5]

In short, the term is medical, and means the purgation or expulsion of something harmful.

---

4. W.K. Wimsatt and Cleanth Brooks, *Literary Criticism: A Short History*, p. 38.
5. *Ibid.*, p. 37.

The second view advanced by Butcher, the most authoritative translator and interpreter of the *Poetics*, is that the term is a religious or moral metaphor, and it implies the "purification or aesthetic depersonalization of our usually selfish emotions of pity and fear." Wimsatt and Brooks support Butcher's view:

> "The second or lustratory view is that adopted by Butcher in his influential essay. It connects more readily with normal modern views about the dignity of the tragic experience and its large enlargement of our souls; it is doubtless nearer not only to what most of us would like to say but to the truth. It has at least the advantage of making the enjoyment of tragedy occur while we are witnessing it, rather than in a sounder sleep when we get home, a relief after emotional orgy."[6]

That tragedy, in addition to delighting and giving aesthetic pleasure, purifies the base emotions of pity and fear, is Aristotle's main thrust on the social function of art and poetry. Plato found poetry unreal and harmful, but Aristotle found it beneficial to mankind as it ennobles our souls.

The Tragic Hero

With the exception of the definition of tragedy itself says Butcher, probably, no passage in the *Poetics* has given rise to so much criticism as the description of the ideal hero in chapter XIII. Professor Butcher's remark, though verging on exaggeration, is very much true; he is quite justified in laying a great emphasis on the importance of the passage on the tragic hero.

The passage is quite long and the characteristics of the hero are interwoven with the plot. The fact is that the actions of the hero form the major part of the plot; his *hamartia*, *peripeteia*, *anagnorisis*, and unusual suffering arouse the emotions of pity and fear, and lead to catharsis. Aristotle enumerates the characteristics of the tragic hero in detail. First, he very precisely eliminates those characters who are unfit to be called tragic.

The tragic hero is not an entirely virtuous man. The downfall of a thoroughly good man will rather arouse anger and

6. *Ibid.*

cause bitterness in the heart of the audience; it will be rather a shocking spectacle to them.

Secondly, if a bad man passes from adversity to prosperity, it will be more alien to tragedy. It will not satisfy the moral sense nor will arouse the emotions of pity and fear. If the reverse is presented, that is, there is the downfall of an utter villain, it will inspire neither pity nor fear. On the other hand, it will satisfy our moral sense. This is because pity is aroused by unmerited misfortune, fear by the misfortune of a man like ourselves. So, the rise of a bad man from adversity to prosperity, or fall from prosperity to adversity is not a tragic event.

The ideal hero then is the character between the two extremes—that of a man who is not eminently good and whose misfortune is brought about, not by vice or depravity, but by some error or frailty. This frailty is his inherent weakness or, now popularly known, *tragic flaw*. Secondly, he is much above the common people, both in position and in intelligence. He has a sense of morality and justice, and is willing to do good to people. He is a renowned and eminent person like Oedipus, Thyestes, or other illustrious men of such families.

In the same passage there are two terms, which require explanation. The first is "misfortune". The hero's misfortune is not ordinary; it is a precipitous downfall from prosperity to catastrophe. The second term, *hamartia* (error) needs a larger explanation. As pointed out by Wimsatt, *hamartia* etymologically means "the missing of a mark with bow and arrow, an unskillful but not morally culpable act". Later on, it began to imply moral responsibility. Socrates, Aristotle's teacher's teacher, said that ignorance is the source of *hamartia*. Aristotle takes *hamartia* to imply moral responsibility, and also to mean a moral lapse, though committed in ignorance. Oedipus' rashness is his frailty or tragic flaw, and his rash act of killing his own father is an act of *hamartia*, a moral error, that leads to his downfall.

The hero's suffering begins with *anagnorisis* (recognition) and *peripeteia* (reversal of situation) that occur in a tragedy in quick succession. The recognition of the error comes to him all of a sudden at a time when he has not even an inkling of it. The realization of ugly truth fills him with remorse. The messenger from Corinth comes to Oedipus when he is a king and is living with his queen and children. But the revelation of his past by the shepherd who had saved his life horrifies him. He is full of remorse that he killed his father and married his own mother. His mother, Jocasta after knowing the grim truth hangs herself. *Peripeteia* follows *anagnorisis* quickly. Oedipus' fall is precipitous. Out of remorse he plucks out his eyes and leaves the throne for penance. The unusual suffering of Oedipus makes the audience feel pity for him, and they are stricken by fear at his fate. They share his suffering because, though he is above the common man, he is more or less like them, and the latent emotions of pity and fear are aroused and shaken violently for catharsis.

Aristotle's tragic hero is a man of eminence and integrity who commits a moral error, and after the recognition of the error and reversal of situation undergoes an unusual suffering and meets his misfortune.

Tragedy, Comedy, and Epic

(a) *Tragedy and Comedy*

The contrast between tragedy and comedy is obvious. Both the genres use the same medium and manner, but differ in the imitation of the object; tragedy imitates actions of noble men, but comedy of ignoble persons. For Aristotle, comedy is an inferior kind of genre, which is concerned with the people, grotesque in appearance and action. In chapter V of the *Poetics* he defines comedy:

> "Comedy is, as we have said, an imitation of characters of a lower type—not, however, in the full sense of the word bad, the ludicrous being merely a subdivision of the ugly. It consists of some defect or ugliness, which is not painful and not destructive. To take an obvious example, the comic mask is ugly and distorted, but does not imply pain."

At other place, he makes distinction between the "old" comedy and the "new" comedy. He says that the "old" comedy is basically lampooning. Aristophanes wrote this kind of comedy and the new comedy was initiated by Menander. Tragedy originated in dithyrambs sung in Dionysiac rituals and comedy in the Dionysiac revels celebrated in villages. He considers Homer to be the source of both tragedy and comedy.

> "Homer first laid down the main lines of comedy by dramatizing the ludicrous instead of writing personal satire. His *Margites* bears the same relation to comedy that the *Iliad* and the *Odyssey* do to tragedy. Lampooners became writers of comedy, and the epic poets were succeeded by tragedians."

When comedy developed, the writers preferred to choose imaginary characters in contrast to the tragedians who wrote plays choosing plots and characters from history. Wimsatt and Brooks write:

> "Both Greek comedy and Greek tragedy decided mainly for the significant name, that of the type or that of the known historic person, the difference between the two being a part of the difference between the meaning of a comic character and that of the tragic."

For Aristotle, virtue and vice are equally important. In tragedy, the focus is on virtue. A virtuous man suffers indescribably for his moral lapses in tragedy, and in comedy, an ignoble man receives minor punishment for his vices. Wimsatt and Brooks explain the difference very clearly in *Literary Criticism: A Short History*.

> "Tragedy and comedy show different, though understandably different relations to the Aristotelian universal. One hinge of this unity and difference is *hamartia*. (The nearly synonymous *hamartima* is the name of the comic flaw in Aristotle's definition of comedy). Tragedy takes *hamartia* literally but magnifies its punishment—and is thus fearful and pitiful. Comedy distorts *hamartia* by caricature, reduces punishment to discomfiture and mortification, and is thus ridiculous."[7]

---

7. Wimsatt and Brooks, *Literary Criticism: A Short History*, p. 50.

Tragedy and comedy, though they have origin in Homer's work, are in sharp contrast. The characters of tragedy are serious and noble, but the characters of comedy are flippant and ignoble. Both commit errors but, whereas the former suffers painfully, the latter escapes misfortune with a light punishment. The audience witnessing the downfall of a tragic hero pity him for the heavy punishment, and fear that they may face a similar fate; but, at the end of a comedy the erring character receives a light punishment, and the way he reacts makes the audience laugh. However, the aim of both tragedy and comedy is the purgation of vice and promotion of virtue. Tragedy is much superior to comedy as it is beautiful, poetic, and grand.

(b) *Tragedy and Epic*

Tragedy and epic both imitate noble characters and their action; the difference between them is that of manner. Aristotle, as has been already said, expresses the view in chapter IV of *Poetics* that

> "...lampooners became writers of comedy, and the epic poets were succeeded by tragedians, since the drama was a larger and higher form of art."

Here the celebrated philosopher and theorist has seen the development of poetry from the biological point of view. As man grows from an infant to a child and then to an adolescent and finally a man; tragedy developed from dionysiac ritual songs (dithyramb) through epic to its present form. A little later, in chapter V, he makes a comparison between the two:

> "Epic poetry agrees with tragedy in so far as it is an imitation in verse of characters of a higher type. They differ, in that epic poetry admits but one kind of metre, and is narrative in form."

The second point of difference he tells is that the range of epic is wider and that of tragedy is narrower. He elaborates this point in chapter XXIV.

> "Epic poetry has, however, a great special quality for enlarging its dimensions, and we can see the reason. In tragedy we cannot imitate several lines of actions

> carried on at one and the same time; we must confine ourselves to the action on the stage...."

In other respects, tragedy and epic are similar. Both may be either simple or complex, ethical or pathetic. The parts also, with the exception of song and spectacle, are the same; for the plot in both requires *hamartia*, *peripeteia*, *anagnorisis*, and scenes of suffering.

Yet, as said earlier, tragedy in Aristotle's opinion is superior to epic in artistic perfection and beauty; besides, its compactness intensifies the intended effect. He writes in chapter XXVI:

> "Tragedy attains its end within narrower limits for the concentrated effect is more pleasurable than one which is spreading over a long time and so diluted."

Illustrating this statement he goes on to say that *Oedipus* of Sophocles would lose much of its effect if it were lengthened to the size of the *Iliad* or the *Odyssey*. In fact, an epic poem furnishes subjects for several tragedies.

Refuting the charge that epic is meant for the civilized audience and tragedy for the inferior, he proves convincingly why tragedy is superior. First, it can be both acted and read by people. Secondly, it contains not only all the elements of the epic but also song and spectacle, the elements specific to drama, for a more pleasurable effect.

Aristotle's Contribution to Literary Criticism

Aristotle is the first and greatest literary critic that the world has seen. He wrote the *Poetics* at the time when poetry was denounced by Plato, the great idealist. Plato's arguments against poetry were so sound and convincing that only a great philosopher and scientist like Aristotle could refute him. He gave a very high and important place to poetry in his philosophical system. Dividing knowledge into three broad categories of theoretical, practical, and productive sciences, he put poetry in the third category, the category of making things. The poet imitates not static human beings but characters in action, guided by their thought, feeling, and emotion. The *concretum* or *synolon* of form and matter is as real as the first idea after which Plato's objects are made. Poetry is as real as the objects made by nature, and like other fine arts is an improvement upon them. This concept of Aristotle was elaborated, later on, by Alexander Pope in *Essay on Criticism*. His definition and interpretation of tragedy and comedy is still unsurpassed, and not only the critics but also all great dramatists have followed him quite faithfully. The foundation he laid for literary criticism is imperishable, and no critic nor any creative writer will ignore him in times to come.

(B) HORACE

Horace wrote *Ars Poetica* in about 68 B.C. Little is known of any work on literary criticism written in the period that lapsed between him and Aristotle. Wimsatt and Brooks introduce him thus:

> "The *Epistle ad Pisones* (in the next century dubbed *Ars Poetica* by Quintilian) is a slick piece of writing, produced by Horace apparently toward the end of his life (65-8 B.C.) after he was the established author of the four books of *Odes*, one of *Epodes*, two of *Satires*, and two of *Epistles*. The whole poetic career of Horace is part of an Augustan and patriotic reaction, and Alexandrian belletristic trends and at the same time against Patrician antiquarianism. But, there is a great difference between the of *Ars* Horace and the *Poetics* of Aristotle or the *Phaedrus* of Plato."[8]

When Horace started writing poetry, Aristotle's theory of poetry was well-established, and a few more genres of poetry had sprung up. His task as a critic, as he felt himself, was to make distinction between different forms, defend the kind of poetry he was writing and, finally, to establish a kind of code for writing good poetry. Propriety or decorum is the focal point of his literary theory. The third aspect of his critical theory is the relationship between form, matter, and the poet.

Decorum

Horace's main focus is on decorum or propriety. His decorum should not be confused with the Indian critic

8. Wimsatt and Brooks, *Literary Criticism: A Short History*, p. 79.

Kshemendra's *auchitya*. Kshemendra is specifically concerned with poetic diction, whereas Horace's horizon is wider and it includes propriety at both social and linguistic levels. His concept of decorum is based on Aristotle's notion of the perfection of tragedy.

His style in *Ars Poetica* is aphoristic with a lot of do's and dont's. In the words of Wimsatt and Brooks:

> "Horace begins his *Ars Poetica* with the negatively Aristotelian example of a mixed species, a beautiful woman sporting a fishtail, and after laughing at this, adds his sufficiently a fishtail, and after laughing at this, adds his sufficiently generalized but nonetheless memorable advice about purple patches and unity."[9]

Horace takes note of the organicity of a work of art and the audience together. He criticises the erring poets, the various kinds of literary pretenders, and the crude audience, and then advises poets to follow decorum.

(a) Five acts, no more, no less.

(b) Only three speakers at a time.

(c) Scenes of butchery offstage.

(d) Hexametre verse for war poems.

The ideal poet is, of course, Homer. He says:

> "Be Homer's works your study and delight,
> Read them by day, and meditate by night."[10]

In modern times, critics have raised the question: Is Horace's notion of decorum based on nature or human convention? The answer that Cleanth Brooks has given is that he was not a profound thinker like Plato and Aristotle. R.S. Crane has hit the point by saying that the decorum of Horace is something affectively and socially oriented—toward the taste and standards of the aristocratic theatre audience of his day rather than toward an Aristotelian or natural objectivity. But, we must remember that by aristocracy is meant the people of high

---

9. Wimsatt and Brooks, *Literary Criticism: A Short History*, pp. 81-82.

10. Alexander Pope's translation.

literary taste, not the only people born in noble and feudal families. Wimsatt and Brooks are worth quoting here:

> "Horace appeals to an audience selected not by social or political standards, but just by literary standards—to his fellow poets and his literary friends, to Maecenas and the other patrons and arbiters of the day."[11]

Since Alexander Pope lived in a period, which was almost similar to that of Horace, he made the Roman classical poet his ideal and wrote *Essay on Criticism*, which is very much based on *Ars Poetica*. In his *Epistle to Augustus*, Horace despises the playwright's dependence on public, and in his tenth *Satire* asserts the sophistication of his satirical standard. And this is what Pope does in his *Epistle to Dr. Arbuthnot*; he, too, criticises the low kind of poetry and defends his stance.

Horace lays stress on feeling and emotion, and, so, considers satire and comedy inferior. He is deeply concerned with the use of language in poetry and makes judicious distinction between the low and the lofty in language. He pays a notable homage to dignity and splendour of diction in poetry. Pope's adapted translation reflects Horace's idea of poetic diction:

> "Command old words that long have slept, to wake,
> Words, that wise Bacon, or brave Raleigh spake;
> Or bid the new be English, ages hence,
> For use will father what's begot by sense."

Horace's idea of decorum in a sentence is that the poet should not be guided by the whims of the pulpit, and be responsible to the really appreciative audience and compose his poetry in a diction where sound and sense are happily blended, and for that he can use even the archaic and obsolete words.

Poiesis, Poiema and Poietes

Even before Aristotle there was the controversy whether *poiesis* (matter) or *poiema* (form) is more important. In simpler words, the question is: Which function of poetry is more important, instruction or delight? Aristotle gave equal importance to both. He said that tragedy should be artistically perfect so as

11. *Ibid*., p. 84.

to give aesthetic pleasure, and the events be so organized as to purgate the emotions of pity and fear. Horace's predecessor Neoptolemus followed Aristotle. Wimsatt and Brooks summarise the long argumentative passage of J.W.H. Atkins:

> "Stoic philosophers followed more or less consistently to the contentual or didactic view. Professional scholars and critics, like Heracliodorous and Eratosthenes, dwelt on diversion and the enchantment of beautiful words. But, Horace's model Neoptolemus adopted what we may call a Peripatetic compromise, Aristotelian in spirit, but more specific than Aristotle, the doctrine that the aim of poetry is two-fold, to charm and at the same time to be a useful teacher."[12]

After referring to Atkins's conclusion, they quote a passage from *Ars Poetica* to support the view that he followed Neoptolemus' Peripatetic view.

> "Either a poet tries to give good advice, or he tries to be amusing—or he tries to be both.... A mixture of pleasure and profit appeals to every reader—an equal administration of sermon and tickle."[13]

Horace is Aristotleian in his views on the relationship between poetry and poet. Earlier it was believed that a poet was born with a divine inspiration. The ancient poets invoked the Muses to inspire them to write poetry. Aristotle, too, made a passing reference to the poet's special sensibility in chapter XVII of the *Poetics*. But, later, he revised his view in *Rhetoric* that certain things are to be learnt either by native insight or by technical training. Elaborating and specifying Aristotle's vague idea on the creation of poetry, Neoptolemus categorically said that both the natural gift and the technical skill are the requisites of composing a poem. Horace follows Neoptolemus faithfully:

> "People like to ask whether a good poem comes natural or is produced by craft. So far as I can see, neither book - learning without a lot of inspiration nor unimproved

12. *Ibid.*, p. 92.

13. Idem.

genius can get very far. The two things work together and need each other."[14]

After saying this Horace goes on advising poets what they should do. The central point of his advice is that a poet should not be commercial, he must gain the wisdom of Socrates and remember the glorious history of poetry and its sacred function. The best poet is one who accepts the advice of a good honest critic and aims at the top.

It is certain that *Ars Poetica* is not a theoretical treatise nor does it have the comprehensiveness and profundity of Aristotle's *Poetics*; yet it is a charming manual for aspiring poets, and of permanent value for its wit and aphoristic style.

(C) LONGINUS

Very little is known about the author of *On The Sublime*, of which the original title is *Peri Hupsous*. R.A. Scott James is of the view that he flourished in the third century A.D. and his name was Cassius Longinus. Other scholars, basing their argument on internal evidence say that he belongs to the first century A.D. Though there is a controversy about his period, the name Longinus has remained unchallenged. Though *Peri Hupsous* is one of the most remarkable books on literary criticism, it remained in dark for quite a long time and was discovered in the sixteenth century only when Robertello edited and published it in 1554.

Longinus was a rhetorician and his main problem was to make distinction between rhetoric and poetry. His predecessor Augustan Caecilius had written on *hupsos*, a quality of elevation or sublimity in writing. Longinus felt that Caecilius had written very little on the subject of *hupsos* and, so, he discussed the subject in detail in *Peri Hupsous*.

In the very beginning of *Peri Hupsous*, he distinguishes poetry from rhetoric: "The effect of elevated language upon audience is not persuasion but transport." There are three words that need explanation—elevated, persuasion, and transport

14. Quoted in Latin and translated by W.K. Wimsatt and Cleanth Brooks, *Literary Criticism: A Short History*, p. 93.

(*ekstasis*). By "elevated" Longinus means roughly charged with emotion, and not a common language spoken in every day life. Besides, it is not the language of an orator. The second word "persuasion" clarifies the difference between poetic diction and rhetorical language. The aim of an orator is to move the audience to come near his own views. He persuades the people to act as he desires. Antony's speech in *Julius Caesar* is a brilliant example of rhetoric. The third word "transport" is distinct from "persuasion". The aim of a creative writer is to lead the reader or audience to *ecstary*, or what the Indian critics say *ananda*.

How is the function of transport performed? Longinus' answer is that it is done by an elevated language, and there are five sources of elevation (*hupsous*). They are:

(a) The power of forming great conceptions (*noēseis*),

(b) Inspired and vehement passion (*pathos*),

(c) Formation of figures (*schēmata*),

(d) Noble diction (*phrasis*),

(e) Dignified and elevated composition (*sūnthesis*).

The first two sources are there in the poet himself. These two sources are not clearly explained in the extant book. Perhaps, they were explained in some other essay which is now lost. Wimsatt and Brooks explain that these two are co-extensive and not coordinate of the last three. In simple words, they cover the area of the poet's art of forming figures, using noble diction, and writing dignified and elevated composition. The following is the diagram given by them showing the relationship between a poet and a poem.

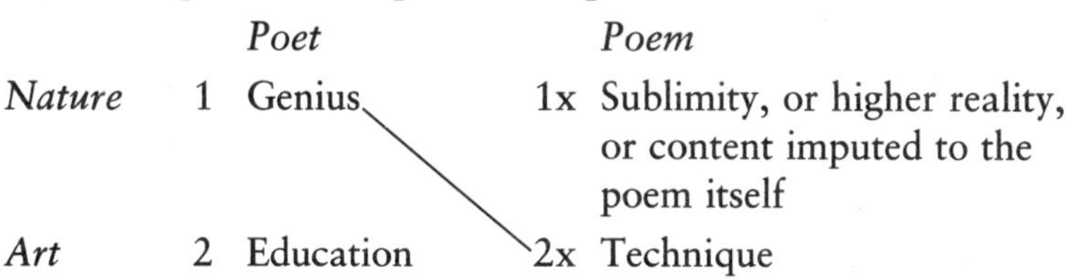

It is clear that the higher ideas and passions play the primary role; the use of figures is for the proper expression of the reality experienced by the writer.

Being a great rhetorician, Longinus has discussed the last three sources, related to the art of writing, in detail. He has taken in account the past Gaeco-Roman conventions and posited his own viewpoint. Nature is important, it is primary, but art perfects it. He writes in chapter II:

> "While nature as a rule is free and independent in matters of passion and elevation, yet she is wont not to act at random and utterly without system. Further nature is the original and vital underlying principle in all cases, but system can define limits and fitting seasons, and can also contribute the safest rules for use and practice."

Longinus' contribution to literary theory is that he has laid emphasis, and rightly so, on the poet's greatness of thought and perception of reality. It is the greatness of idea and world outlook that makes a poem great. The *Iliad*, the *Odyssey*, the *Ramayana*, and the *Mahabharata* are great poems as they contain great ideas as they are written by great souls. But ideas must be suitably expressed for transport (*ekstasis*). Besides, they please all and always. We read Shakespeare's plays not once but again and again as they are perennial source of pleasure. Longinus' greatness has been succinctly assessed in a few lines by Wimsatt and Brooks:

> "One of the most extraordinary features of the essay on *The Sublime* is the variety of criteria, the number of approaches to poetry, which it manages to include—not only the main three, the transport of the audience, the genius of the author, the devices of rhetoric—but in passing the democratic idea that great poetry is that which pleases all and always (in chapter VII) and again a further variation on the subject-object relation, the most spectacular or operative part of the essay (in chapters IX and XXXV), the idea of physical grandeur as the counterpart of the psychic."[15]

---

15. Wimsatt and Brooks, *Literary Criticism: A Short History*, p. 107.

3

BRITISH CRITICISM UPTO THE EIGHTEENTH CENTURY

English literature uptill the time of Chaucer was laden with knight-errantry and supernatural beliefs. The arrival of renaissance changed the thought-process of the English intellectuals. The knowledge of Greece and Rome came like the first rays of the sun that dispersed the thick fog of superstition and false beliefs that covered the entire nation. Secularism and humanism became the dominant ideas in the fourteenth century. It was not only philosophy and science that influenced the English people greatly but also the Greek and Latin literatures. With the beginning of the sixteenth century a new kind of literature, secular and humanistic, began to be written. Chaucer and Langland had heralded the new era in the fourteenth century. The new thrust came with Thomas Wyatt and Earl of Surrey. The poets included in the famous anthology *Tottle's Miscellaney* wrote a new kind of poetry centring on man, his feelings, emotions, problems, and aspirations, and the focus shifted from the supernatural to the human.

If Aeschylus, Sophocles, Euripides, Aristophanese, Homer, Virgil, Horace, Bion, and Petrarch influenced the English poets, the three great literary theorists—Aristotle, Horace, and Longinus—refined their critical insight. No doubt, poets learn from their illustrious predecessors, but critical theories perfect their art of writing. Besides, criticism explains the nature, function, and value of poetry in man's life. Sir Philip Sidney, a poet of great merit (unfortunately he died in a battle field at a very young age), was the first critic who explained lucidly why poetry is of great value to humanity. We can say he is the first important critic from England.

(A) SIR PHILIP SIDNEY: AN APOLOGY FOR POETRY

Sir Philip Sidney wrote *An Apology for Poetry* in reply to Stephen Gosson, a Puritan priest, who denounced poetry saying that it was immoral in a pamphlet titled *School of Abuse: Containing a pleasant invective against Poets, Pipers, Players, Jesters and such like Caterpillars of a Commonwealth*, and dedicated it to "The Right Noble Gentleman, Master Philip Sidney, Esquire." By that time Sidney had got his sonnets to Stella and the romance *Arcadia*. Since, the pamphlet was dedicated to him, he gave a befitting reply to Gosson in a gentlemanly manner. His *Apology for Poetry* is not an invective. On the other hand, it is a scholarly piece of writing and there is no need to know even the fact that it has any relation to Gosson's pamphlet.

Although it was written as early as 1585, it was published in 1598. Because there were two publishers, it was published under two titles: *Defence of Poesie* and *An Apology for Poetry*. The second title *An Apology for Poetry* is more common in our days and only a few anthologies have printed it with the first title. Sidney's aim is to refute Gosson's charge that poetry is immoral, debilitating, and provocative of debauchery. The essay can be divided into three broad headings: (a) Definition of Poetry, (b) The Poet as Maker and Teacher, and (c) Poetry, History, and Philosophy.

Definition of Poetry

In the beginning of the essay Sidney repeats Aristotle's idea of the function of poetry that its aim is to delight and instruct. In other words, poetry gives not only pleasure, it teachers us also, that is, it has a higher form of function and it cannot be immoral or debilitating.

He defines poetry almost repeating the great Greek philosopher:

> "Poetry, therefore, is an art of imitation, for so Aristotle termeth it in his word *mimesis*, that is to say, a representing, counterfeiting, or figuring forth, so to speak metaphorically, a speaking picture, with this end—to teach and delight."

Sidney is quite clear in stating that poetry is not a carbon copy of the objects it imitates. He uses the words "represent" and "counterfeit", which mean "not an exact imitation", and allows the creative writer to add something from his own or deviate from the original because the ultimate end of poetry is to delight the audience and lead them to the path of morality. This idea of his is further explained when he compares poetry with philosophy and history.

He, then, describes the criteria that distinguish poetry from other modes of writing.

The first criterion is verse. A poem is not written in prose. Metre and stanza forms are its basic components. The poet takes liberty with the syntax of the language and makes use of rhyme and figures of speech for the desired expression of his feelings and ideas. Inversion, changes of number, person, tense, periphrasis and rhetorical question and deletion of conjunction are some of the important devices that make verse poetry and distinguishes it from prose. Apart from these, there are simile and metaphor that are the grand features of a good composition.

Secondly, poets use fable, that is, an invented story. It means that while describing an event or scene, a poet employs his imagination and invents something, an event or character, for delight and instruction. The fable may be a pure product of imagination for a fictionalised form of an experience.

Thirdly, there is passion which can be termed as forceful and moving expression. In the words of David Daiches, it means that "imaginative literature can be justified if it communicates historical or philosophical or moral truths in a lively and pleasing manner." But it is difficult to agree with his interpretation. Passion literally means a great, uncontrollable emotion, to do something noble even at the cost of one's own life. The passion of Christ is well-known and so are the Passion plays that dramatize his life. Sidney, in our opinion, refers to passion as a noble emotion very much moral in its aim and is very much near to Longinus on this point.

Sidney, himself a poet, places poetry on a high pedestal and sets a high ideal for all poets and gives a befitting reply to the author of *School of Abuse*.

The Poet

Taking from Aristotle and Horace the idea that poetry delights and teachers, Sidney combines the idea of teaching with the Greek idea of making. The poet (*poietes*) plays the role of maker and teacher at the same time. He sees the world of reality and makes a new world in his poetry to delight and instruct the reader. The world he makes is not very much different from our world, but it is an ideal world where justice and righteousness prevail. He writes:

> "Only the poet...lifted up with the vigour of his own invention, doth grow in effect another nature, in making either better than nature bringeth forth, or quite a new, forms such as never in nature..., so he goeth hand in hand with nature."

The world that a poet creates is not an altogether an ideally perfect world; it is a world peopled with both good and bad characters. But, what happens in this world is that good people come out with flying colours at the end and the bad people suffer punishment for their sinful acts. It is, perhaps, from here the idea of "poetic justice" began. Therefore, the poet is a teacher who leads people to the path of morality by showing off a new world created by him.

Poetry, History, and Philosophy

Sidney makes a comparison between poetry, history and philosophy. As we shall see, his argument that poetry is superior to both is very much based on Aristotle's view expressed in a passing manner in the *Poetics*.

At first, poetry and history are compared. History, says Sidney, simply describes events that occurred in the past. Realistic in nature, it occasionally tells the victory of the bad over the good. This is not the way to teach people live a virtuous life. Poetry, on the other hand, never allows the wicked to win; it always allows the virtuous to win in their struggle against evil.

The argument that history is more real than poetry is not valid. It is said that the poet invents but the historian does not do so, and he describes the events as they have occurred. Yet, it is to be known that there are very few historians who were present in a battlefield, for example. Besides, historians write about those events which had happened long before they were born. Their history is based upon the narration of other people who, too, were not born at the time when a battle was fought. The truth is that both poets and historians invent, but poets teach and historians describe. Naturally, poetry is superior to history.

The same case is there with philosophy. Poetry is superior to it. Philosophy is abstract, but poetry is concrete and based on experience. Sidney writes:

> "The philosopher teaches a disputative virtue, but I do an active virtue.... He teacheth virtue by certain abstract considerations, but I only bid you follow the footing of them that have gone before you."

The total argument of Sidney in favour of poetry is that philosophy teaches us moral values and the path of a virtuous life, but it is abstract, dull, and dry, where as poetry, on the other hand, does the same things in a lively and delightful way. The language of poetry is the language of the concrete.

(B) JOHN DRYDEN

With Dryden began English literary criticism. No doubt, there were critics like Sir Philip Sidney[1] and Ben Jonson who wrote authoritatively on the theory of literature, but inspite of their genius they failed to bring in the "native element" that was the need of the time in England. Sidney followed the classical principles in spirit, but interpreted them in the romantic vein, and Ben Jonson, the great dramatist, adhered to those principles in such a rigid way that he failed to do justice to the contemporary English drama. It was left to John Dryden to apply the classical principles in the analysis and interpretation of the English drama that began in the sixteenth century and reached its height during the Elizabethan and Jacobean periods. He modified the classical

1. In fairness to Sidney, it can be said that Sidney died young at the young age of thirty two.

principles and applied his own critical acumen, an acumen evolved from the study of both the Greek and British plays. He judged Ben Jonson and Shakespeare rightly and we, even today, appreciate his sound and balanced opinion on drama and dramatists. He very rightly deviated from the hackneyed path followed by his contemporaries and predecessors, and these words of his still ring in our ears:

> "It is not enough that Aristotle has said so, for Aristotle drew his models of tragedy from Sophocles and Euripides; and, if he had seen ours, might have changed his mind."

It is clear that Dryden thought originally on the theory of drama. He was fully aware of the fact that Shakespeare and Marlowe wrote the best kind of tragedy, though they did not follow Aristotle to the letter. Being himself a creative writer, Dryden knew that he could not write plays on the beaten lines and, so, made experiments with the form of the drama.

He followed, of course, the principles of literary criticism enunciated by Aristotle and Horace, but modified them in the light of the works of Chaucer, Spenser, Marlowe, Shakespeare, Ben Jonson, and the Jacobean dramatists. His wide learning and open-mindedness enabled him to analyse objects and judge their quality with sympathy and impartiality, and call a spade a spade. He was the first English critic who, adhering to the basic tenets of classicism, formulated a new line of poetics, which we may call neo-classicism.

In his masterpiece *An Essay of Dramatic Poesy*, he not only answered the charges levelled by the French critic Sorbiere against the English plays but also formulated a sound theory of drama, which is still held in high esteem by both critics and playwrights. He defined drama:

> "...a just and lively image of human nature, representing its passions, and its humours, and the change of fortune to which it is subject for the delight and instruction of mankind."

If we compare Dryden's definition of drama with that of Aristotle, we find that he has included both tragedy and comedy, whereas the old master confined himself to tragedy to the maximum and discussed comedy as an inferior form of drama. The reason for doing so is that Aristotle had the plays of Aristophanese and the new comedy of Menander only. Had he seen Shakespeare's comedies, especially *Measure for Measure*, *The Merchant of Venice*, *As You Like It*, *A Winter's Tale*, and *The Tempest*, he would have defined drama in a different way. Dryden's greatness lies in the independence of mind.

The other important aspect of Dryden's critical theory is that the *Essay* maintains a balance between delight and instruction. A creative work is superficial if it is artificial or devoid of morality. A play should be a lively image of human nature, that is, it should present human life in an entertaining manner, but it should lead people to the path of morality. This is why poets and playwrights after Dryden assumed the social responsibility and made efforts to chasten morality with ridicule.

Dryden praises Shakespkeare in the *Essay* as he was able to fuse pleasure and morality together. He praises him in glowing words:

> "Shakespeare was the man who of all moderns, and perhaps ancient poets, had the largest and most comprehensive soul...." And at other place,
>
> "Shakespeare was the Homer, or father of our dramatic poets."

The next important contribution to literary criticism is his concept of the heroic tragedy. Before him, the heroic play was considered the dramatization of the epic or heroic poem. He introduced the elements of "courtly wit" and "admiration" at the place of "fear" and wrote the play *All For Love*, accordingly. However, he was proved wrong in the formulation of his new concept of tragedy.

The idea that "wit" is a very important element in poetry and drama, was received well by his contemporaries and younger writers. Pope followed him and so did the playwrights of the Restoration Comedy.

Adhering to the basic tenets of classical criticism, Dryden formulated his theory of literature emphasizing the importance of morality, wit, polished language, and heroic couplet in poetry and drama. He emphasized the importance of poetic justice so strongly advocated by Sir Philip Sidney. It is really of great credit that when all critics preceding him thought it their duty to repeat almost blindly the classical principles to the letter, Dryden opened a new path for the appreciation of the Elizabethan and Jacobean drama. He said about himself very humbly:

> "I have only laid down some opinion of the Ancients and Moderns, and of my own...which I thought probable."

What he said "probable" was certainty, and this is why T.S. Eliot commented:

> "The great work of Dryden in criticism is that at the right moment he became conscious of the necessity of affirming the native element in literature."

An Essay of Dramatic Poesy

Dryden's fame as a critic rests chiefly on *An Essay of Dramatic Poesy*. He wrote the book in dialogue form during the plague years of 1965-6 when he had retired to the country as a precautionary measure. The adverse remarks of a French diplomat, Samuel Sorbiere, made on the English plays, especially the comedies, that they paid scant regard to the unities of time, place, and action, provoked Dryden to write the *Essay*.

Well conversant with the writings of Corneille, Dryden meditated over Sorbiere's comments but did not give a direct reply to the charges. Formulating a sound theory of drama, he defended the plays written by the dramatists of his time. *An Essay of Dramatic Poesy* is a discussion on the theory of drama by four friends—Crites, Eugenius, Lisideius, and Neander—who board a barge and drift slowly to the Thames to hear the gunshots better in the battle between the English and the Dutch. Since, it is an imagined voyage, they forget the battle and are soon engaged in a literary discussion, the subject, of course, being poetry and drama.

Crites[2], the first speaker, expresses the extreme classical view that the Greeks and Romans fully discovered and illustrated the perennial laws of drama to which the moderns cannot offer

2. Crites is, perhaps, modelled after Sir Robert Howard, Dryden's brother-in-law.

anything new, and that they must conform to the classical views. He further says that there are not any significant differences between the Elizabethan drama and the drama of his time. However, the Elizabethan drama is superior to the contemporary drama except in versification.

Eugenius, possibly Dryden's friend Charles Sackville, takes the other side and says that the ancient poets failed badly in the application of the rules prescribed by their critics. Let us remember that Dryden has deliberately invented the name Eugenius as it is related to the science eugenics that tries to improve the quality of a species by controlled breeding. It follows then that the new generation is better than the old generation, and this is what Eugenius says in his speech.

The third character Lisideius, Sir Charles Sedley in real life, accepts the premises of Crites and Eugenius that the classical rules for imitation of nature as prescribed by Horace in *Ars Poetica* are the basics of dramatic creation. Then, he advances his argument that the best kind of drama is not written by the contemporary English playwrights but by the French dramatists. He, thus, echoes Sorbieres' argument and follows the French critic Corneille.

At this stage when these three have taken three different stands, each negating the other in his conclusion, Neander, meaning the new man who is Dryden himself, intervenes. He accepts Lisideius' definition of the drama and dilates on the words, "lively" , "human nature", "delight", and "instruction":

> "A just and lively, image of human nature, representing its passions and humours, and the changes of fortune to which it is subject, for the delight and instruction of mankind."

The former speakers had put enough stress on the word "just". Now, Neander collocates this word with "lively" and "instruction". He says that the dramatist presents people in action, not static pictures as the French do. Secondly, the word "lively" is closely related to lifelikeness, that is, *verisimilitude* we know today. The English dramatists, he says, present characters who are real human beings, people whom we meet in our everyday life, with the purpose of teaching the audience moral values. Besides, he accepts the principle of the unities of time, place, and action for the purpose of *verisimilitude*.

At the end of the discussion, Neander while praising the importance of rhyme concludes that the classical principles formulated by the Greeks and Romans are still valid and the contemporary English plays conform to those rules better than the French plays. He, in this way justifies the elements of morality or poetic justice, liveliness or verisimilitude, the humours and passion in the plays, both tragedy and comedy, of his time. By the same principles, he indicates the nobleness of the Elizabethan and Jacobean plays, especially of Ben Jonson, Shakespeare, and Fletcher. His remark on Shakespeare and Jonson are of great interest:

> "Shakespeare was the Homer, or father of our dramatic poets; Jonson was the Virgil, the pattern of elaborate writing; I admire him but I love Shakespeare."

The *Essay* ends with the four friends coming quietly to the shore of the river at the foot of Somerset Stairs. Though, they have not reached the points of agreement on certain issues, they part with mutual courtesy. The readers are left free to form their own opinion.

The great merit of *An Essay of Dramatic Poesy*, apart from its balance between feeling and reasoning, is its wit, politeness, and open-endedness. All the characters are allowed to speak their mind without constraint and no one is undermined, though, we all know, Neander is Dryden himself. Dryden's ability to retain openness to contrary arguments makes the *Essay* an enduring piece of criticism. F.R. Leavis has very correctly assessed it and remarked: "*An Essay of Dramatic Poesy* exemplifies that kind of pseudo-platonic dialogue, which during the next seventy-five years became one of the most prevalent neo-classic forms in England."

(C) ALEXANDER POPE

Pope did not write his theory of poetry in prose and, so, he is not a critic in the sense Sidney and Dryden are. He, like

Horace, is essentially a poet whose views are expressed in *An Essay on Criticism* and *An Essay on Man*. Pope's great quality is that he viewed poetry as the expression of an individual's feelings, problems, and aspirations not in isolation but in a social set up. His poetry and poetics deal with man in society. What is more significant is that his writings epitomise the leading ideas of the eighteenth century. The salient features of his critical theory are discussed in brief.

Nature and Art

Pope followed the eighteenth century concept of the relation between nature and art. The Italian renaissance changed the old model of the universe. Milton, although he made use of the classical model of the universe in *Paradise Lost*, was well aware of the views of Copernicus and Galileo. The eighteenth century intellectuals made a compromise between the old religious ideas and the new discoveries of science. They made it clear that the universe is God's creation and nature is His Art. The laws of nature are universal, and there are regularity, order, symmetry, and harmony in its system.

Art is an imitation of nature and, so, it must contain regularity, order, symmetry, and harmony. It is imperative on the part of poetry to follow nature as it is God's art:

> "First follow Nature, and your judgement frame,
> By her just standard, which is still the same:
> Unerring Nature, still divinely bright,
> One clear, unchang'd, and universal light:
> Life, force, and beauty, must to all impart,
> At once the source, and end, and test of art."

The forest is a product of nature, and when man plants trees in an orderly way, he makes a garden, which a work of art.

> "Where order in variety we see
> And where, tho' all things differ, all agree."

Art while imitating nature maintains its variety and within that variety there are unity and harmony. Art is nature, but created with a method and contains a pattern amidst differing elements.

"Those Rules of old discover'd, not devis'd
Are Nature still, but Nature methodis'd."

Man and Poetry

Man is a bundle of contradictions; he is always in diffidence and doubt. There are two main principles in human nature: the first is self-love and the second reason. Self-love drives man to action, which may be good to him and others, or good to him but bad for others. If his action is right and proper, it will be beneficial for all. Righteousness and propriety in action can be achieved by reason, which controls self-love. Now, reason must follow the ways of God. If man follows reason and the ways of God, he will find true happiness in this world. He advises in *An Essay on Man*:

"Remember, man, the Universal Cause
Acts not by partial, but by general laws,
And makes what happiness we justly call
Subsists not in the good of one, but all."

And a little later in Epistle IV of *An Essay on Man*, he writes aphoristically:

"God loves from whole to parts; but human soul
Must rise from individual to whole."

Pope accepts the Aristotelian principle that poetry delights and instructs. His emphasis is on both. Wit is the main instrument of delight:

"What oft was thought, but ne'er so well exprest."

The second function, instruction, is given in detail in *An Essay on Criticism* and *An Essay on Man*. The emphasis is on the content of morality. Man's morality is to be guided by reason, which follows the ways of God. Poetry should instruct how man can get happiness as a social being. The task of poetry is noble as it teaches man how he can establish order, symmetry, and harmony within his self and in the society of which he is a member.

Wit, Versification, and Diction

i. *Wit*

The word "wit" has three meanings: (a) the capacity for inventive thought and quick understanding, (b) a natural aptitude for using words and ideas in a quick and inventive way to create humour, and (c) a person with this aptitude. Wit alone does not make a person a good poet. Reason should control it. As nature is orderly and systematic, and its rules are specific to symmetry and harmony to maintain unity in variety, the poet too should be guided by reason to maintain a balance between wit and judgement.

"Some to whom heaven in wit has been profuse,
Want as much more, to turn it to its use;
For wit and judgement often are at strife,
Though meant each other's aid, like man and wife."

ii. *Versification*

Pope considers the iambic metre the best as all great classics are written in that metre. If there is rhyme in two lines and they form a couplet, it is much better. In other words, the heroic couplet is the best kind of versification. The iambic metre is slow and majestic in movement, and in the pentametre, the third foot balances the preceding and following feet. The rhyme gives an impressive effect in the heroic couplet. Pope makes a plea for the heroic couplet as it is regular, symmetrical, witty, and pleasing to the ear.

But, he says, the handling of heroic couplet is delicate. A slight mistake may spoil the desired effect. First, there should be proper rhyme in a couplet. The rhyme should be meaningful too. Meaningless rhyme may destroy its beauty. He also warns the danger of the use of unnecessary open-vowel endings and use of expletives.

"These equal syllables alone require,
Tho' oft the ear the open vowels tire;
While expletives their feeble aid do join;
And ten low words oft creep in one dull line."

He demonstrates how a long metre can be adroitly used for both slow and fast paces. The first is the example of slow movement:

"A needless Alexandrine ends the song
That like a wounded snake, drags its slow length along."

The second example is of fast movement:

> "Not so, when swift Camilla scours the plain
> Flies o'er th' unbending corn, and skims along the main."

Pope's ideals are Homer, Horace, Quintillian, and John Dryden, the great masters of heroic couplet.

> "Be Homer's works your study and delight
> Read them by day and meditate by night."[3]

iii. *Diction*

Pope' concept of the language of poetry is rather narrow. He assumes that the kind of diction used by Horace and Dryden is the ideal. We can say that he is in favour of the language used by the aristocracy in London and the universities of Oxford, and Cambridge. Within this narrow range he expresses his views on poetic diction and style. He says that a poet imitates nature faithfully and dresses the sublime thoughts in a sparkling diction. But, if he is more interested in language and not in the sublimity of thought, his poetry becomes a luxuriant tree without fruit. Abundance of words or verbosity is a disqualification and, so, it is always advisable to express great ideas in plain words. He explains how verbosity is a defect.

> "Others for language all their care express
> And value books, as women, men, for dress
> Their praise is still—the style is excellent,
> The sense, they humbly take upon content.
> Words are like leaves; and where they most abound,
> Much fruit of beneath is rarely found."

There must be a proper correlation between sound and sense. More sound is empty of meaning and the reader or the listener wonders what the poet is saying.

The diction of a poem should correspond to its subject matter and emotion. The words should be soft and gentle while describing the spring season, be highly formal while making comments; ridicule should not be vulgar and must be tinged with subtle irony, and while expressing wrath they should be

---

3. Translation of Horace's words in *Ars Poetica*.

hoarse and coarse, "like the torrent roar/when Ajax strives some rock's vast weight to throw."

Pope's ideal is his predecessor John Dryden who varied his style to match the subject-matter and the emotion. He admires Dryden that he had the ability to express his ideas in fewest words possible. Pope is humble enough not to refer to his own lines, which are the best examples of brevity and sparkling wit.

(D) SAMUEL JOHNSON

Samuel Johnson, popularly known as Dr. Johnson, is the greatest figure in the English literary history. The first authoritative lexicographer, eminent scholar, great literary theorist, essayist, and poet, Dr. Johnson stands as a tower before us. He is the first critic who following Aristotle's concept of the universal, combined the author's biography with his works, the method that was adopted by Sigmund Freud and his followers in a specialized and scientific way. Even today, his *Rasselas, Preface to Shakespeare*, and *Lives of Poets* are read with the same interest as they were in the eighteenth century. Here, the main points of his critical theory are explained in brief.

The Theory of the Universal

The Greek philosopher Plato propounded the idea that abstract forms are more basic than material things. Aristotle also accepted his teacher's concept of the universality of forms. The material objects of the world are made after the form or idea. They differ in appearance as they are imitations of the Form. In other words, Form or Idea is universal. Dr. Johnson accepting the viewpoints of the Greek philosophers says that poetry is imitation of both the particular and the universal, and that the universal or general is portrayed through the study of the particular. General nature is what is found in most people in most ages. Its opposite is the idiosyncratic, the eccentric behaviour of only a few people in a few places in few times. He writes in *Life of Cowley*:

> "Great thoughts are always general, and consist in positions not limited by exceptions, and in descriptions not descending to minuteness."

As poetry is primarily concerned with general ideas, its main task is to imitate them in a language, which aims at universality.

> "It is a general rule in poetry that all appropriated terms of art should be sunk in general expressions, because poetry is to speak a universal language."

Imlac, the main character in *Rasselas*, expresses the same idea more explicitly:

> "The business of the poet...is to examine, not the individual, but the species; to remark general properties and large appearances; he does not number the streaks of the tulip, or describe the different shades in the verdure of the forest. He is to exhibit in his portraits of nature such prominent and striking features, as recall the original to every mind.... He must dirvest himself of the prejudices of his age or country; he must consider right and wrong in their abstracted and invariable state; he must disregard present laws and opinions, and rise to general and transcendental truths, which will always be the same."

Dr. Johnson's ideal is quite high. He expects great literature to transcend the limits of a country or nation, and be universal in respect of time and space. However, he is cautious enough to give importance to the individual also. If poets represent only the general in human nature, all works will be almost identical. This is why he expects a writer to create an individual that will represent his species also. The creative writer should embody the universal traits in his characters. It is for this reason that he praises Shakespeare in *Preface to Shakespeare*:

> "Shakespeare's characters are not modified by the customs of particular places, unpracticed by the rest of the world; ...they are the genuine progeny of common humanity.... His persons act and speak by the influence of those general passions and principles by which all minds are agitated, and the whole system of life is continued in motion. In the writings of other poets, a character is too often an individual; in those of Shakespeare it is commonly a species."

Dr. Johnson's view that a character should have individual traits and universal qualities as well is very much that of Engels and Gorky who expressed the view that a character must have its own individuality, yet look like a member of its social group or species.[4] It is important to note that this view was expressed by Dr. Johnson one hundred years ago.

The Biographical Method

Dr. Johnson's biographical method is best illustrated in his monumental *Lives of the Poets*. He begins the evaluation of every poet with a selective sketch of his life, especially his social and moral disposition, and then correlates the ideas developed by him in his poetry. What is significant is that the literary achievements of the author in *Lives* are interpreted and judged from social, moral, and critical points of view.

David Daiches is of the view that Dr. Johnson's method is different from that of the nineteenth century biographers like Edward Dowden who adopted the biocritical method. But, we have to aceept the fact that the nineteenth century biocritical method has its origin in *Lives of the Poets*. Now, after significant contribution of Freud to literary criticisim, an author's biography is being considered a good source for understanding of the meaning of her/his work, especially the unconscious meaning. Besides, the French structuralists also consider it important to have a good knowledge of an author's life for understanding the development and shaping of her/his mind.

The Comparative Method

Johnson followed Dryden's comparative method more elaborately under his biocritical method. Like Dryden, he felt that no writer would be properly evaluated in isolation, and it is necessary to compare him with other authors. Purely normative criticism cannot go very far giving awards to each work measuring it with a scale. Secondly, it is to be assessed in comparison with other works of the same genre. This method

4. Engels wrote "Each of them is a type [in Minna Kautsky's novel *Old Ones and the NEW*] but at the same time also a definite individual, a *Deiser*, as old Hegel would express himself, and that is how it should be."

was adopted by R.S. Crane in his analysis and interpretation of Shakespeare's *Macbeth*.

Thus, Dr. Johnson used his comparative method at two levels: first, the comparison between two authors, and second between the given text and other texts belonging to the same genre. Since, the first level of comparison is primary, he paid more attention to it in *Lives of the Poets*, where he made a comprehensive comparison between different poets, especially in *Life of Pope*. In this study, he, while comparing Pope and Dryden, included biographical data as a part of the comparison. He established the literary characters of Pope and Dryden, their habits of mind, and their poetic faculty's working, before he went to discuss and evaluate their literary achievements.

Evaluation of Shakespeare

Dr. Johnson followed Dryden to a large extent in his appraisal of Shakespeare. Yet, we should not assume that he copied Dryden's line of criticism. If Shakespeare is great, it is because he fulfils all conditions of the theory of the Universal. Of course, his plays are the models of Dryden's famous definition of drama as given in *An Essay of Dramatic Poesy* as they are the faithful mirrors of manners and of life as it is. The characters are not affected by the customs of particular places, unpractised by the rest of the world. They are a part of the teeming humanity. Johnson praises Shakespeare's universality:

> "In the writings of other poets a character is too often an individual, in those of Shakespeare it is commonly a species."

As the main task of poetry is to delight and instruct, a poet should not be a mere entertainer. Shakespeare's plays, Johnson says, are delightful, no doubt, but they instruct also. "Instruction" he writes, "can be derived from his wide extension of design. His plays are filled with axioms and domestic wisdom."

Shakespeare's heroes are not heroes of the classical period of Greece and Rome. They are people like the common Englishmen. Hamlet or Othello is not different from John or Jack. The remarkable quality of the dramatist is that "he approximates the remote and familiarises the wonderful."

Johnson criticises Shakespeare on the ground of his defiance of the principle of poetic justice, because he sacrifices virtue to convenience occasionally. Sometimes, he is so much engrossed in pleasing the coarse audience that he forgets to instruct them the lose sight of morality principle of poetic; Cordelia should not have met her tragic end.

Metaphysical Poetry

Johnson is rather harsh on metaphysical poets, guided by the spirit of the age, he favours the classical tradition and criticises deviation from it. John Dryden accused Donne of affecting "metaphysics where nature should reign" and perplexing the "minds of the fair sex with nice speculations of philosophy, when he should engage their hearts with the softness of love."

Johnson criticises the metaphysical poets on three counts:

(i) The metaphysical poets were men of learning and their entire endeavour was to exhibit their knowledge. They showed their learning in rhyme-scheme and far-fetched imagery, and thus wrote verse, not poetry. Their poetry is an exercise of fingers to count stresses. Because of their unusual rhythm, they fail to appeal to the ear.

(ii) They imitated neither nature nor life. What Johnson means here is that the metaphysical poets went against the norms, the English society had set up. As such they were far away from the reality of life and failed to imitate it as it is.

(iii) They had wit but did not have natural thought. They could not express their ideas and feelings in a natural way; on the other hand, the most heterogeneous ideas are yoked by violence together.

Milton's *Lycidas* and Pastoral Poetry

Dr. Johnson like Dryden moved freely from grand generalisations about the form and content of poetry to their practical application. Although his arguments are strong and convincing, they occasionally suffer from his strong likes and dislikes. His judgements on the merit of a poem are marred by a narrower and biased taste occasionally. As he never liked pastoral poetry, his analysis of Milton's *Lycidas* is tinged with a biased attitude to its theme, form, and metre.

He criticises *Lycidas* for the reason that it is a pastoral poem, which does not progress because of its limited range. The second reason for its being a poem of inferior quality is that a poem should be a part of the poet's experience but, in *Lycidas* Milton is not the sufferer. As the poem is not the result of Milton's own experience, it lacks "true passion" and, hence, devoid of truth and vulgar in taste. He writes in *Life of Milton*:

> "In this poem there is no nature, for there is no truth; there is no art, for there is nothing new. Its form is that of pastoral, easy, vulgar, and, therefore, disgusting."

In the same *Life*, he comments on its diction and metre disapprovingly:

> "One of the poems on which much praise has been bestowed is *Lycidas* of which the diction is harsh, the rhymes uncertain, and the numbers uncertain."

Dr. Johnson has been criticised for his harsh judgement on *Lycidas*, but in fairness to him it can be said that he, after all, was the product of his age and carried with him the literary taste of the time. He was tuned to diction and metrical forms of the classical age, and any kind of deviation from the established convention and the standard rhythm of the period seemed harsh and vulgar. Secondly, he was not prejudiced against Milton the poet. He did praise *Paradise Lost* lavishly, because he found it a superb poem. The truth is that he had his own touchstone and tested every literary text objectively.

4

BRITISH CRITICISM: THE NINETEENTH CENTURY

(A) WILLIAM WORDSWORTH

Soon after, Dr. Johnson, creative writers began to react against the classicism of Dryden and the eighteenth century. They found that the regular use of the heroic couplet and neglect of other stanza forms especially rhyme royal, spenserian stanza, quartet, terza rima, and ottava rima was not fair, and that the eighteenth century poets made the stream of poetry an artificial canal. Besides, the restraint of emotion in poetry, they found, was undesirable. The first poet who showed this mood of transition from classicism to romanticism was Thomas Gray who made a break with the tradition in *Elegy Written in a Country Churchyard*, *The Bard*, and *Progress of Poesy*; William Collins wrote *Ode to Evening* and William Blake *Songs of Innocence* and *Songs of Experience*, the poems that could never be written and appreciated in the age of Dryden and Dr. Johnson. The theory behind the new kind of poetry was given by William Wordsworth in "Preface" to the *Lyrical Ballads*, a collection of poems, almost all by Wordsworth himself and his friend Samuel Taylor Coleridge, in the year 1798.

The great shift, as M.H. Abrams has pointed out and discussed at length in *The Mirror and The Lamp*, was from the view of imitating reality to showing it. Uptill the eighteenth century, all literary theorists said that poetry was a mirror where reality was reflected, Wordsworth and Coleridge called it a lamp that showed reality and that it had its own existence, a thing in itself. It was this new concept of poetry that was developed by the New Critics of America.

Wordsworth's Poetic Theory

Wordsworth sharply reacted against the eighteenth century literary theory which rested upon the classical idea of imitation or *mimesis*, which envisages that the poet is an imitator of "general nature", and strictly adheres to the perceived reality. In the strife between fancy/imagination and reason, the latter has upper hand. In other words, reason is like a rider who controls the horse of fancy. Pope wrote in *An Essay on Criticism*:

> The winged courser, like a generous horse
> Shows true mettle when you check his course!

Wordsworth's definition of poetry is just the opposite.

> "I have said that poetry is the spontaneous overflow of powerful feelings: it takes its origin from emotion recollected in tranquillity: the emotion is contemplated till...the tranquillity gradually disappears and an emotion, kindred to that which was before the subject of contemplation, is gradually produced...."

By this definition Wordsworth means that a poet does not write a poem just on the scene of an event or experience, which he is watching or experiencing. The event or experience moves him deeply and he recollects it when he is alone at a peaceful place. During contemplation, the tranquillity passes away and the past emotion takes him over. He writes poetry in that state. Reason has no place in the composition of a poem; the word *overflow* suggests that the poet is a container who cannot hold the powerful emotions recollected in tranquillity for a long time and they will surge up to flow out in the form of poetry.

This definition clearly marks a shift from the mimetic depiction of external objects under the control of reason to the spontaneous and unrestrained expression of emotions. The poet transmutes all his sense perceptions into poetry with the help of imagination.

Some interpreters of Wordsworth's poetic theory in order to simplify his definition are content with the phrase "emotions recollected in tranquillity" and leave the clause "till...the tranquillity gradually disappears." Yeats says that a poet creates poetry in a trance and Wordsworth is in some other way near to

Yeats when he says that a poet is seized by the emotion he had in the past. Here imagination plays the most vital role in bringing back the experience of the past and creating a mood in which a successful composition generally begins.

"The Daffodils" best illustrates Wordsworth's definition of poetry and the process of composition. Wordsworth felt a great pleasure when he saw a large number of daffodils by a lake. But, he did not compose the poem sitting in a corner. It is only after his return from the place and passage of time that he composed "The Daffodils" in tranquillity:

> "For oft when on my couch I lie
> In vacant or in pensive mood;
> They flash upon that inward eye
> Which is the bliss of solitude.
> And then my heart with pleasure fills,
> And dances with the daffodils."

The last two lines suggest that the recollection of the daffodils stirs the poet to his depths and overwhelms him with the original ecstatic emotion. It is this recreated emotion, which is transmuted into poetry. Professor Garrod has very succinctly remarked:

> "It is this hour of passionate awakening, which is the hour of poetry."

Of great critical interest is Wordsworth's concept of imagination as a creative power. The eighteenth century critics and poets did not make difference between fancy and imagination, and said that "fancy [is] the power of forming ideal pictures." Wordsworth and Coleridge gave more importance to imagination, and defined it as a power

> "...of higher import, denoting operations of the mind upon those objects, and process of creation or of composition governed by certain fixed laws."

It is a creative power that acts upon the objects of the world. It is the most active agent of the poetic process that transmutes the sense impressions into poetry by recreating it.

Wordsworth's poetic theory best harmonised the ideas of the romantics like Coleridge, Byron, Shelley, and Keats, and the precursors of romanticism like Gray and Collins, and showed a new path to the younger generation of writers. His rejection of the mimetic theory that poetry is a mirror of reality and positing the new theory that it is a lamp that shows reality is of paramount importance in the development of literary criticism in the western world, especially England.

Subject-matter and Theme of Poetry

Wordsworth declared in "Preface" to the *Lyrical Ballads* that he would choose for the subject-matter of his poetry "incidents and situations from common life." He further wrote that the "poet is a man speaking to men". Wordsworth's "man" is different from Dryden's or Pope's "man". Pope, no doubt, wrote "The proper study of mankind is man", but his "man" is the urban man inhabiting the city of London. In fact, the eighteenth century poets seldom went beyond the precincts of the city wall and remained happy with focusing their attention mostly on the town life. As Professor Sutherland has pointed out, even nature for them meant human nature, or the immutable laws governing the universe, or the rules of art extracted from the works of the ancients.

Wordsworth's view on the subject-matter and theme of poetry is quite different from that of the eighteenth century poets. Nature for him is a patronising force that leads man to perfection. Spectacular sights as blue hills, snow-clad mountains, meandering rivers, sparkling waves, a host of blooming flowers are physical manifestations of nature, which is a spirit that guides man to ennoble his soul. This is why he considered:

> "...man and nature as essentially adopted to each other, and the mind of man as naturally the mirror of the fairest and most interesting properties of nature."

Man is not the lone subject of poetry. It is the interaction of man and nature that gives rise to appropriate subject-matter of abiding interest. Wordsworth, thus, made improvement upon the diction of Pope and postulated that "poetry is the image of man and nature." He wrote in *The Recluse*:

> "On Man, on Nature, and on Human life,
> Musing in solitude, I oft perceive

Fair strains of imagery before me rise
Accompanied by feelings of delight
Pure, with no unplacing sadness mixed."

As opposed to his predecessors, Wordsworth decided to choose humble and simple rural life for poetic treatment and discarded the false refinements of the towns-people. He proposed to relate the incidents and situations from common life in simple and plain idioms and trace in them "the primary laws of our nature." In his poems he took up such humble characters as a leech-gatherer, an insane mother, an idiot boy, an old beggar, and a solitary reaper. He explained in the *Preface* that he chose such characters for the reason that they were nearest to nature and quite unsophisticated, and hence suited to poetic treatment.

> "Humble and rustic life was generally chosen because in that condition, the essential passions of the heart find a better soil in which they can attain their maturity, are less under restraint, and speak a plainer or more emphatic language...."

The quoted passage indicates Wordsworth's conviction that the common and humble humanity, which toils and loves and shares the general heritage of smiles and tears, is the only subject of permanent interest. Naturally, Wordsworth's themes and subject-matter are the common people who live simply in the company of nature, and not the joys and sorrows of princes and renowned heroes.

Historically speaking, Wordsworth's experiment in respect of the new themes of poetry is highly significant. Breaking the barriers of the eighteenth century tradition and taking inspiration from Gray's *Elegy*, he opened a new vista for "the great and important extension of literary sympathies and subject-matter." James Sutherland paid him a glowing tribute when he wrote:

> "It has been customary to assume that to any real poet not only the meanest flower that blows but the humblest man that walks the earth, ought invariably to give thoughts that do lie too deep for tears."

To Wordsworth, therefore, must go the credit for introducing such themes into English as are essentially democratic in nature.

In this respect he is an innovator and trend-setter. He is the first to assert and demonstrate that the depiction of the common man and his humble world, his hopes and fears, his weal and woe, his natural and human surroundings may be a source of great aesthetic pleasure and moral instruction.

Poetic Diction

No part of Wordsworth's *Preface* has been of greater critical controversy than that which deals with poetic diction. Wordsworth is chiefly concerned, apart from the subject-matter, with the language of poetry. A careful study of the *Preface* (1800) and *Appendix* on poetic diction reveals his abiding interest in the question of the language of poetry. He fulminates against the glossy, unfelling and stilted diction of the preceding age and proposes to substitute for it "the language really used by men." This is the upshot of his observations on the subject, and herein consists his most remarkable experiment in the realm of poetic theory. To put in the words of Rene Wellek:

> "All the emphasis is put on Wordsworth's rejection of eighteenth century diction, on his identification of 'language of prose' with that of metrical composition, and of the language of poetry with the language spoken by the middle and lower classes of society."

The question of poetic diction is as old as poetry itself; Aristotle made comments on the language of drama, and Horace and Longinus much more. Longinus made distinction between rhetoric and poetry, and laid emphasis on the emotive aspect for "transport". In England, the eighteenth century poets and critics raised the question of poetic diction and discussed it in detail. They protested against the poetic diction that was latinate, pedantic and affected, and appealed for polite idiom, the educated spoken word. Alexander Pope wanted poetic diction to be precise and polished, or in modern terms, cultured:

> "True wit is Nature to advantage dress'd
> What was oft thought, but never so well express'd."

The romantic poets led by Wordsworth, too, reacted against pedantry and affectation, but their appeal was for the primitive, the native, the directly passionate, the natural spoken word. Wordsworth went further when he asserted that there is no difference between the language of the common man and that of poetry, practically:

> "..., there neither is, nor can be, any essential difference between the language of prose and metrical composition."

He repudiated Thomas Gray's pronouncement that "the language of the age is never the language of poetry." His concept of poetic diction is related to his notion of the subject-matter of poetry. He declared that he would choose "incidents and situations from common life" to write poems. He argued that as man and nature are "essentially adopted to each other, and the mind of man is naturally the mirror of the fairest and most interesting nature", the poet should study the life of the common people and "relate or describe them throughout as far as possible in a selection of language really used by men."

Wordsworth's rejection of the elaborate and highly decorative urbane diction of his lesser contemporaries and plea for plain language led to a great controversy as well misunderstanding. His friend and collaborator S.T. Coleridge refuted Wordsworth's view of poetic diction. He argued that if Wordsworth meant that poetry and prose have the same vocabulary, or dictionary, on which to draw, he simply uttered a truism. Secondly, if a poet writes bad poetry, the fault lies in him not in the language he is using. And thirdly, the uneducated rustic never speaks a poetic language; it is the educated poet who changes it into poetry. The reading public found that Wordsworth himself did not follow his own principles in his masterpieces, like *The Prelude, Ode on Intimations of Immortality* and *Tintern Abbey.*

In fairness to Wordsworth's concept of diction, it can be said that in the enthusiasm of his youth he made big pronouncements hurriedly, and did not give second thought to them. Besides, he did not criticise Spenser, Milton, and Pope, the poets who created English poetic diction. He targeted the now anonymous contemporary poets who wrote the melange of dictions. He criticised, indirectly, the unhealthy tradition that used a too decorative diction, completely devoid of sincerity of feeling what the poets of the eighteen-nineties did fifty years later. He stressed the need for using words, phrases, and images from the everyday life of the common people who lived in calm, serene, and green surroundings, far away from the smoky lanes of London and other big cities. Being far away from the artificial life of the town, they thought plainly and spoke the language of the heart. His assertion that "the language of conversation in the middle and lower classes of society is adopted to the purposes of poetic pleasure" anticipates J.M. Synge's use of the language of the Aran Island's people in his world class plays.

The Importance of "Preface" to *Lyrical Ballads*

Wordsworth wrote the *Preface* to the second edition of the *Lyrical Ballads* that was published in 1800, two years after the first edition. The *Preface*, writes Rene Wellek, is usually considered the manifesto of English Romantic Movement, the signal for break with the age of Neo-Classicism. No doubt, a close study of the *Preface* confirms the remark of Rene Wellek that Wordsworth has broken a new ground of English poetic theory, yet we should be aware of the fact it is not an out and out novel or experimental critical work having no affinities with the neo-classical postulates against which he reacted so sharply. No poet can demolish tradition completely; all that he does is to make certain innovations to enrich it. Wordsworth corrected a few extremes of the neo-classical period and revived some of the best of Elizabethan poetry that was most congenial to his age.

The eighteenth century poets focused their attention on wit and reason. They disliked the upsurge of emotion and pleaded for its reasonable control. They made excessive use of the heroic couplet which resulted in monotony and dullness. The great virtue of Wordsworth's *Preface* is that it propounded the idea that poetry is basically an expression of feelings that overwhelm human beings being subjective in nature. The various faculties of the mind—sensation, emotion, imagination, and contemplation—work in harmony and contribute towards poetic creation. On the point of contemplation, he is very much like Matthew Arnold who defined poetry as a criticism of life. The following passage gives us a good idea about the process of poetic creation where contemplation plays an important role.

> "I have said that poetry is the spontaneous overflow of powerful feelings: it takes its origin from emotion recollected in tranquillity: the *emotion is contemplated*[1] till.... The tranquillity gradually disappears and an emotion, kindred to that which was before *the subject of contemplation*, is gradually produced."

Wordsworth's experiment with regard to the subject-matter of poetry is of great historical importance. Though, poets like Blake and Gray had written about the common people and their poor neglected life, it was Wordsworth who gave a theoretical base for such kind of poetry. And what he wrote in the *Preface*, he actually did in his poetry and produced such immortal poems like "Lucy Gray", "The Solitary Reaper", "The Leech-gatherer", "The Cuckoo", "The Rainbow", "We Are Seven", "Michael", and many poems like these, especially "The Lucy Poems".

The second important point of discussion in the *Preface* is the language of poetry. In the first place it underlines "the absurdity of decorating and dressing poetry with unnecessary embellishments to the neglect of genuine poetic inspiration". Wordsworth does not accept an "art" that outgrows and overtops "nature". Secondly, he has propounded a great principle of not only poetry but all creative writing that the medium should be adequate to the idea and that the highest art lies in "the perfect harmony of thought and form". Thirdly, the language of everyday life can be successfully employed in poetry. That the language of conversation and the language of poetry can be brought together has been advocated by Eliot in his famous essay "Poetry and Drama" and experimented in *Murder in Cathedral*. However, Wordsworth takes an extreme point of view when he says that there is no difference between the two kinds of language. As I.A. Richards has pointed out there are two uses of language: referential and emotive, the language of the common people is generally referential. When the poet uses it, he makes it poetic by organizing the words in a

1. Italics mine.

special way. The simple words form an image or become metaphors and symbols.

In the *Preface*, Wordsworth is quite explicit in defining the function of poetry and is at one with the neo-classicists. He very clearly states that poetry is not an end in itself and that it should be used as a vehicle of moral teaching. He differed from the eighteenth century writers and pleaded for the refinement of sensibilities to render them more humane and compassionate. It is difficult to say how much he was influenced by Rousseau, but it is certain that he pleaded in the *Preface* that poetry should not be artificial and it is not manners but sensibility that is to be refined and purgated by poetry. It is this view of Wordsworth that influenced Matthew Arnold and John Ruskin who held the view that "poetry is the application of noble and profound ideas to life" and that "the art of a nation...is an exponent of its ethical state."

Lastly, Wordsworth's views on practical criticism contain the seed for much later literary criticism. He affirms that the reader should not allow an outside authority to over-ride his critical opinion. His view that a new work of art should be judged with reference to classic examples influenced Arnold in the formation of his "touchstone method." The *Preface* is in addition, forerunner of Walter Pater's view that the merits of a work of art should be judged on the basis of one's own impressions.

The "Preface" to the *Lyrical Ballads* is of great historical importance for its revolutionary ideas on the theory of poetry, diction, and practical criticism. It created a new taste in reading poetry and influenced the younger generation of creative writers to compose a new kind of poetry, which is still unsurpassed despite the hostile criticism of T.S. Eliot and F.R. Leavis.

(B) SAMUEL TAYLOR COLERIDGE

S.T. Coleridge laid the foundation of modern criticism. Imbibing the concepts of Kantian and Hegelian philosophy he introduced a new meaning of imagination and placed it high above "fancy" that was almost synonymous with it in the eighteenth century. Taking Kant's concept of "the thing in itself" he maintained that a poem has its own identity and autonomy, an idea that was later developed and perfected first by Eliot and, later on, by the New Critics of America. Following are the basic concepts of his critical theory.

Poetry is an Organic Whole

There is a great similarity between Kant's concept of the "thing in itself" and Coleridge's notion of a poem. In a legitimate poem, the relation between the parts and the whole is intimate and organic, and there is a total harmony of expression and form, and content become different aspects of the same thing. Secondly, the total is more than the sum total of its parts, and has its own existence and meaning. He writes in *Biographia Literaria*:

> "A poem is that species of composition, which is opposed to works of science by proposing for its immediate object pleasure, not truth.... It is discriminated by proposing itself such delight from the whole, as is compatible with a distinct gratification from each component part."

Of course, Coleridge repeats what Aristotle said in *Poetics*. The components, too, support the whole. The difference between the two is that Coleridge observes the difference between science and poetry, and says that the whole poem gives us delight or aesthetic pleasure whereas science provides us truth.

Later on, he comes to the kind of truth poetry shows to the reader. Science and philosophy are concerned with differentiation of objects for the discovery of truth. For them the communication of truth is the immediate purpose. On the other hand, the immediate purpose of poetry is pleasure and the ultimate end is truth, moral or intellectual.

In what way is a poem an organic whole? Coleridge explains that the contents of prose and poetry are the same. The difference between the two is that of combination. A poem makes use of metre and rhyme but a prose passage does not. A particular pleasure is felt when the sounds are harmonised and when a prose piece contains that quality, it, too, becomes poetry. In other words, all compositions that have the chain of the recurrence of sounds and numbers superadded become poetry, whatever may be their contents. Secondly, poetry is best words in best order. The deletion or alteration of a word or phrase way make it disjointed. The organicity of a poem lies in its emotive sequence of words.

Poetry and Poet

Coleridge considers poetry the activity of the poetic genius. He writes:

> "What is poetry? is nearly the same question with, what is a poet. That the answer to the one is involved in the solution of the other. For it is a distinction resulting from the poetic genius itself, which sustains and modifies the images, thoughts, and emotions of the poet's own mind."

The poet, in ideal perfection, brings the whole soul of man into activity. Coleridge makes distinction between poetry and poem. In fact, he should have used the word verse at the place of poem. The Sanskrit scholars Dandin and Bhamaha had made this distinction in the eighth century, and said that even a prose passage could be poetic. Coleridge says that poetry is not confined to metrical language only; it can be, in a larger sense, engaged by painters, philosophers, and scientists.

Since, poetry is a creation of the poet and imagination is the magical power to balance or reconcile the opposites and discordant qualities, the poet employs it for composing a good poem. Fancy is also there but it, at best, helps to produce a bad or inferior poem.

Imagination and Fancy

Fancy and imagination were synonymous upto the eighteenth century. The romantic movement began first in Germany when A.W. Shlegel published his *Lectures of Dramatic Art and Literature*. A little later, Hegel in his *Lectures on Aesthetics* classified the development of art and poetry into three stages:

symbolic, classic, and romantic.[2] Coleridge, himself a philosopher, accepted the German concept of romanticism and combined it with imagination.

Wordsworth was the first person to make distinction between fancy and imagination. He wrote in the *Preface* about "fancy".

> "Fancy depends upon the rapidity and profusion with which she scatters her thoughts and images... or she prides herself upon the curious subtlety and the curious elaboration with which she can detect their lurking affinities."

He quoted his friend the famous essayist, Charles Lamb, who had defined imagination explicitly:

> "Imagination draws all things to one...it makes things animate or inanimate, beings with their attributes, subjects with their accessories, take one colour and serve to one effect."

Coleridge made the distinction between the two clearer and better than what Wordsworth had done. He divided imagination into primary and secondary, and distinguished them from fancy.

> "The imagination then, I consider either as primary, or secondary. The primary imagination I hold to be the living power and prime agent of all human perception, and as a repetition in the finite mind of the eternal act of creation in the infinite I am. The secondary imagination I consider as an echo of the former, co-existing with the conscious will, yet still as identical with the primary in the *kind*, and differing only in *degree* and in the *mode* of its operation, It dissolves, diffuses, dissipates, in order to recreate; or where the process is rendered impossible, yet still at all events it struggles to idealize and to unify. It is essentially vital as all objects (as objects) are essentially fixed and dead."

---

2. symbolic = the art of Egypt in the pyramid period; classic=the art and poetry of Greece in the classical period; and romantic=modern art and poetry.

What is the relation between these two forms of imagination? we may ask. Coleridge says that the imagination has two stages. In the primary stage (manifestation) it is the great ordering principle. It is the agent, which enables us to both discriminate and order, separate and synthesize, and make perception possible. The secondary imagination is the conscious human use of this power. When a person employs his primary imagination, he does not make a conscious effort. He simply exercises the basic faculty of his awareness of his self and the external world. The secondary imagination is more conscious and less elemental, but it does not differ in kind from the primary. It projects and creates new harmories of meaning. The employment of the secondary imagination is, in the larger sense, a poetic activity.

Fancy is not that rich and powerful and harmonizing power, and hence inferior to imagination. Coleridge writes:

> "Fancy, on the contrary, has no counters to play with, but fixities and definites. The fancy is indeed no other than a mode of memory emancipated from the order of time and space; while it is blended with, and modified by that empirical phenomenon of the will, which we express by the word CHOICE. But equally with the ordinary memory, fancy must receive all its material ready made from the law of association."

Since fancy is related to fixities and definites, it does not have the ability to harmonize the discordant variables. Naturally, it is inferior to imagination. Imagination is the right instrument of poetic creativity.

Thus, Coleridge made a clear cut distinction between imagination and fancy and placed the former on a higher pedestal. Of course, as he himself admitted, he was highly indebted to his friend William Wordsworth—who had acknowledged his indebtedness to Charles Lamb, the famous essayist.

(C) PERCY BYSSHE SHELLEY

Shelley, can best be compared with Sir Philip Sidney. Like Sidney, he wrote "A Defence of Poetry" and like him died young. But there is a difference; Sidney was with the establishment while Shelley was a rebel. For Sidney, poetry delights and teaches, but for Shelley, it is a means to achieve a goal more noble than mere teaching morality, the transformation of this sorrowful world into a happy world. For him, poetry has a social function, apart from giving aesthetic pleasure and moral values to an individual.

"A Defence of Poetry" can be divided into three parts. In the first part Shelley defines poetry. He says that there are two mental faculties in man: reason and imagination. Reason is concerned with the inter-relationship of thoughts whereas imagination colours those thoughts with its own light like the sun. It composes from them other thoughts, each containing within itself the principle of its own integrity. It means that imagination is superior to reason. He writes:

> "Reason is to imagination as the instrument to the agent, as the body to spirit, as the shadow to spirit."

Poetry being a form of higher thought is "the expression of the imagination".

For Shelley, poetry is not meant for delight and instruction only. Its task is the transformation of the world. The functions of poetry determine its form and content. Therefore, the components of poetry are: language, colour, form, and religious and civil habits of action. As such a poem is "the very image of life expressed in its eternal truth".

The second part discusses the nature of the poet. The poet is like an Aeolian lyre. The lyre changes its melody according to the drive of the wind. Likewise, the poet in as instrument over whom a series of external and internal impressions are driven. His melody changes according to the nature of the impressions he receives. He, a member of society, partakes the pleasures, sufferings, and aspirations of his fellow men, and produces an augmented treasure of expressions, harmoniously. Yet, the poet is not a passive receiver of impressions; he has a greater role to play in society. He is an "institutor of laws" and "founder of civil society." He is a legislator or prophet. The work of a poet, as it changes the thought process of the readers, cannot be recognized instantly as that of a politician or legislator. He is like a nightingale, which sings in darkness to cheer its own solitude with sweet sounds. Its listeners, entranced by the melody of an unseen musician, feel that "they are moved and softened, yet know not whence and why". This idea of his is expressed in "Ode To A Skylark" where these line occur:

> "Like a poet hidden
> In the light of thought,
> Singing hymns unbidden,
> Till the world is wrought."

To sympathy with hopes and fears it heeded not.

In the third part he discusses the functions of the poet and poetry. He says that he has already stated that the first function is to move the heart of the listeners and readers. The second function is more important. Poetry awakens and enlarges man's mind "...by rendering it to the receptacle of a thousand unapprehended thoughts, it lifts the veil from the hidden beauty of the world and makes the familiar objects be unfamiliar as if they were not familiar".

Here, Shelley anticipates the Russian formalist Viktor Shklovsky who considers the art of *defamiliarization* as the prime principle of literariness.

Thirdly, poetry creates new materials of knowledge, power, and pleasure, and the desire to reproduce and arrange them in a rhythm or order, which is beautiful and good. He goes beyond John Keats who remains satisfied with beauty and truth only. Shelley is very much like the Indian poets who speak of *satyam*, *shivam* and *sundaram* as the three functions/aspects of poetry. He too declares that poetry has three components: the beautiful, the truth, and the good. Great poetry is something divine and is at once the circumference and centre of knowledge. He writes:

> "A great poem is a fountain for ever-flowing with the waters of wisdom and delight."

Robert Frost, perhaps, has taken Shelley's words and incorporated in his famous essay "The Figure A Poem Makes", where he has written the sentence: "A poem begins in delight and ends in wisdom". Since, poetry is an eternal fountain of delight and wisdom, Shelley concludes:

> "Poetry is the record of the best and happiest moments of the happiest and best minds."

The poet as he authors the highest wisdom, pleasure, virtue, and glory ought personally to be the happiest, the best, the wisest, and the most illustrious of men.[3] He must have the vision of an ideal world, a world of beauty and wisdom because "poetry turns all things to happiness". The task of a poet is to change the present world to a better world and this he does with his poetry. The essay ends with the sentence: "Poets are the unacknowledged legislators of the world".

Shelley is not a critic in the traditional sense. His *Defence* is neither a discussion on literary forms nor evaluation of poetry and poets. What he hits at is the function and goal of poetry. He has written this essay as if he was in a trance and envisioned what poetry should be and what it should aim at. The idea that its main task is to change the world may seem to academic critics something Utopian, but it was actually concretized during the French Revolution and the struggle for independence in Afro-Asian countries in the twentieth century. The Indian poets, especially Kazi Nazrul Islam, Subramanya Bharati, Vallatol, Maithili Sharn Gupta, Jayashankar Prasad wrote poetry that aroused revolutionary feelings in Indians during the British regime.

(D) MATTHEW ARNOLD

Wordsworth, Coleridge, and Shelley added new elements to the British criticism and made it independent of the influence of classicism. If Wordsworth and Coleridge laid stress on the role of imagination, Shelley added the social dimension. Although highly critical of Shelley's poetry, Arnold could not turn his eyes away from the problems of the English society that had recently entered the new era of industrial revolution. Arnold found, in his own way, everything topsy-turvy, and loss of faith and culture.

Dr. Johnson evaluated literature on the principle of universal, and Coleridge on Kantian philosophy, especially *The Critique of Pure Reason*, and Shelley on his principle of transformation of

3. W.B. Yeats also expresses the idea that artists or poets are gay in "Lapis Lazuli". It is difficult to guess whether he read Shelley's essay or not.

society. Matthew Arnold widened the range of criticism by linking it with culture.

Arnold's concept of culture is not traditional; it is complex and consists of rigorous religious discipline and open-minded intellectual inquiry accompanied with the sweetness of manner. He named these two qualities *Hebraism* and *Hellenism*. According to him sweetness of temperament and light of wisdom are the special features of culture, which is a blend of an analytic mind and hebraic discipline.

Arnold defines poetry that it is "a criticism of life". If poetry is a criticism of life it may be pertinently asked, what is criticism? Arnold has answered the question in the essays "The Function of Criticism in the Present Time" and "The Study of Poetry". The first essay is a theoretical consideration of the nature and function of criticism, and the second of its practical application.

Criticism and its Function

Arnold defines criticism that it is "a disinterested endeavour to learn and propagate the best that is known and thought in the world".

The keywords in this definition are "disinterested", "endeavour", "known", and "thought". These highly formal words enhance the serious nature of criticism. It is not an effort or attempt but *endeavour* which is associated with earnestness and industriousness. The adjective "disinterested" means "not influenced by personal advantage" or "impartial". The words "known" and "thought" refer to the contents of literature. Thus, this definition tells us that criticism is an earnest and industrious activity of studying the best known ideas of the world and spread them among people. The question arises, what are those best ideas and where can they be found? The answer is: Poetry.

Arnold defines poetry more elaborately in "The Study of Poetry":

> "Poetry is a criticism of life under the conditions fixed for such a criticism by the laws of poetry and poetic beauty."

He says that the discovery, and analysis of new ideas is the work of a philosopher or a scientist, and their synthesis and exposition is the grand work of the poetic genius. At other place he writes:

> "It is undeniable that the exercise of a creative power, that is, a free creative activity is the highest function of man; it is proved to be so by man's finding in it true happiness."

The production of literature depends upon two factors: the first, the writer who creates it and carries it to the people, and the second, a proper atmosphere for creation of great literature because it is great ideas that make literature great. The great works of Aeschylus and Shakespeare were created in great epochs, the epochs of high culture.

The function of criticism is to evaluate works disinterestedly and carry them to people. It is a creative activity and it is this quality that makes it alive and active. And to remain alive it must be sincere, simple, flexible, and ever widening its knowledge.

The Touchstone Method

In the essay "The Function of Criticism in the Present Time", a theoretical consideration of poetry and criticism, and their function are discussed. "The Study of Poetry" deals with the methods of evaluating literary works.

In the beginning of the essay Aronld quotes Wordsworth's view of poetry that it is "the impassioned expression which is in the countenance of all sciences" and that it is "the breath and finer spirit of all knowledge". After quoting and explaining Wordsworth he says that in short, poetry contains the great ideas of science, philosophy, and religion. As such this high destiny of poetry demands a high standard. The best kind of poetry has a power of forming, sustaining, and delighting us as nothing else can. Therefore, criticism, which is a disinterested study of poetry, must have a high standard of estimating creating works.

There are three kinds of estimate: personal, historical, and real. The personal and historical estimates are fallacious as they fail to evaluate the "high truth" and "higher seriousness", the basic qualities of good poetry.

The personal estimate lacks disinterestedness. It is marred by an individual's prejudices. If an individual evaluates a work according to his personal likes and dislikes, he will never do justice to it. Subjectivity is the bane of criticism and, so, a good work may be condemned and an ordinary work overpraised.

The historical method, too, suffers from certain limitations. The basic postulate of historical estimate is that poetry has progressed gradually and a poet's work is a stage in its development. If the critic thinks on this line his conclusion is that the new poets are better and if there is a gradual decline, the old writers are better. The truth is at a far distance. The quality of a poet cannot be judged by his age; it is the intrinsic value of his works that makes him great or ordinary.

Criticism cannot be subjective. A critic is a man of culture, as defined in *Culture and Anarchy*. He should adopt the *touchstone method*, which is the real estimate. A goldsmith tests gold on his touchstone. The touchstone is objective and will immediately show whether the metal tested is gold or brass or some other metal. The works of Homer, Aeschylus, Virgil, Dante, and Shakespeare are touchstones. They contain both "high seriousness" and "high truth". The other books may be evaluated by the standards set by these great classics. They are the touchstones.

Applying his touchstone method Arnold finds Chaucer that he is "father of English poetry", "well of English undefiled", poet of "liquid diction" but lacking in "high seriousness". Dryden and Pope are poets of prose of "our indispensable eighteenth century", Gray a minor classic and Shelley "a beautiful ineffectual angel beating his luminous wings in the void in vain". The English poets who are praised for high seriousness and high truth are Spenser, Shakespeare, Milton, and Wordsworth, but Keats with reservations.

Arnold's inclusion of culture in the creation of poetry is of great importance. The eminent critics who followed this idea are F.R. Leavis and Raymond Williams, though a bit differently. That great classics are the touchstones for evaluation of new poets, was also said by old Sanskrit literary critics, especially Anandavardhana and Abhinavagupta.

5

MODERN BRITISH CRITICISM

Upto the time of Matthew Arnold literary criticism in England was basically aesthetic in its approach to literature, and it cherished the Christian values. Of course, it imbibed the aesthetics of Schlegel, Goethe, and Schiller, and philosophy of Kant and Hegel, yet it remained basically English. Towards the end of the nineteenth century the avant-garde literature of France torpedoed the Victorian conventions of writing, and the English writers began to study the new trends in French literature. Arthur Symons's *Symbolist Movement in Literature* was the first book of literary history that aroused interest in the avant-garde poets of France. Ezra Pound and T.S. Eliot were the first young poets who studied French literature and literary criticism seriously, and propounded a new theory of literature, which is generally known as Impersonal Theory of Art. Soon after Eliot came I.A. Richards, basically a teacher, with his *Principles of Literary Criticism* and *Practical Criticism*, which were followed by William Empson's *Seven Types of Ambiguity* and *The Structure of Complex Words*. Dr. F.R. Leavis, accepting Arnold's idea of the relationship between culture and poetry, edited the influential journal *Scrutiny* and created a new taste of literature. His *New Bearings in English Poetry*, *Revaluation*, and *The Great Tradition* set a very high standard of criticism.

The waves of the influence of Eliot, Richards, and Empson crossed the Atlantic and reached America. The New Critics, John Crowe Ransom, R.P. Blackmur, John Spingarn, W.K. Wimsatt, Cleanth Brooks, R.S. Crane, and John Penn Warren, all hailed these two British critics (Eliot was already there) and accepted their new theories of literature.

(A) THOMAS STEARNS ELIOT

It is said that Eliot's criticism best explains his own poetry. Perhaps, the reason for this kind of allegation came from that group of critics who, unaware of the literary movements in the continent, had little idea of modernism that began in the eighties of the nineteenth century. They did not know about Ibsen, Flaubert, Zola, Mallarmé, and Baudelaire. Eliot learnt a lot from the French symbolists and critics like Remy de Gourment. The fact is that his "Tradition and the Individual Talent" has its source in Gourment's writings and a few passages in the essay are paraphrase of the French original. Eliot's greatness as a critic lies in his contribution to the enrichment of English criticism and creating a new taste for literature. The main features of his criticism are briefly explained.

Autonomy of Poetry

Upto the eighteenth century, English critics and poets considered "delight" and "instruction" the main functions of poetry. Wordsworth, in the beginning tried to modify this view but later on followed the old path. It was Shelley who first assigned poetry the task of changing the world and, for this purpose, laid emphasis on its autonomy. Unfortunately, he remained the lone critic throughout the century and principles of Christianity prevailed over it. Eliot, in a systematic way, argued for the autonomy of poetry. He emphatically said that poetry should be judged by its own principles, not by the principles of other branches of knowledge. In the essay "Dante and Shakespeare", he very clearly wrote that these two poets are not to be read for their religious views or some other kind of ideas. A poem is to be read as a poem, and should be judged as a work of art. He also wrote that Dante's poetry cannot be said to be superior to Shakespeare's only for the reason that the former has a coherent philosophy behind his work, whereas the latter lacks it.

The idea that poetry is autonomous and it should be judged by its own principles made a great impact on the New Critics of America. They advocated the idea that a poem is an independent entity. We need not read a poem for meaning and instruction only. It is a work of art and every line, every phrase, and every word is an integral part of the whole, and our task is to trace their lineaments. A poem like a painting has its own existence and autonomy, and every colouration enhances its total poetic effect.

Theory of Impersonality

For Wordsworth, the poet and poetry are inseparable, that is, poetry is an expression of the poet's personality. The eighteenth century poets spoke through a persona and never addressed the audience directly. The romantics threw away the mask and wrote freely about their personal feelings and ideas.

Eliot separates the two and says that the writer's personality should not be visible in his writings, it must be merged in his works. Poetry is autonomous and can be best analysed, interpreted, and evaluated in its own terms, and therefore it is necessary that the author's personality should not have its independent existence in the created work. He writes in "Tradition and the Individual Talent":

> "The emotion of art is impersonal. And the poet cannot reach this impersonality without surrendering himself wholly to the work to be done."

It follows then that a successful work of art should have its own entity and the author's personality must not lurk behind it. These lines in the same essay reject Wordsworth's definition of poetry that it is "a spontaneous overflow of powerful feelings".

> "Poetry is not a turning loose of emotion, but an escape from emotion; it is not the expression of personality, but an escape from personality."

What Eliot means here is that a poem is a totality, a whole, in which the poet's identity is fully merged. The following lines advance the idea further.

> "The poet has not a "personality" to express, but a particular medium, which is only a medium, not a personality, in which impressions and experiences combine in peculiar and unexpected ways."

Eliot here goes back to the eighteenth century poets with some modification. The neo-classicists did not like to express their views subjectively; they wore a mask. Eliot says that the poet is like a medium in a seance. The medium, almost in a trance, delivers the message of the invoked spirit. The poet also composes poetry in the same way and his personality is not discernible in the created work.

That the poet is a medium has been emphasized by W.B. Yeats and C.G. Jung. Yeats, as has been explained a few lines before, is of the view that a poet while composing a poem is in a state of trance, that is, his conscious personality is almost dormant. Jung says that a great work of art is the expression of our forefathers' wisdom, and since at the time of composition, the collective unconscious is functioning, the creative writer's conscious is silent and so, he becomes a medium, and the created work is independent of his personality.

Finally, Eliot reiterates Coleridge's idea that a poem is an organism that has its own entity. In "Introduction" to the *Sacred Wood* (1928 edition) he writes:

> "We can say that a poem, in some sense, has its own life; that it parts from something quite different from a body or neatly ordered biographical data; that the feeling, or emotion, or vision, resulting from the poem is something different from the feeling or emotion or vision in the mind of the poet."

Yvor Winters did not appreciate Eliot's view that a poet is a medium and accused him of reducing the poet to an automaton. But, Winters's charge is not valid. Keats had spoken of "negative capability" of the poet, which is very near to Eliot's idea that the poet is a medium. We have already seen that Jung and Yeats also called the poet a medium and the independent existence of a great poem. Eliot's theory of impersonality is quite valid and in a good poem the poet is seldom visible.

Objective Correlative

Related to the theory of impersonality is Eliot's concept of *objective correlative*, which explains how the poet merges his personality in the structure or wholeness of his poems. In the essay titled "Hamlet and his Problems", he called the play an artistic failure as Shakespeare had too much of himself in the hero. As such there is much subjectivity in *Hamlet* and the author's personality is not merged fully in the play. Eliot explains the term objective correlative:

> "The only way of expressing emotion in the form of art is by finding an *objective correlative*[1]; in other words, a set of objects, a situation, a chain of events, which shall be the formula of that particular emotion; such that, when the external facts, which must terminate in sensory experience, are given, the emotion is actually evoked."

It follows from this statement that a poet or playwright should not state his feelings, emotions, and ideas plainly. He should create appropriate situations or a chain of events to convey them. This idea was further developed by Ransom in a different way. He says that apart from a set of objects, there are images, metaphors, and symbols for the expression of emotions.

The Waste Land is one of the best examples of objective correlative where the poet has taken the help of ancient myths discussed in Jessie Weston's *From Ritual to Romance*, and James Frazer's *The Golden Bough*. The reference to the myth of King Fisher and his desert kingdom is the objective correlative of the feeling of the spiritual dryness of post-war Europe.

Dissociation of Sensibility

Eliot used the phrase "dissociation of sensibility" in his famous essay "The Metaphysical Poets", which he wrote as a review of Herbert Grierson's *Metaphysical Lyrics and Poems of the Seventeenth Century*. Praising Donne and other metaphysical poets for fusion of thought and feeling in their poetry, he wrote the famous sentence:

> "A thought to Donne was an experience; it modified his sensibility."

Of course, he wrote this sentence under the influence of Mallarmé who had coined the phrase *unified sensibility*. A little later, he writes in the essay that there was unification of thought and feeling in the poetry of Donne and other seventeenth century poets, but after some time, there began the dissociation of the two:

1. Italics mine

> "In the seventeenth century a *dissociation of sensibility* set in, from which we have never recovered; and this dissociation of sensibility, as is natural, was aggravated by the influence of the two most powerful poets of the century, Milton and Dryden."

After making this bold and shocking statement, he explains the phrase that it is opposite of "unified sensibility", the fusion of thought and feeling. In the unified sensibility, a poet feels and thinks at the same time, that is, they are the two components of the same experience. The poets who succeeded the Elizabethan poets "possessed a mechanism of sensibility, which could devour any kind of experience". But, poets like Milton and Dryden and their successors thought and felt by fits and became unbalanced in their verse. They performed certain poetic functions well, but the bright language concealed their feeling and they reflected more. Thomas Gray's *Elegy* is an example of dissociation of sensibility. Shelley in *The Triumph of Life* and Keats in *Hyperion* struggled for the unification of thought and feeling, but they died young.

The term "dissociation of sensibility" became much more popular than Eliot would have anticipated. A host of critics evaluated the established poets on the touchstones of objective correlative and dissociation of sensibility. Eliot may not be right in the application of this principle of poetic process in the cases of Milton and Thomas Gray, but he is quite justified that a poet must have unified sensibility and that dissociation of sensibility is a fault. The fusion of thought and feeling produces a good poem, and their separation makes the expression of feeling highly subjective.

(B) I.A. RICHARDS

I.A. Richards is, by far, the most influential critic on both sides of the Atlantic. No doubt, T.S. Eliot pioneered modernism in poetry and F.R. Leavis defended it, it was I.A. Richards who formulated the principles of "close reading" and "practical criticism" that changed the old methods of teaching and appreciating poetry. Secondly, he is the first British critic who studied and analysed poetry from language point of view. The

New Critics of America hailed his theory and practice, and followed him almost truly and developed his literary theory to new heights. Thirdly, Richards shall be ever remembered for his pedagogical approach to literary criticism, an approach that bridged the gap between the learner and the scholar, between the beginner and the expert. His main concepts are present in *Meaning of Meaning*, *Principles of Literary Criticism*, and *Practical Criticism*. These are the basic points of his theory and practice.

Theory of Value and Synaesthesis/Synthesis

In chapter IV of *Principles of Literary Criticism*, Richards writes:

> "The two pillars upon which a theory of criticism must rest are an account of value and an account of communication."

It means that poetry or literature has two aspects: communication and value. A literary work communicates the writer's ideas emotively. The ideas, a generalisation of the experiences of the writer's own and of others, are communicated to the reader to evoke responses. It may be asked why is the reader expected to read the work and respond to the ideas embedded in the text? Richards's answer is: value. The next question is: What is value? He answers:

> "Anything is valuable, which will satisfy an appetency without moving the frustration of some equal or more important appetency."

The term "appetency" needs explanation because it has been used in a special sense in the quoted sentence. The word is archaic and its general meaning is longing or desire. Richards considers it an aspect of impulses. He divides impulses into appetencies and aversions, the first positive and the second negative. Our appetencies are aroused when we read a poem, a play or a novel, and if the text satisfies us at the end, we say that it is valuable.

The arousal and satisfaction of appetencies is a complex process. An experience involves the arousal and interplay of various impulses, but in the experience of beauty our impulses are organized in a special way. In this peculiar organization, the rivalry of conflicting impulses is avoided, not by suppressing them but by allowing them free play. The harmonization of the conflicting impulses is the state of synaesthesis, an equilibrium, the state of experiencing beauty. A successful poem arouses appetencies, the positive impulses. They are in conflict in the middle and are happily synthesised at the end, and give the reader the pleasure of beauty.

Richards's concept of synaesthesis (later on, he changed the word and wrote *synthesis* in *Principles of Literary Criticism*) is basically the affective theory of Aristotle of Greece and Bharata of India. Richards is concerned with the phenomenon of effect of a literary text on the reader. Aristotle says that tragedy gives aesthetic pleasure as it is organized in a special way. Bharata is very near to Richards when he says that a *bhava* (emotion) dormant in the reader is aroused and is changed into *rasa* (the total poetic effect) by the mixture of *vibhavas, anubhavas,* and *vyabhicharibhavas*, and as Abhinavagupta has added to Bharata's theory, the transformation of the *bhavas* into *rasas* is made in such a way as to give aesthetic pleasure to the reader. All the three, Aristotle, Bharata, and Richards, arrive at the same conclusion, though their paths are slightly different from the other.

Context Theory

Basically a philosopher, like Ernst Cassirer, Richards is interested in the communicative aspect of language: how meaning is carried. Since the word is the smallest unit in communication, he has paid more attention to it like the German and French philosophers, and answered the two basic questions related to it. The questions are: What does a word mean and from where does it derive its meaning? His answer is that a word may mean something in isolation, but its final meaning is determined by its context. In other words, the source of the meaning of a word is the context in communication. Wimsatt and Brooks have neatly summarised the basic arguments of the context theory.

(i) Words interanimate one another. They are qualified by the whole context in which they figure. This context derives its power from the other contexts in the text.

Therefore, the meaning of the entire text depends upon the relationship of the words in the contexts that complete the whole. This idea that words, their contexts, and the text are inextricably woven leads to "close reading" of texts as practised first in *Practical Criticism* and then in Empson's *Seven Types of Ambiguity* and the New Criticism of America.

(ii) The meaning of a poem does not consist in a line or stanza. Even a very important line or statement, say Milton's line "They also serve who only stand wait" in "On His Blindness", gains its meaning in its relationship with other elements in the text. In other words, no single element is the most important in a poem; it is the poem as a whole which is important.

(iii) A poet makes experiments in language when he explores his meaning. Words do not form a mosaic pattern by themselves; they are "resultants which the poet arrives at only through the interplay of the interpretative possibilities of the whole utterance."

(iv) Fourthly, the reader, like the writer, finds the meaning through a process of explanation. This explanation may be said an inference or guesswork. It follows then that there is no final meaning of a poem. This view of Richards was further developed by Stanley Fish, which we now know as Reader's Response Theory.

(v) Finally, metaphor is a typical instance of the merging of contexts. It is not a mere comparison; it is a linchpin that joins two contexts. The two contexts may seem quite distant, but the bold and appropriate metaphor gives a new meaning as we see in the poems of Donne, Herbert, and Eliot.

Two Uses of Language

In *Principles of Literary Criticism*, chapter XXXIV, Richards defines the two uses of language: the referential and the emotive.

> "A statement may be used for the sake of the reference, true or false, which it causes. This is the scientific use of language. But, it may also be used for the sake of the

> effects in emotion and attitude produced by the reference, it occasions. This is the emotive use of language."

Richards's distinction between the referential and the emotive use of language is clear and of great practical use in teaching literature and also distinguishing it from other modes of discourse. Referential use of language is the base of the kind of the language, which describes matter of fact things, say the language of science. For example, "Two plus two is four," or "The sun rises in the east". But, when William Blake writes, "O rose, thou art sick!" or Shelley writes "If winter comes, can spring be far behind!", there is the use of emotive language.

In scientific or referential use of language "a difference in the references is a failure. The end has not been achieved". Further, in the scientific use of language, the reference to the object must be correct, and, not only this, other references related to it should also be correct. It means that there must be logical relationship between the references.

On the other hand, such logicality is not required in the emotive use of language. What is important is the effect of language on attitude and emotion. Richards concludes:

> "...what matters is that the series of attitudes due to the references should have their own proper organization, their own emotional inter-connection, and this often has no dependence upon the logical relations of such references as may be concerned in bringing the attitudes in being."

Statement and Pseudo-statement

These two terms were first explained in *Science and Poetry* (1926), which was later renamed *Sciences and Poetries.* Elaborating and improving upon the idea of the previously coined terms—referential and emotive uses of language—Richards explains the kind of language made use of in poetry. He says that words work in a poem in two main fashions, as sensory stimuli and as symbols. It is the second function, which is more significant. Using metaphors and symbols, poetry makes symbols. He defines the term:

> "A pseudo-statement is a form of words, which is justified entirely by its effect in releasing or organizing our impulses and attitudes. When Blake writes, "O Rose, thou art sick!" he makes a pseudo-statement, the veracity of which is determined by our attitude. A statement on the other hand is justified by truth, i.e., its correspondence, in a highly technical sense, with the fact to which it points."

It follows then that the truth of a statement is literally correct, and there is no underlying meaning, but in a pseudo-statement, the underlying meaning is the real meaning, and the surface meaning is only a covering. When Wordsworth says in "The Daffodils", "Ten thousand saw I at a glance", he means that the flowers were large in number. The following lines of *The Waste Land* are a brilliant example of pseudo-statement.

> "Then I saw one I knew, and stopped him, crying: Stetson
>
> You who were with me in the ships at Mylae!
> That corpse you planted last year in your garden.
> Has it begun to sprout? Will it bloom this year?"

The truth of these lines is different from the literal meaning and it can be realised by our emotional attitude and the context.

Four Kinds of Meaning

Perhaps, the most useful book for teachers and students of English literature is *Practical Criticism*. While teaching poetry at Cambridge University, Richards found that the undergraduate students made stock responses to the poems he had given them to appreciate. The poems, which he has named "protocols" in *Practical Criticism*, did not bear the poets' names nor the titles. Finding that their interpretation was subjective and far from the facts in the protocols, he devised a new method of reading for proper understanding of poetry in general. This method is now famous as "close reading".

"Close reading" means the method of reading in which the linguistic relationship between words, phrases, and sentences in the poem are under study. The reader must not try to find those things in a poem, which do not exist there. The total meaning of a poem rests upon *sense, feeling, tone*, and *intention*, which Richards calls the four kinds of meaning.

(i) **Sense.** Every writer has something to say. He will not be read if he writes something meaningless. By sense, Richards means the literal meaning of the text. While writing on a subject the poet conveys his ideas through words, which have a definite meaning, usually the dictionary meaning. The argument of the poem is the sense. In addition, the words, as they are organised in a special way, evoke the kind of emotion in the reader, the poet himself has felt.

(ii) **Feeling.** Feeling is the second aspect of meaning. The poet makes statements, but he is not mechanical nor emotionally detached to the object or idea he is writing about. He has some kind of feeling attached to it; it may be love, hatred, anguish, anger, sadness, and likewise. There is the feeling of wonder in these simple lines:

> "Twinkle, Twinkle little star
> How I wonder what you are."

Feeling, in short, means the author's attitude to the subject of the created work.

(iii) **Tone.** Tone means the general character of sound and also a modulation of the voice expressing a feeling or mood. In our daily life we never speak in a flat tone; the pitch and quality of sound varies continually to give additional meaning to the words being spoken. In poetry also, the tone is varied according to the mood and feeling of the poet. The variation of tone is easily discernible in Yeats's famous poem "Easter 1916". Tone and feeling are inextricably woven and the former suggests the feeling of the poet, and tone is changed for the appropriate expression of feeling.

Secondly, tone refers to the writer's attitude to the listener also. He always has in his mind the kind of audience he is going to address through his poetry. The tone may be formal or informal or sometimes a mixture of the both. The tones used by metaphysical poets of the seventeenth century and Robert Browning vary continually as they shift from the listener to the subject, and from the subject to the listener. So is the case with

Eliot in poems like "Love Song of Alfred J. Prufrock", "Gerontion" and *The Waste Land.*

(iv) Intention. Every writer has a purpose behind her/his writing. This purpose may be overt or covert. Antony's famous speech in *Julius Caesar* has the purpose of arousing the listeners' wrath against Brutus. Richards explains all the four meanings in this sentence:

> "Finally, apart from what he says (sense), his attitude to what he is talking about (feeling), and his attitude to listener (tone), there is the speaker's intention, his aim, conscious or unconscious, the effect he is endeavouring to promote."

The romantic poets are very clear in the expression of their intention. Wordsworth speaks overtly against materialism and advises his readers to go back to nature, Shelley wants the world of sorrow to be changed into a happy world, and Keats speaks of the permanence of beauty. Modern poets are rather subtle. Philip Larkin is never direct in stating his intention, and so is the case with Eliot and Donald Davie. It is the task of the reader to trace out the writer's intention in the poem he/she is reading for full understanding.

(C) F.R. LEAVIS

F.R. Leavis, popularly known as Dr. F.R. Leavis like Dr. Johnson, is the most influential English critic of the twentieth century. His great contribution to literary criticism is that he, playing the role of an iconocdast, raised its standard and created a taste for really good intellectual poetry in England. Never elevated to the post of Professor, he had a large number of followers who became Professors in different universities in England and America.

He followed T.S. Eliot theoretically and Richards's technique of "close reading". The learned journal the *Scrutiny*, which he edited from 1931 till its demise in 1953 remained the single force in creating the new literary taste in English, a taste for modern and experimental creative writings of George Eliot, Henry James, Joseph Conrad, James Joyce, John Donne, Gerard Manley Hopkins, T.S. Eliot, and Ezra Pound. His denunciation of Milton, the romantic and Victorian poets was the sting pronouncements that created widespread controvesy, but his method of analysis and logic of argument was so sound that his opponents calmed down soon and followed his line.

Following are the main features of his literary criticism.

Emphasis on Culture

Like Arnold he considers literature as a vital part of culture. It is a product of culture and enriches it. His emphasis is on Englishness of culture, and in this respect, he lacks the universality of Oliver Goldsmith, the eighteenth century writer of *The Citizen of the World*. He defines his stand in *Revaluation* and *The Great Tradition*, where he enumerates the elements that have contributed to the growth and development of English literature and made it great. He is all praise for Chaucer and Shakespeare who made English poetry stand on its own. John Donne gave it vitality. Englishness is present in the novels of Jane Austen, George Eliot, Henry James, Joseph Conrad, and D.H. Lawrence who raised its intellectual height and perfected the art of the novel. His analysis of Eliots' *The Waste Land* and Ezra Pound's *Hugh Selwyn Mauberley*, the first and best, shows how English poetry reached a new height in the twentieth century and, representing the English culture, enriched it plentifully.

Poetry and Sensibility

Dr. Leavis' lays stress on sensibility. The poet must have the sensibility to feel and understand the reality around him. The poets of the eighteen-nineties, the Edwardian and the Georgian periods, harped back on those things that existed in the Victorian age and did not see the new things that sprang up in the beginning of the twentieth century. Poetry has a serious relation to reality. The slogan "art for art's sake" raised by the *fin de siécle* poets from their ivory tower did a substantial harm to poetry. Literature is rooted in life, and any attempt to remain aloof from the realities of life will end in writing poetry, which is dreamy and unsubstantial. The modern age, Leavis observed, began with a new note, the danger of the rising power of Kaiser and the growing darkness of the impending war. The Victorian optimism and prudery were outdated and, so, poetry had to be written in a new way expressing the modern sensibility. He, therefore, hailed Eliot and Pound who expressed the new reality in their poetry.

Poetry and the Reading Public

Leavis makes distinction between good poetry and bad poetry, and poet and poetaster. The other term he uses is "undergraduate poetry", which is for the immature minds, or the kind of poetry, which is devoid of serious thoughts.

By good poetry Leavis means the poetry, which expresses "the true voice of feeling", a phrase coined by the eminent critic Sir Herbert Read. The poet must not write those things of which he has neither experience nor adequate knowledge. He agrees with Mallarme and Eliot that there should be unified sensibility in poetry. Secondly, there is a difference between poetry and verse. Poetry expresses intensity of feeling, whereas verse is nothing but prose in rhyme and metre. The poetry of A.C. Swinburne, John Drinkwater, and John Masefield lacks in intensity of feeling and sounds hollow; there is a wide gap between sound and sense.

The third important aspect of poetry is that it is intellectual. It means that both content and form (including language or diction) are of the best quality. The organization of words, the tropes, and ideas are all woven in the texture of poetry deftly and skilfully. The content is not related to common place things, but of things that are well thought over. For example, in Donne's poetry, contrasting ideas may be violently yoked together in the opinion of Dr. Johnson, but the fact is that it was the great capacity of Donne's genius that he blended them together with his unified sensibility.

The word "undergraduate" is used for that kind of literature which is conventional, stereotyped, and written in a plain language so as not to jolt the reader. One reading is sufficient. Great literature is intellectual, innovative, and contains new serious ideas that force the reader to read it again and again, and make an intellectual exercise for its full understanding. George Eliot's *Middlewarch*, Hopkins's poetry, and T.S. Eliot's

The Waste Land are such pieces of literature, which demand careful reading and which compel us to think in a new way.

The Critic as Complete Reader

Leavis speaks of "the common reader" in the "Introduction" to *The Common Pursuit.* His concept of "the common reader" (in fact, the ideal reader) is very much like that of *sahridaya* in Indian poetics. According to Indian critics, a *sahridaya* is fully acquainted with the art of poetry and responds fully to *Kavya.* Leavis, too, expects complete responsiveness from the common or ideal reader. He emphatically says that "the ideal critic is the ideal reader." In his famous essay "Criticism and Philosophy", he writes that complete responsiveness is the first quality of a critic.

> "The critic's aim is, first, to realize as sensitively and completely as possible this or that, which claims his attention; and a certain valuing is implicit in the realizing."

He lays stress on academic criticism and advises all literary critics to be a part of a collaborative community that exists in universities. The university culture, refined in taste and enriched by the contribution of the ideal reader-critics "will be post-graduate in understanding and humane in its approach to life."

Inspite of being a controversial figure, doctrinaire in his critical theory, crude and invective in his denunciation of critics and creative writers, Leavis has raised the level of English literary criticism and the readers of literature. It is another matter that we may not always agree with him.

American New Criticism

American New Criticism has its roots in the critical theories of T.S. Eliot and I.A. Richards. Taking cue from the French critic-poet Remy de Gourment, Eliot propounded the impersonal theory of art in his famous essay "Tradition and the Individual Talent", and asserted the independent existence of poetry. He compared the poet to a catalysist, a medium, that combines emotions and feelings together to make poetry. In "Dante and Shakespeare", he refuted the idea held by older critics that a great philosophy is absolutely necessary to make a poem great and said that Shakespeare's poetry is, without a base in a well-recognized philosophy, as great as that of Dante. In the "Introduction" to 1928 edition of the *Sacred Wood*, he defined his notion of the autonomy of poetry and art.

> "We can only say that a poem, in some sense, has its own life; that its parts form something quite different from a body of neatly ordered biographical data; that the feeling or emotion, or vision, resulting from the poem is something different from the feeling or vision in the mind of the poet."[2]

I.A. Richards, too, maintained the independent entity of poetry and, after his experiments with the undergraduates students of Cambridge University where he was a teacher, came to the conclusion that the disclosure of the author's name distorts our understanding of his works. He, therefore, suggested that we can best understand a poem if we pay full attention to its sense, feeling, tone, and intention. The other significant contribution of his to literary criticism is the distinction between scientific truth and poetic truth. Science, he said, makes statement and poetry pseudo-statement. The "truth" of a scientific statement can be verified in a laboratory, but the "truth" of a poetic statement (i.e., pseudo-statement) depends on our feeling and attitude. Related to it is his distinction made earlier in *Principles of Literary Criticism* between the uses of language: referential and emotive. The first is the language of science and the second of poetry.

Eliot and Richards evoked responses from the American critics whose leader was John Crowe Ransom. They largely accepted the new poetics of England but, as original thinkers they were, they made certain corrections and developed a new approach to literature, which is now universally known as New Criticism. The New Critics soon divided into two groups, one followed the aesthetics of Kant and Coleridge, and the other Aristotle's poetic method, though both the groups acknowledged their indebtedness to Eliot and Richards. Handy and Westbrook have called them the Formalists and the Neo-Aristotelians/

2. Quoted by Wimsatt and Brooks, *Literary Criticism: A Short History*, p. 665.

Genre critics. The nomenclature "genre critics" is not proper as Aristotle himself was not that kind of critic, and also because all people follow the classification of literature into genres and make distinction between different forms of each genre.

(D) FORMALIST CRITICS

The leading critics of Formalist criticism are John Crowe Ransom, Yvor Winters, R.P. Blackmur, Robert Heilman, Allen Tate, W.K. Wimsatt, Cleanth Brooks, and Robert Penn Warren. John Crowe Ransom criticised in *The New Criticism* the affective theory of I.A. Richards, especially his concept of synaesthesis, and levelled the same charge against T.S. Eliot. He found Richards's relevant poetic structure not only hypothetical but also highly subjective; for if the balanced poise is in our response, not in the structure of the poem, our analysis will certainly be erroneous and whimsical. In *The World's Body* he discussed the poetic structure in detail and argued that a poem has the *logical structure,* which is its argument[3], and the *irrelevant local texture*, which is its imagery, metaphor, symbolism, and other local details that make a poem a rich composite. Poetry is, therefore, not purely a pseudo-statement; the logical structure contains some scientific truth and hence objectivity.

The principles which Ransom laid down in *The New Criticism*, and *The World's Body* became the starting point for all modern American critics. The New critics negate the Victorian and neo-humanist emphasis on the moral uses of literature[4], the historical tradition and the biography of the author. They also refute Roger Fry's concept of pure form and regard poetry as a valid source of knowledge that cannot be communicated in terms other than its own. They follow fully the principle of the principality of the text under study, and reject the things, which are not there.

What is important for the formalist critic is a close reading of the text in terms of its form (metre, stanza, rhyme, and

---

3. Ransom has used "argument" in the sense Milton has done at the beginning of each book of *Paradise Lost*, that is, the main idea or theme of the poem.
4. Robert Frost changed the word "instruction" to "wisdom": "A poem begins in delight and ends in wisdom".

rhythm) and the materials (simile, metaphor, image, allusion, and symbol) it is made of because it is the concretum of the logical structure and irrelevant local texture. The method of analysis is like that of G. Wilson Knight, F.R. Leavis, L.C. Knights, and William Empson.

Cleanth Brooks, Robert Penn Warren, and Robert Heilman deviated from Ransom in their approach to literature. Ransom and Winters held that the logical or cognitive aspect of poetic apprehension was necessary because a poem contains scientific truth also, but these three maintained that a poem is an organic composition of images and, so, the reader is concerned with the poetic truth only.

Secondly, praising I.A. Richards's emphasis on irony, Brooks redefined irony that it is "the obvious warping of a statement by the context", and maintained that irony or paradox is the principle of poetic structure.[5]

They demonstrated their method of analysis in *Understanding Poetry* (1938), *Understanding Fiction* (1943), and *Understanding Drama* (1945). Robert Penn Warren was Brooks's collaborator in the first two books and Robert Heilman in the last one. Brooks made the exposition of his theory in the essay "The Formalist Critic" (1951), which made the younger generation name his group Formalist Critics and the theory Formalist Criticism. The method developed by these three Formalist Critics is so penetrating, exhaustive, and comprehensive that it is yet to be surpassed by scholars and critics in the U.K. and the USA, and no student of literature can spare herself/himself from studying these three monumental works.[6]

(E) NEO-ARISTOTELIANS/CHICAGO CRITICS

Handy and Westbrook named the literary theory of the Chicago School of critics *Genre Criticism* on the ground that "any critic who concentrates on formal distinction in literature may be called in the loose sense of the term, a Genre Critic", but soon they hastened to add "the study of Genre Criticism, in any

5. C.f. Dandin, Bhamaha, and Kuntaka on *Vakrokti*.
6. David Perkins, James Reeves, and H. Coombes, the writers of the sixties, have followed Richards and Brooks almost to the letter.

sense of the term, is best begun with a study of Aristotle and of the use of the inductive method as a foundation for literary criticism." In my opinion it is rather erroneous to name the neo-Aristotelians or Chicago critics Genre Critics as all people follow the classification of literature into genres according to form. It is better to call R.S. Crane (the leader), Elder Olson, Wayne C. Booth, and John Mckeon neo-Aristotelians as they all follow Aristotle almost to the letter and apply his method in the analysis of texts, or Chicago School of critics as they all belong to Chicago. Of course, they all follow Eliot and Richards as do Ransom and Brooks.

Elder Olson in his classic essay "The Poetic Method of Aristotle: Its Powers and Limitations" has reinterpreted Aristotle's *Poetics* in the light of the *Politics*, the *Physics*, and the *Rhetoric*, and we personally feel it is the best exposition of Aristotle's poetic theory.

Placing *Poetics* in the general scheme of Aristotle's philosophy, Olson concludes that poetry, painting, and music belong to the category of productive sciences. The art of poetry is the art of making like music and painting, but differs from them in respect of medium. The genres of poetry differ from one another in respect of either object or manner, though their medium is the same, that is word. The poet, the painter, and the musician are all makers. While imitating an object in action, they produce a concretum of form and matter, which is a work of art. For example, a sculptor makes a statue of Venus. The matter is a piece of marble and the form is of the goddess of love, but the statue is neither marble nor Venus; it is a work of art, quite different from its material and the object it has imitated.

After interpreting Aristotle's *Poetics* and poetic method thus, neo-Aristotelians under the leadership of R.S. Crane have criticised Cleanth Brooks on two grounds. The first is that the Formalist critic's method is, because he has already taken it for granted that irony or paradox is the principle of structure, basically deductive, whereas a critic should use both inductive and deductive methods, and start his analysis of the given text using the inductive method first. The second argument against Brooks is that Formalist criticism does not make distinction between two genres of poetry. Crane says that even two texts of the same genre are not alike. In a brilliant analysis of *Macbeth* he demonstrates how *Othello* and *Macbeth* both written by Shakespeare are different from the other. *Othello* is on the pattern of the Greek tragedy as defined by Aristotle, but *Macbeth* is a play between *Othello* and *Richard III*; the latter could be very well rejected by Aristotle on moral grounds. No critic can do justice to *Macbeth* unless he defines its place in the history of tragedy, differentiates it from other tragedies, and then analyses it first inductively and next deductively to understand its structure, and the way the author has organised it.

The basic difference between Formalists and neo-Aristotelians lies in their concepts of critical method and nature of art. The neo-Aristotelians follow the great Greek philosopher when they state that knowledge is based on systematic analysis. The subject under study may be amorphous or even be irregular, yet the principles of its study must be systematic and scientific. It follows then that literature, which is a product of imagination may be subjective hence partly wayward, but its study, criticism, must be scientific. The Formalists, on the other hand, say that the study of poetry is ontological, not scientific.

Secondly, the Formalist who follows Kant's aesthetic "The Thing-in-itself", believes that knowledge can be derived from the poem under study alone, and there is no need of knowing the history of its genre nor of its author's biography. The neo-Aristotelian says that the knowledge of a thing cannot be discovered within the framework of the thing itself. The adequate knowledge of a thing, thereby a literary text, can be gained when we place it in the system in which it exists.

However, these differences, although fundamental and of far-reaching consequences, are made on the philosophical plane; in practice both employ the same technique[7]. However, the neo-Aristotelians have widened the precincts of the Formalists who remained confined to the text only.

---

7. Cf Elder Olson's analysis of "Sailing to Byzantium" and Cleanth Brooks's "Ode on a Grecian Urn".

6

CONTEMPORARY CRITICISM

Upto the first half of the nineteenth century literary criticism was mainly concerned with the aesthetic and moral aspects of literature. Shelley was the first poet-critic who threw light on the more important function of poetry: transformation of society. Hippolyte Taine in his *History of English Literature* pointed out that literature is the product of time, race, and milieu. His point was that these three factors contribute to the growth of an author. The defect in his theory was that he had a mechanical view of life, and never saw that history does not move in a cyclical way and that the same kind of literature is never written again.

Marx and Engels, the German economists and philosophers, refuted Taine's mechanical point of view and said that literature is a human activity, not a purely material activity. Engels remarked that he learnt more from Balzac's novels than from many French historians and economists about the socio-economic conditions of France. A new kind of criticism sprang up from their writings, which we now know as *Marxist Criticism.*

If Marx and Engels were tracing social reality in literature, the other German, Sigmund Freud, was studying literature to understand the functioning of man's psyche. Fully interested in the abnormal behaviour of man, he discovered that there are two layers of the psyche: the conscious and the unconscious. It is the unconscious, which plays a great role in creative writing as authors find a free play of their repressed desires in the world of fantasy. He maintained that a creative writer is usually a neurotic afflicted by the harsh realities of life. Unable to cope up with the realities he weaves a fantasy where he becomes a triumphant and happy man. Therefore, a literary text can be successfully interpreted if the author's personal experiences, especially the experiences still hidden to people, are correlated with it. His famous essay "Creative Writers and Daydreaming" and other writings are the foundation on which psycho-analytic criticism is built.

Jung broke away with Freud on the latter's interpretation of the unconscious and the sexual drive. He refuted Freud's concept of libido that all constructive activities have their source in the instinct of sex. Secondly, he proved that man's unconscious has two layers: the surface layer, which constitutes an individual's personal experiences, and the deep layer, which contains the wisdom of man's forefathers. A creative writer under the influence of the collective unconscious delivers the wisdom of the ancient people through his creative writing. His two essays "Psychology and Literature" and "Archetypes of the Collective Unconscious" form the basis of *archetypal criticism*. His ideas were applied by his disciple Maud Bodkin in her *Archetypal Patterns in Poetry* (1935). It was a neglected book till the nineteen-fifties, but now it is read widely.

A little later, anthropology, made its presence felt through Sir James Frazer's voluminous *The Golden Bough*. Gilbert Murray established relationship between ancient mythical characters and literary characters in the essay "Hamlet and Orestes". It can be said that *myth criticism* began with Murray. Northrop Frye combined Jung's and Frazer's ideas in *Anatomy of Criticism: Four Essays* and the famous essay "Archetypes of Literature" published a few years earlier. The name *myth criticism* has become more popular after Frye's interpretation of myth and archetype, and the name *archetypal criticism* is seldom used these days.

Developments in modern linguistics have widened the horizons of criticism. Ferdinand de Saussure's division of philology into Diachrony (Historical linguistics) and Synchromy (Descriptive linguistics), the concept of language as a system and distinction between langue and *parole* made a great impact on the study of language. That the relationship between word (signifier) and meaning (signified) is based on convention, not on logic inspired his disciples to study literature from the linguistic point of view. The Russian linguists and critics, especially Viktor Shklovsky, Boris Eichenbaum, Roman Jakobson, and Jurij Tynyanov took the lead. Their critical theory is now known as Russian Formalism. They rejected the age-old mimetic theory that literature mirrors reality, and posited the view that it is a semiotic mediation of reality, that is, reality is embedded in the text itself. Secondly, they made distinction between literary criticism and literary history on the pattern of descriptive linguistics and historical linguistics, and pointed out that literary criticism is the study of texts and literary history the chronological description of literature through different ages.

Later on, Roman Jakobson, after leaving the then USSR, collaborated with the French anthropologist Claude Lévi-Strauss. Combining linguistics and anthropology they analysed Baudelaire's "Les Chats". Their new approach to literature laid the foundation of Structuralism. The impact of French structuralism and post-structuralism made a great impact on English, American and Continental criticism. At present, structuralism and its later form post-structuralism (including Deconstruction) have pervaded all modern critical theories, such as marxist criticism, feminist criticism, and post-colonial theory of literature.

Feminist criticism has its roots in the writings of Aphra Behn, Mary Woolstonecraft, John Stuart Mill, Virginia Woolf, and Simone de Beauvoir. Now, it is an acknowledged theory of literature and so is the case with Post-Colonial Theory of Literature that began with Edward Said's *Orientalism* (1978). Though limited in scope and an offshoot of Marxist Criticism, it has become quite popular in Afro-Asian and Latin countries that suffered the heavy yoke of imperialism for a long time.

Recent critical theories are intermingled. No theory is pure. Feminist criticism has taken the ideas of Marxist Criticism, Post-Colonial Theory and Post-Structuralism (including Deconstruction). Marxist Criticism is highly influenced by feminism and Post-Structuralism and so is the case with Post-Colonial Theory of Literature. Julia Kristeva, Helen Cixous, Catherine Belsey, Gayatri Chakravarty Spivak, Terry Eogleton, and Aijaz Ahmed have taken help of other critical theories, though they have stuck to their own theories. As science has been collaborative on the global level, criticism, also, is on the way to becoming global.

(A) MARXIST CRITICISM

Marxist Criticism has, as the name indicates, its origin in the writings of Marx and Engels. These two philosophers and social scientists were deeply interested in literature as were Kant, Hegel, and Freud. Marx considered literature as an important activity of man in society. Marx was himself a poet in his youth and a great admirer of Shakespeare and Goethe. Engels read literature from the sociological point of view. In order that we can understand their idea of literature, it is important to know their concept of the universe, the human society, and the individual man.

Mark and Engels are known for their dialectical materialism. They accepted Hegel's concept of the dialectical progress of history: thesis, antithesis, and synthesis of the opposing ideas at a higher level. But, they refuted the postulate that idea precedes matter and said that as the world is made of matter man too is made of matter and all his ideas stem from his material needs and material activities. In "Preface" to *A Contribution to the Critique of Political Economy*, Marx wrote:

> "The general result at which I arrived and which served as a guiding thread for my studies, can be briefly formulated as follows:
>
> In this social production of their life, men enter into definite relations that are indispensable and independent of their will, relations of production, which correspond to definite stage of development of their material productive forces. The sum total of these relations of production constitutes the economic structure of society, the real foundation, on which rises a legal and political super structure and to which correspond definite forms of social consciousness. The mode of production of material life conditions the social, political, and intellectual life process in general."[1]

---

1. Marx and Engels, *Selected Works,* vol. I (Moscow: Progress Publishers, 1980), p. 50.

That man's thought process is determined by his material activity (that is, his economic behaviour in society) is very clearly stated in the long essay *The German Ideology*.

> "The production of ideas, of conceptions, of consciousness, is at first directly interwoven with the material activity and the material intercourse of men—the language of real life. Conceiving, thinking, the mental intercourse of men at this stage still appear as the direct efflux of their material behaviour. The same applies to mental production as expressed in the language of politics, law, religion, morality, metaphysics, etc. of people."[2]

Marx's idea of social structure and the place of literature as its component can be diagrammed thus.

<table>
<tr><th colspan="2">SUPER STRUCTURE</th></tr>
<tr><td colspan="2">• Religion and Morality
• Philosophy and Ethics
• Political System, State Power, and Law
• Education, Literature, and Art</td></tr>
<tr><th colspan="2">MODE OF PRODUCTION</th></tr>
<tr><td colspan="2">Relation of Production and Distribution</td></tr>
<tr><td colspan="2">Forces of Production and Distribution</td></tr>
<tr><td>Instruments of Production and Distribution, and Technology</td><td>Productive Forces: Man</td></tr>
<tr><th colspan="2">BASE STRUCTURE</th></tr>
</table>

Literature like law, religion, metaphysical, and politics is a mental production. It is a mental product because a writer has "something" to say in his created work and that "something" is his ideas, his view of life, and perception of the reality he has

2. B. Krylov, ed., *Marx and Engels: On Literature and Art* (Moscow: Progress Publishers, 1978), pp. 42-43.

experienced in the world he lives in. His outlook of the world and his own life are not entirely based on his own experience; they are also based upon the philosophies propounded in the past and the challenges of life in the present. Naturally, it is a superficial view to think of literature a means of mere entertainment or delight. On the other hand, it is a specific form of social consciousness and embodies man's feelings, emotions, aspirations, and struggle for a better world.

Man's prime motive is to satisfy his basic material needs—food, cloth, and shelter—which sustain his life in this world. All his thinking is determined first by these three, which force him to come into relationship with others, who, too, like him are human beings constantly labouring for their existence. Man's material activity, in relationship with others, forms the economic or base structure on which the super structure rests. A change in the base structure causes changes in the different components—law, religion, metaphysics, politics, and education (including literature)—of the super structure. In "Preface" to the *Critique of Political Economy*, Marx explained his concept of the relationship between base structure and super structure.

To explain it in a simple language how a change in the base structure revolutionises the super structure, the differences in the different stages of evolution of human society can be taken as an illustration. In the hunting stage, when man had primitive tools of production, his religion and law were of one kind, which changed when he entered the pastoral stage. Further, changes came in the agricultural stage and in the industrial age. The industrial revolution demolished monarchy and aristocracy completely, and ushered in the dawn of democracy and internationalism.

The idea that the super structure is absolutely dependent on the base structure is not correct, and some theorists have oversimplified Marx's concept of the social structure. Engels very specifically wrote to W. Borgius:

> "Political, juridical, philosophical, religious, literary, and artistic developments are based on economic development. But, all these react upon one another and also upon the

> economic base. It is not that the economic situation is cause, solely active, while everything else is only a passive effect."[3]

In the famous letter to Joseph Block, Engels wrote:

> "According to the materialist conception of history, the ultimately determining element in history is the production and reproduction of real life. More than this neither Marx nor I have ever asserted. Hence, if somebody twists this into saying that the economic element is the only determining one, he transforms that proposition into a meaningless, abstract, senseless phrase. The economic situation is the basis, but the various elements of the super structure...also exercise their influence upon the course of the historical struggles and in many cases preponderate in determining their form."[4]

It follows then that literature, being a part of the super structure of society is a specific form of social consciousness, and changes in its content and form are largely caused by men's material activity or the base structure. Literature is not a passive onlooker. It also reacts and causes changes in the base structure and other components of the super structure, such as law, religion, and politics.

The next important point is the position of the creative writer and the role of the ideas he expresses in his writing. According to Marx and Engels, literature is a conscious effort of the writer to recreate his perception of reality. His perception and realization of reality are mostly determined by his encounter with different forces in his worldy life and the components of the super structure, viz., law, religion, morality, philosophy, education, politics, and literature.

The components of the base structure are never at one. The hitherto known history has been the history of class-struggle. The human society, since the days of primitive communism, has remained divided between two broad classes of the rulers and

---

3. Marx and Engels, *Selected Works,* vol. III, p. 502.
4. *Ibid.*, pp. 487-88.

the ruled, and each class with its own hierarchy. In the words of Marx and Engels:

> "There two classes, whatever has been their form, have stood in constant opposition to one another, carried on an uninterrupted, now hidden, now open fight that each time ended, either in a revolutionary reconstitution of society at large, or in the common ruin of the contending classes."[5]

The progress of history has its seed in this class struggle. The ruling class that has control over the means of production labours hard constantly to develop and revolutionise its base and maintain the upper hand by all means. The ruled class also works continuously to develop and revolutionise its base. The ruling class as it does not want the ruled class to reach its level imposes its ideas on the ruled class. Thus, the ideas of the ruling class become the dominant ideas of every epoch. Marx writes in *A Critique of Political Economy*:

> "The ideas of the ruling class are in every epoch the ruling ideas, i.e., the class which is ruling the material force of society, is not at the same time its ruling intellectual force."[6]

Surprisingly, the ruling class always considers its own ideas to be universal to all, although its ideas are meant for revolutionising its own base. Besides, it tries to convince the ruled class of the universality and permanence of its ideas. Anwar Abdul Malek took up this idea of Marx and applied it in the analysis of the relationship between the colonisers and the colonised people during the colonial period, and Edward said applied it in the interpretation of literary texts.

It is obvious, then, that literature written in a classbase society projects the ideas of the class to which the author belongs. Aeschylus wrote *Oresteia* where he propounded the strange idea that the son is not a blood-relation of his mother. Engels in his scholarly analysis of the play has proved that the

5. Marx and Engels, "Manifesto of the Communist Party", *Selected Works*, vol. I, p. 109.
6. Marx and Engels, *Selected Works*, vol. I, p. 47.

playwright had defended the patriarchal form of society and subjugation of women. Now, science has proved that the largest number of blood cells of a son match his mother's, not father's, and she is the best donor to her son or daughter in kidney or liver transplant.

As literature is an imaginative re-creation of the social reality, no literary text can remain untouched with the ideas of the class to which the author belongs. Terry Eagleton has very clearly summarised the relationship between literature, the writer, and his society.

> "Literary works are not mysteriously inspired, or explicable simply in terms of their author's psychology. They are forms of perception, particular ways of seeing the world; and as such they have a relation to that dominant way of seeing the world which is the social mentality or ideology of an age."[7]

In brief, the development of literature is constantly governed by the development of social laws. The dominant ideas of an epoch are challenged by the new emerging class and when the old weak ruling class is overthrown, the new ideas take the place of the old ideas. However, the replacement is not wholly done. There is a synthesis of the old and the new at a higher level, the new ideas more domineering. The same social law operates in the development of literature. The old ideas of the old epoch give way to the new ideas in the creative writings of the new epoch. In the beginning, kings, princes, and knights were the main characters, but with the rise of the middle class in the nineteenth century people from the middle class became heroes and heroines in novels, and after the industrial revolution and rise of the proletariat, the factory workers became protagonists of novels and short-stories.

II

Within this framework of Marx's model of social structure and social development are the foundations of Marxist Criticism. For Marx and Engels, a literary work is the product of the

7. Terry Eagleton, *Marxism and Literary Criticism*, (London: Routledge and Kegan Paul, 1976), p. 5.

author who is a member of the human world, which is still divided into the broad division of two classes. Here are given the basic concepts of Marxist Criticism, irrespective of Soviet and European trends, which occasionally conflict and contradict each other.

The Basic Concepts

1. Literature is a specific form of social consciousness

Marxist criticism says that literature is the product of an individual in society. Although, he records his own experiences and the experiences of other people, his ideas are not purely his; they are all formed under the influence of the social forces. B. Krylov comments:

> "The essence, origin, development, and social role of art can only be understood through analysis of the social system as a whole, within which the economic factor—the development of productive forces in complex interaction with production relations—plays the decisive role."[8]

The social system from the beginning of the pastoral age has never been monolithic. Each social group, formed by its economic status, has had its own ideas and concepts of law, religion, politics, and morality. The writer as a member of a social group, while writing about himself writes about the feelings and aspirations of his group or class. The novel has its origin in the rise of the middle class. George Eliot's and Charles Dickens's novels represent the feelings, problems, and aspirations of the middle class of Victorian England and the folk-tales of the common people all over the world.

2. Literature is a product of labour, not a divine inspiration

In the beginning man's hand was very much like that of an ape. It became different and more flexible when he started making tools. Engels writes:

8. B. Krylov, "Preface", *Marx and Engels: On Literature and Art,* (Moscow: Progress Publishers, 1978), p. 17.

> "In the constant efforts of improving the tools, the hand became not only the organ of labour but also the product of labour."[9]

This flexibility of the hand helped man invent pictogram and later on ideograph to record the vocal symbols on stones and develop the writing system. He began to imitate the momentous events of life in the form of dance, song, and rituals. The momentous events mainly affected his material life such as the rise and setting of the sun, the waxing and waning of the moon, the changes in the seasons, harvest, birth, marriage, death, and victory and defeat in battles. Man celebrated them the way they affected his material life. Through myths he tried to explain the phenomena of nature, and composed hymns to please gods and practised magic to drive away the evil spirits.

3. The laws of social development determine the course of the development of literature

The development of literature, the rise and fall of a genre, changes in themes and forms, and the world outlook of writers can be explained in terms of the changes in the social structure. The laws that operate behind the social changes determine the laws of developments in literature. Since the day man progressed from the stage of primitive communism, that is, the hunting stage, there has been a fierce competition among different social groups for the control over the means of production. The social group or the class that gained the economic power also controlled the super structure. It created law, religion, morality, government, and the contents of education in its own interest to solidify its position. The other class struggled hard for economic freedom. Thus, there were two kinds of literature, one of the ruling class and the other of the ruled. As the ruling class had the upper hand, its literature was considered superior and literature of the age.

Yet, it would be a vulgar representation of Marx to say straightway that the development of literature is solely dependent on the laws of social development. The laws of the development of literature are autonomous and they function in their own

9. Marx and Engels, *On Literature and Art*, p. 128.

way, and are not always subordinate to economic laws. Krylov has very precisely summarised this view of Marx and Engels.

> "They [Marx and Engels] were in no way inclined to qualify art as a passive product of the economic system. On the contrary, they emphasized that the various forms of social consciousness—including, of course, artistic creation—actively influence the social reality from which they emerge."[10]

4. Autonomy of art and individual creativity

Literature, like other components of the super structure, is autonomous and influences the base structure. It can solidify, strengthen, revolutionise, or change the base or economic structure. The court poets usually tried to solidify and strengthen the economic structure that suited the ruling class, but the poets who were unhappy with the current system wanted to change it. Poets like Blake, Shelley, and Hugo challenged the ruling ideas of their age and, to a large extent, changed the economic structure.

Related to the autonomy of literature and art is the individual creativity. In the words of Parkinson, "The creative writer is not a passive reflector of social consciousness."[11]

Individual creativity plays a big role in making art and literature autonomous. Apart from making innovation in form and technique, he expresses his own vision of life, which may be different from held by the conventional people and, which may attack the current system that suits the ruling class. Swift's *The Drapier's Letters* attacks the profit motive of the British government and defends the interest of the Irish people. Swift, Shelley, Gorky, and Premchand are writers who did not subscribe to the views of the ruling class and opposed its policy of exploitation. Marx and Engels clearly say that it is not necessary for the creative writer to defend the dominant ideas of the epoch developed and protected by the ruling class. He may criticise them and present new ideas that are good for the entire humanity. They refute the mechanical

---

10. B. Krylov, ed., *Marx and Engels: On Literature and Art*, p. 19.
11. G.H.R. Parkinson, *Georg Luckacs*, (London: Routlege and Kegan Paul, 1977), p. 85.

interpretation of literary history that a work of literature is the product of time, race, and milieu, and there is little scope for individual creativity. Great writers write for the entire humanity and expose the contradictions in society.

5. Reality and artistic truth

Marxist criticism lays emphasis on the correlation between reality and artistic truth. Artistic truth is reality presented in a special way. The artist must be a truthful observer of life and present it in all its details. There cannot be an opposition between artistic truth and scientific truth as both are concerned with the welfare of mankind. Vassily Novikov, a leading Marxist critic, lays stress on the relationship between artistic truth and scientific truth:

> "Literature, like science, is concerned with truth, truth which is historical, empirically verifiable, and which is within the experience of the human mind. The Marxist is not confined to technique only; his aim is to examine the faithfulness with which reality is presented in the text."[12]

Charles Dickens revels in the art of exaggeration, but the reality he presents in his novels is as true as the scientific truth. Similarly, Ralph Ellision's *The Invisible Man* is a good example of the ideal relationship between artistic and scientific truth.

6. Realism and socialist realism

The concern with reality and artistic truth leads to the concepts of realism and socialist realism. Engels defined the term realism in his letter to Margaret Harness:

> "Realism to my mind implies, besides truth of detail, the truthful reproduction of typical characters in typical circumstances."[13]

In his letter to Minna Kautsky he explained the term "type".

> "In both spheres, the characters exhibit the sharp individuation so customary in your work. Each of them

12. Vassily Novikov, *Artistic Truth and Dialectics of Creative Work*, (Moscow: Progress Publishers, 1988), p. 90.
13. *Marx and Engels: On Literature and Art*, p. 90.

> is a type, but at the same time also a definite individual, a deiser (this one) as old Hegel would say and that is how it should be."[14]

He named Leo Tolstoy, George Eliot, W.M. Thackeray, Charles Dickens, Henri Balzac, and Emile Zola as the writers of realism who observed contradictions in society and drew people's attention to them. He also explained that by "type" is meant the character who while maintaining his individuality represents her or his class.

Maxim Gorky added the adjective "critical" to the term realism and expressed the view that the literature of critical realism was born when the bourgeois system began to crash under the pressure of its own contradictions, and when the proletariat grew strong enough to challenge the bourgeoisie, "socialist realism" came into existence. The British Marxist critic Arnold Kettle has defined the term critical realism thus:

> "[It is] literature written in the era of class society, from a point of view which, while not fully socialist, is nevertheless sufficiently critical of class society and to contribute to the feeling of human consciousness from the limitations, which class society has imposed on it."[15]

Socialist realism came when mankind further marched on to the path of the classless society and the proletariat began to challenge the bourgeois system. Kettle defines it:

> "It is a literature written from the point of view of the class-conscious working class, whose socialist consciousness illuminates their whole view of the nature of the world and of potentialities of mankind."[16]

The writers of socialist realism depict the struggle of the working class with the hope of emancipation from the chains of exploitation at the global level. Novelists like Maxim Gorky, Premchand, H.G. Wells, John Steinbeck, Mikhail Sholokhov and Graham Greene and poets such as Pablo Neruda, Mayakovsky, and Faiz

14. *Ibid.*, p. 87.
15. Arnold Kettle, "Dickens and the Popular Tradition", *Marxists on Literature*, ed. David Craig, (London: Penguin, 1973), p. 214.
16. Idem, p. 214.

Ahmed Faiz, and playwrights like Bernard Shaw, John Galsworthy, Bertolt Brecht Arthur Miller, and Arnold Wesker are the great names among the writers of socialist realism. The other great writer, downgraded by the Russian Marxist critics, is Jean Paul Sartre who has blended Existentialism and Marxism in his literary and philosophical works and maintained a proper balance between the individual and society.

The great contribution of Marxist criticism to the study of literature is that it has explained the hitherto unknown, or neglected, relationship between literature and other components of the super structure (law, religion, politics, and morality) and also how the laws of social development influence the laws of development in literature. It is only a luxury to conceive literature as a means of aesthetic pleasure only. Literature is a serious mental activity and a perenniel source of knowledge, and its aim is to study the problems of man in society and envision a world free from all kinds of suffering. It is this outlook of Marxist criticism that has influenced the recent feminist criticism, which aims at both woman and man to be treated on equal footing.

(B) PSYCHO-ANALYTIC CRITICISM

Psycho-analytic criticism has its roots in Sigmund Freud's psycho-analysis and his views on creative writing. Like Karl Marx, Sigmund Freud was a German and deeply interested in literature. The big difference between the two is that, whereas the former found literature an important source of social reality, the latter the hidden feelings and emotions of the individual. A fully qualified doctor, Freud found some of his patients although in good health suffering from abnormality. Their abnormal behaviour led him to trace the source in their psyche. For the discovery of the causes of neurosis, he studied the life history of the patients first by means of hypnotism and, later, by "free association." He studied literary works of the past and present, myths and legends of Greece, Italy and Germany. His psycho-analysis made a great revolution in the field of psychology. It also made a great impact on both creative writers and literary criticism. These four concepts of psycho-analysis—unconscious, dream, fantasy, displacement, and symbol—are of paramount importance in literary criticism.

The Unconscious

Freud divided the human psyche broadly into the *conscious* and the *unconscious*. The conscious part consists of reason and conscience, and the unconscious the repressed desires. The conscious is active in a normal person when he/she is awake and the unconscious when a sleep. The repressed desires are usually violative of morality or social taboos. When a person is asleep and the conscious is at rest the unconscious begins to function. Its functioning results in dream in normal people and neurosis in the mentally sick. The unconscious dominates the conscious of the neurotic.

Dream and Fantasy

Dreams are the works of the unconscious. The repressed desires are fulfilled in dreams. In other words, dreams are a kind of wish fulfilment. The violent experiences and terribly morally violative desires cause nightmares.

Fantasy is a kind of dream. The difference between the two is of occurrence and duration. Dreams come when we are asleep and the conscious is fully at rest. Fantasy is day dreaming. Creative writers fantasise and so do the neurotics. The difference between the two is that the creative writer commands his/her fantasy, but the neurotic is commanded by it.

Displacement and Symbol

The objects desired, the objects obstructing the wish, and the means to gain the object do not come as real objects in a dream; they come in some other form. The change of one form to the other is *displacement*. The transformed object or the new form is a *symbol*. Freud says that a pointed object in dream is the symbol of phallus. People believe in India that the snake is a symbol of death or wealth in one's dream.

Freud's discovery of the unconscious and concepts of dream, fantasy, displacement, and symbol have had a far-reaching impact on literary criticism. His famous essay "Creative Writers and Daydreaming"[17] is the very foundation on which the edifice of psycho-analytic criticism is built.

---

17. Printed in *20th Century Criticism: A Reader*, ed., David Lodge (London: Longman, 1972).

The essay begins with the following questions:

(a) From what sources does the creative writer draw his material?

(b) How does he manage to make such an impression on the readers?

(c) How does he arouse in us emotions of which, perhaps, we had not thought ourselves capable?

Freud emphatically says that the writer himself cannot answer these questions. The literary critic or a good reader can answer them if he/she is able to discover an affinity between people's day-to-day activities and creative writing. Creative writing is an imaginative activity and all human beings are endowed with imagination. The first traces of imaginative activity can be found in childhood. The child at play behaves like a creative writer. He takes the world of his play seriously. The stick he rides is a real horse for him. Then what is the relation between play and reality? The answer is that the play is a displacement of real life. A child cannot ride a horse. The stick is a displacement of the horse. For adults it is a symbolical representation of the horse.

The world, a creative writer fantasises is a displacement of the real world in which he lives and the reality he encounters in his life. There is a close similarity between a child's play and a creative writer's fantasy; both are imaginative activities, but the matter does not end here. An adult who was once a child, crushed under the heavy burden of life, looks back with intense seriousness on the games played in his/her childhood. He/she can win the high yield of pleasure back by equating the serious occupations of the present with his/her childhood games to throw off the too heavy burden. But, the adult male and female cannot play the games of their childhood. Naturally, fantasy takes the place of childhood games.

Freud, then, makes difference between fantasy/day dream and play. The first difference is that the child does not hide its play, but the grown-up is ashamed of his/her fantasies and conceals them; it is easier for him/her to confess his/her misdeeds, weaknesses, and desires in plain words. Secondly, a child's play is determined by the wish to be big and grown up; on the other hand, the grown-up is torn between the opposites of the world of reality and the world of fantasy.

There are two questions to be answered. The first is, why does an adult weave a fantasy? The second is, what kind of person is he? Freud's answer is that only an unsatisfied person fantasises. A happy person will not do so. The motives of fantasies are unsatisfied wishes and every simple fantasy is the fulfilment of a wish. The wishes can be ambitious wishes, which serve to elevate the subject's personality, or they may be erotic ones. The fantasies are neither stereotyped nor unalterable; they are variables and their relation to time is very important.

The three moments of time—present, past, and future—are inter linked. Present means the current impressions. Some event, some remark, some person, or some picture may provoke the adult and arouse her/his major wishes. Past means that the unsatisfied person looks back at her/his past and recollects the experience (an infantile one, usually) in which her/his wish was fulfilled. Then comes the future. The adult creates a situation relating to the future, which represents the fulfilment of the wish. Freud gives the example of a poor orphan boy employed in the house of a rich person fantasises to marry his only beautiful daughter and be the heir of his property. He says that all romantic novels are fantasies and a kind of wish fulfilment.

After describing the nature of day dream/fantasy he discusses the connection between the creative writer and the daydreamer. Everybody is a daydreamer. But, all people are not creative writers. People daydream when they are in a difficult situation or when their desires remain unsatisfied. Creative writers are a kind of neurotic people. They weave fantasies to get rid of neurosis, as the creation of a work of art has a therapeutic effect.

Freud says that his theory is best applicable to the "lesser" (inferior) writers. These writers are of two types. The writers of the first type make use of ready made materials, and of the second type make stories after their experiences. The "lesser" writer chooses a hero who is the centre of interest. He tries to win the reader's sympathy for the hero by every possible means.

He places him under the protection of special providence. All the women in the novel are in sympathy with him and the most beautiful is almost mad after him. The characters are sharply divided into good and bad people. The people who support the hero or have sympathy for him are good characters, and those who do him harm are bad people. Such type of novel is a kind of wish fulfilment, a fantasy to escape the harsh reality of the present or an effort to get rid of neurosis.[18]

At the end of this long essay Freud summarises his arguments.

A strong impression or experience awakens in the memory of the creative writer an earlier experience, usually an infantile one. A strong wish stems from that experience. The creative writer fulfils his wish in the created work. This created work, like a day-dream, is a continuation and a substitute for what was once the play of childhood. The writer usually handles a readymade material, the popular treasure-house of myths, legends, folk-tales and fairy-tales. Myths and legends are "distorted vestiges of the wishful fantasies of whole nations, the secular dreams of youthful humanity." Because of this characteristic, young neurotic writers find them easy to handle and equally easy to identify their selves with those of the heroes and heroines in them. The study of a creative work reveals the personal character of its author. Readers experience a great pleasure in such writings, because the writer softens the character of his/her egoistic daydream by altering and disguising it, and gives an artistic touch for aesthetic pleasure.

This brief analysis of Charles Dickens's David Copperfield will illustrate Freud's psycho-analytic approach to literature.

David Copperfield

When Dickens began writing this novel, he was already an established novelist, well-settled in life with his wife and six children.

Twelfth Night party was celebrated at Devonshire on 2nd February, 1849. During that moment of happiness a few parallel

18. We can add that most of the romantic films follow this pattern and the famous television serial *Mungerilal Ke Haseen Sapne.*

events reminded him of the sad and painful experiences of the past. They were:

(i) At the age of 37 his father had collapsed under debt, was arrested and sent to Marshalsea Jail.

(ii) Twelfth Night was celebrated for his son Charley's birth. At this age, Dickens had been sent to work in the blacking factory.

(iii) In the spring of 1848, John Forster had casually mentioned that Charles Wentworth Dilke, the manager of the *Daily News*, had seen Dickens in boyhood and had given him half a crown while he used to sit at the window of the blacking factory. This was a severe jolt for Dickens and he confided everything to Forster, especially his mother's desire that he should continue working in the blacking factory.[19]

(iv) On May 7 in 1848, Dickens wrote to Forster, "This day eleven years, poor dear Mary died." We all know that she was his wife's sister and Dickens had great affection for her.

(v) The death of Fanny in the autumn of the same year added poignancy to the recollection of the sad and painful events of the past: Forster's words triggered the blast.

Thus, *David Copperfield* is a fantasy created by Dickens after being jolted by the harsh and painful realities of life. This is what Freud has said that a strong impression or experience awakens in the memory of the creative writer his/her early experiences.

Dickens, a great novelist that he was, did not present his biography in a simple and straightforward manner. The novel is a wonderful transformation of Dickens's early life into a work of art. Dickens himself wrote:

> "I really think I have done it ingeniously and with a very complicated interweaving of truth and fiction."

19. Dickens said, "I never afterwards forgot, I never shall forget, I never can forget, my mother was warm for my being sent back."

The truth is disguised, of course, but it is easily traceable, especially in the episodes of the Micawber family and their imprisonment, Urania cottage and Emily, and the experiences of young David in the factory. Besides, Dora is Mary Hogarth who died in 1837, or Maria Beadnell.

The second half of the novel is patterned after the famous story of Cinderella. Miss Betsey Trotwood, the old grand aunt is a kind of the old woman in fairy-tales. As the old woman turns out to a benevolent beautiful fairy who saves good poor children who are in dire need of help and turns their bad fortune into a good one. Miss Trotwood saves David from utter collapse and provides him the opportunity and all kinds of help for his revival and a better life. Besides, the second half of the novel is a kind of wish fulfilment. Mr. Micawber who was jailed for not paying loan becomes a magistrate, and David a successful and fully satisfied author. Let us remember that at the time of writing the novel, Dickens was still young.

David Copperfield is a novel occasioned by the words of Forster who, indirectly opened the valve of Dickens's pent up emotions of pain and anguish stored in his heart. He wrote the novel to get rid of the memories of the miserable past and put all his labour into it to make it a work of art. The material he used is the experiences of his life and of the story of Cinderella. The novel is not a biography, but for its proper understanding, the knowledge of its author's biography is highly rewarding and also how deftly he has made use of the ready made material of a fairy tale. The writing of the novel must have had a therapeutic effect on the troubled Dickens.

II

Dr. Ernest Jones has applied Freud's concept of Oedipus complex in the essay "Hamlet" where he traces this complex in Prince Hamlet and arrives at the conclusion that the main reason for his softness to his mother and hostility to his new father is Oedipus complex. Freud's analysis of *King Lear* is brilliant. He argues that the main cause of Lear's tragedy is his unability to control his libido and renounce the royal life, which he had decided earlier and live a simple life till the end.

Perhaps, the best critic in England is Sir Herbert Read who has followed Freud's psychology innovatively. His *Wordsworth* is a searching analysis of Wordsworth's psyche and poetry. His essay "Freud and Literature" is a judicious evaluation of Freud's approach to literature and life.

According to Herbert, poetry is a method of thought but the poet does not think in abstract terms, which are highly rational. His/her expression of ideas is emotional and for this he/she makes use of figures of speech, especially metaphor. "Psycho-analysis is a science of tropes of metaphor and its variants, synecdoche and metonymy. The unconscious in its struggle with the conscious always turns away from the general to the concrete and finds the tangible trifle more congenial than the large abstraction." Psychoanalysis helps the reader to interpret the metaphors produced by the author's unconscious.

Jacques Lacan is the most important modern critic who has followed and developed Freud's psycho-analysis in his literary theory. He has combined linguistics with psycho-analysis and shown the limitations of the both branches of knowledge in his famous lecture. "The Insistence of the Letter in the Unconscious". His view is that the unconscious is structured like language, and that before anything else, language was present in the unconscious. In the beginning of the lecture, he says:

> "As our title suggests, beyond what we call the word what the psycho-analysis discovers in the unconscious is the whole structure of language."[20]

A little later, after defining the term "letter" that it is the material support, which concrete speech borrows from language, he makes the point that language exists prior to any mental development.

> "For the primary reason is that language and its structure exist prior to the moment at which each individual at a certain point in his mental development makes his entry into it."[21]

20. Jacques Lacan, "The Insistence of the Letter in the Unconscious", *Modern Criticism and Theory*, ed, David Lodge, (London: Longman, 1988), p. 82.

21. *Ibid.*

Accepting Ferdinand de Saussure's concept of language, he points out the limitation of the concept of "signifier" and "signified." A simple word in isolation signifies a particular concept. For example, the signifier "tree" signifies the concept of *tree*. But, in the case of the signifier "Ladies" written on the door of room, the word does not signify the concept of *ladies*; it signifies that the room is meant for ladies. What Lacan means by giving the example of two rooms before which the words "ladies" and "gentlemen" are written and the difference in their meanings is that Saussurian linguistics cannot explain the metaphors, images, symbols, and other tropes in literary works. He, therefore, makes a fusion of psycho-analysis and linguistics.

Lacan's critical theory is a new approach to literature. He has modified both Freud and De Saussure. Freud's view is that a literary text reveals its author's mind and the symbols, images, and metaphors are the products of the unconscious. For De Saussure, language is a product of the conscious. Lacan argues that the role of the unconscious is equally important in the creation of a literary text, which is a linguistic structure. His followers interpret literary texts on these three basic premises:

(i) The unconscious is structured like language.

(ii) The "letter" (the material support which concrete speech borrows from language) is present in the unconscious before any mental development.

(iii) The meaning of a text cannot be discovered by solely applying Saussurian principle of signifier and signified, and their arbitrary relationship. For proper understanding, the psycho-analytic explanation of tropes is essential. It is exigent that structuralism and psycho-analysis are combined together for the analysis of literary texts.

Lacan's addition of linguistics to psycho-analytic criticism has opened a new vista in the interpretation and evaluation of modern literature, especially post-modern poetry, novel, and drama.

(C) MYTH CRITICISM

Myth criticism (also called archetypal criticism) has its base in anthropology and psychology. Like New criticism, it uses all the methods of close analysis and like the Neo-Aristotelians, it accepts the development of different genres, yet its main focus is on cultural and psychological patterns that underlie a text. "In every age", writes Northrop Frye:

> "Poets who are thinkers (remembering that poets think in metaphors and images, not in propositions) and are deeply concerned with the origin or destiny or desires of mankind—with anything that belongs to the larger outlines of what literature can express—can hardly find a literary theme that does not coincide with a myth."[22]

As a literary text is a part of culture, the main aim of the critic is to trace the thematic relationship between the text under study and the original myth, which is its source. The second task is to explain the reason why creative writers compulsorily return to ancient myths. When the critic is able to do it successfully, he/she "makes us understand the corresponding place that a work of literature has in the context of the whole".[23]

Myth criticism has its origin in the writings of Giamb-attista Vico, Edward Tylor, James Frazer, Sigmund Freud, and Carl Jung, the first three cultural anthropologists and the last two psychologists who studied ancient myths, legends and folk-tales seriously and gave a psychological interpretation of their nature, meaning, and function. The anthropologists differed from the psychologists in their interpretation of myths, legends, and folk-tales; for them they are imaginative interpretation of the natural phenomena. On the other hand Freud defined them as projections (displacement) of the desires and fears of the primitive man stored in his unconscious, and for Jung they are manifestations of the archetypes of the collective unconscious.

Before Tylor and Frazer, Vico used myths and legends as clues for explaining man's cultural and intellectual history. He discovered that the gods, goddesses, heroes, and heroines of the ancient societies are the expressions of the human nature and

---

22. Northrop Fyre, "Myth , Fiction and Displacement," *Twentieth Century Criticism,* ed. W.J. Handy and Max Westbrook, (Delhi: Light and Life Publishers, 1977), p. 166.

23. *Ibid.*, p. 168.

behaviour. Freud interpreted myths from the psychological point of view. Vico's interpretation is cultural and it reaches the conclusion that the primitive man created a god out of fear and projected his troublesome desires on him; his emphasis is on the social customs and institutions, which develop out of the human beliefs and desires that myth discloses. Basically there is no contradiction in the conclusions of Vico and Freud; the only difference is of the areas they have focused on.

Edward Tylor made cultural anthropology more scientific and comprehensive. Influenced by Charles Darwin, he developed on evolutionary relationship between primitive and modern cultures, stressing the cultural achievement of the entire humanity from the savage to the civilized state. It is remarkable of him to propound the theory that all human races belong to one species, the theory scientists vindicated in the last decade of the twentieth century.

Following Tylor's theory that myths are basic to all human races, and that all human societies have developed from the primitive or savage state to the stage of civilization, James Frazer posited the theory that all societies have progressed from the state of magic to the state of religion and have finally reached the state of science, and that the gods and heroes of myths are the vegetative deities. J.B. Vickery has summarised the conclusions of Frazer's voluminous *The Golden Bough*:

> "First, the evolutionary view appears with his notion that man develops socially and psychologically through three stages. While early man moves historically from a society founded on the hunt through a pastoral order to an agricultural state, he also progresses from a psychological state controlled by magic to one under the sway of religion and finally to a scientic view of life. Second, ... that primitive deities were primarily vegetative spirits rather than solar gods."[24]

Professor Gilbert Murray, perhaps, the first myth critic analysed some of the classics of old Greek and English literatures

24. J.B. Vickery, *The Literary Impact of the Golden Bough*, (Princeton; New Jersey: Princeton University Press, 1973), p. 67.

in the light of Frazer's thesis. In the essay "Hamlet and Orestes", after a comparative study of the classical Greek literature, Saxo's *History of the Danes*, especially the Amlodi/ Amlehtus saga, Shakespeare's *Hamlet*, and the ancient Greek myth of the birth of Zeus he arrives at the conclusion that Hamlet, Orestes, Gertrude, Clytemnestra, Agamemnon, and Laius have the elements of the vegetative deities and have their origin in the rituals of death and rebirth of the ancient deities connected with the cycle of seasons. After establishing the connection between Orestes and Hamlet, Claudius and Aegisthus, Gertrude and Clytemnestra he comments:

> "There is clearly a common element in all these stories and the reader will doubtless have recognised it. It is the worldwide ritual story of what we may call the golden-bough-kings. That ritual story is, as I have tried to show elsewhere [*Euripides and His Age*, 1913], the fundamental conceptions that form the basis of Greek tragedy, and not Greek tragedy only."[25]

In short, Clytemnestra, Jocasta, and Gertrude are Earth Mother; Agamemnon, Laius, and King Hamlet are the dying-god, and Orestes, Oedipus, and Hamlet have the elements of winter in them. It is difficult to agree entirely with Murray, but his argument that these figures have their origin in myths and rituals celebrating the cycles of seasons and vegetative deities is very much true.

According to Freud, the creative writer, especially of the ordinary kind, creates the world of his/her fantasy, which is based upon the readymade and familiar material available in "the popular treasure house of myths, legends and fairy-tales". Though, he accepted the idea that the whole nation has "wishful fantasies", which find their expression in myths, he never believed in the existence of the "collective unconscious". His disciple Carl Gustav Jung who broke away from him on this point refuted him in his long essay "Archetypes of the Collective Unconscious" and wrote:

---

25. Gilbert Murray, "Hamlet and Orestes", *Five Approaches of Literary Criticism*, ed. Wilbur Scott, (Toronto: Collier-Macmillan Ltd. 1962), p. 272.

> "For Freud, accordingly, the unconscious is of an exclusively personal nature, although he was aware of its archaic and mythological thought forms."

After making this statement he propounded the concept of the collective unconscious. According to him, the unconscious has two layers: the superficial or personal and the deeper or collective. The personal unconscious rests upon the collective unconscious, which is inborn and universal. In contrast to the personal unconscious, the collective unconscious has contents and modes of behaviour that are more or less the same everywhere and in all individuals. Whereas "the contents of the personal unconscious are chiefly the feeling-toned complexes constituting the personal and private life, the contents of the collective unconscious are the archetypes or primordial images, which find their expression in dreams, myths, fairy-tales, and folk-lore."[26]

The archetypes are the experiences of the race stored in the collective unconscious, which is like a pool of water, and when the individual has a complete breakdown in his personal life and is unable to adjust in the social life, the collective unconscious, the store house of wisdom, comes to his/her rescue in dreams. The archetypes are altered by becoming conscious and by being perceived, and they take their colour from the individual consciousness in which they happen to appear. The archetypes were formed in the very beginning of man's coming upon the earth and stored in the unconscious with the passage of time. Man perceived the events that affected his material and emotional life subjectively and imaginatively, and correlated them together. Jung writes:

> "Primitive man is not much interested in objective explanations of the obvious, but he has an irresistible urge to assimilate all outer sense experiences to inner, psychic events. It is not enough for the primitive man to see the sun rise and set; this external observation must at the same time be a psychic happening; the sun in its

26. C.G. Jung, "Archetypes of the Collective Unconscious", *Twentieth Century Criticism: Major Statements*, ed. W.J. Handy and Max Westbrook, (Light and Life Publishers, 1977), p. 205.

> course must represent the fate of a god or hero who, in the last analysis, dwells nowhere except in the soul of man."[27]

The main archetypes are:

i. Lake
ii. Shadow
iii. Nixie (anima for men and animus for women)
iv. The black and the white magicians
v. The wise old man

i. *The Lake*

It is the archetype of the collective unconscious. The dreamer sees the collective unconscious as a pool of water. The contents of the lake are the nixie, the magicians, and the wise old man. Water is an object of fear and regeneration at the same time. Only the brave and the inquisitive can face it and dive into it to know the meaning of life in the moments of spiritual crisis.

ii. *The Shadow*

When the dreamer approaches the lake, the surface of the collective unconscious, he/she is terror-struck by the shadow, which is her or his reflection, the reflection of her/his true self. If he/she understands the true nature of the shadow and is not terrified by the reflection, the dream will continue. The true self is not what the dreamer sees in a mirror or has formed a false opinion about her/him; it is something different, ugly and deformed as the old woman sees it in Sylvia Plath's "Mirror":

> "Now I am a lake.....
> ....
> In me she has drowned a young girl, and in me an old woman
> Rises toward her day by day, like a terrible fish."

iii. *The Nixie*

The nixie is the archetype of the principle of life. It is anima for male and animus for female. It can take the shape of a mermaid/siren or horse. When the dreamer is not afraid of the

27. C.G. Jung, "Archetypes of Collective Unconscious," *Twentieth Century Criticism: Major Statements*, p. 207.

shadow, the archetype of her/his self, she/he enters the lake and discovers the nixie. The nixie, a horse or mermaid, will take her/ him to a strange place.

iv. *The White and the Black Magicians*

The dreamer carried by the nixie to a strange place meets the white and the black magicians who are the archetypes of good and evil. The magician in white is dark in colour and the magician in black is fair, and hence the confusion in the mind of the dreamer whom to choose. It is difficult for her/him to know who is really white and who is really black as the dress confuses her/him. In other words the dreamer is unable to make distinction between right and wrong, good and evil. This is the spiritual crisis.

v. *The Wise Old Man*

Finally, the wise old man, archetype of the meaning of life, comes to the rescue of the dreamer. He explains the crisis and the way to overcome it. The spiritual crisis is overcome and the dreamer reaches the state of equilibrium and becomes happy again.

In the famous essay "Psychology and Literature", Jung specifically discusses the relationship between literature and psychology, and stressing the role of the collective unconscious reaches a conclusion, which is diametrically opposed to Freud's conclusion in "Creative writers and Day dreaming". Jung says that the creative writer in his creative process is guided not only by his personal experiences but also by the racial experiences. There is an inextricable tie between the writer, the wisdom stored in the collective unconscious, and the created work. The writer is a medium who, like the priest of Delphi, delivers the wisdom and experiences of his/her forefathers. Jung writes:

> "As a human being he may have moods and a will and personal aims, but as an artist he is "man" in a higher sense, he is "collective" man—one who carries and shapes the unconscious, psychie life of mankind."[28]

---

28. C.G. Jung, "Psychology and Literature", *20th Century Criticism: A Reader*, ed, David Lodge, p. 186.

It is, therefore, useless to look into the personal life of the artist to explain his work; art in fact, forces upon him and he is only the efficient cause. In the concluding paragraph of the essay he affirms the impersonality of the writer and supremacy of the racial wisdom.

> "This is why every great work of art is objective and impersonal, but nonetheless profoundly moves us each and all. And this is also why the personal life of the poet cannot be held essential to his art, but at most a help or hindrance to his creative task."[29]

This view of Jung that a great work of art contains the wisdom of the writer's forefathers and the writer functions like a medium is very much similar to that of W.B. Yeats who said that a poet creates poetry in trance and functions like a medium who delivers reality realized in a vision.

II

After the pioneering works of cultural anthropologists and psycho-analysts, myth criticism came to its own in the critical works of Gilbert Murray, Maud Bodkin, Northrop Frye, Lilian Feder, Leslie Fiedler, and Richard Chace. These critics combined anthropology and Jungian psychology, and formed the modern myth criticism. Laying a great emphasis on mythology and its structure, Northrop Frye wrote:

> "Mythology as a total structure defining as it does a society's religious beliefs, historical traditions, cosmological speculations...in short, the whole range of its verbal expressiveness is the matrix of literature and major poetry keeps returning to it."[30]

Leslie Feder almost echoes Frye when he writes:

> "The task of the critic is to discover the deepest meanings, meanings which extend beyond the single work to a whole body of books, the archetypal symbols to which...writers compulsively return."[31]

29. *Ibid.*, p. 188.
30. Northrop Frye, "Myth, Fiction and Displacement," *Twentieth Century Criticism: Major Statements*, p. 166.
31. Quoted by Wilbur Scott, "Introduction", *Five Approaches of Criticism*, p. 249.

The first critic who applied Jung's theory of literature is Maud Bodkin. Her book *Archetypal Patterns in Poetry* (1934) did not receive the attention it deserved as it was purely a new approach, quite away from the track of Eliot, Richards, Leavis, and New Critics of America. The book drew the attention of critics and scholars after the second world war when the entire Europe and America were passing through a spiritual crisis. *Archetypal Patterns is Poetry* is a brilliant and original analysis of some of the great poems in English literature and successfully explains why certain symbols and images, simple though they may appear, move the reader more emotionally than other symbols and images. The reason, she gives, is that these symbols and images are related to the archetypes of the collective unconscious. She states her method and objective in the Preface:

> "An attempt is here made to bring psychological anlaysis and reflection to bear upon the imaginative experience communicated by great poetry, and to examine those forms or patterns in which the universal forces of our nature there find objectivization."[32]

Referring to Jung's article "On the Relation of Analytical psychology and Poetic Art", she comments:

> "The special emotional significance possessed by certain poems—a significance going beyond any definite meaning conveyed—he attributed to the stirring in the reader's mind within or beneath his conscious response, of unconscious forces, which he terms *primordial images* or *archetypes*. These archetypes he describes as psychic residue of numberless experiences of the same type, experiences which have happened not to the individual but to his ancestors, and of which the results are inherited in the structure of the brain, a *priori* determinants of individual experience."[33]

Her analysis of Coleridge's *Rime of the Ancient Mariner,* Eliot's *The Waste Land*, Shakespeare's *Hamlet*, and Dante's

32. Maud Bodkin, *Archetypal Patterns in Poetry*, (London: Oxford Univ. Press, 1934), p. 1.

33. Idem, p. 1.

Divine Comedy throws a new light on the structure and meaning of these classics. Her discovery of the archetypal patterns or motifs enlightens us greatly and we learn the most profound and universal experiences, and concerns of the human race.

Narthrop Frye is the greatest exponent and practitioner of myth criticism. His essay "Archetypes of Literature" and treatise *Anatomy of Criticism: Four Essays* form the base of modern myth criticism. *Fearful Symmetry: A Study of William Blake* (1947), *The Well-Tempered Critic* (1963), *The Secular Scripture* (1976), *The Great Code: The Bible and Literature* (1982) and *Northrop Frye on Shakespeare* (1986) are the practical application of his literary theory.

Following Aristotle and Marx, he affirms that literature is animation of "infinite social action and infinite human thought." The deviation from the greek philosopher to Karl Marx is significant as Frye is concerned with man in society through different ages. He writes in *Anatomy of Criticism*:

> "The study of literature takes us toward seeing poetry as the imitation of infinite social action and infinite human thought, the mind of a man who is all men, the universal creative word which is all words."[34]

Frye follows Edward Tylor who said that all human races have their origin in one species, not different species. He stresses the fact that all human beings of the world have the same pattern of feeling, thinking, and social action and, therefore, all great works of literature return to ancient myths for their material, and only archetypal and anagogic criticism can best explain the nature, origin, and forms of literature. His concept of criticism can be briefly described thus.

Literary criticism is like physical sciences that study nature systematically and try to explain the order by interpreting different phenomena, which are seemingly diverse but are governed by certain laws fixed and regular. It is the task of literary criticism to be like physical sciences in its methodology

34. Northrop Frye, *Anatomy of Criticism: Four Essays,* (Princeton: New Jersey: Princeton Univ. Press, 1957), p. 125.

and find out a system in literary texts. He explains why criticism has to be systematic:

> "It is clear that criticism cannot be systematic unless there is a quality in literature, which enables it to be so, an order of words corresponding to the order of nature in the natural sciences."[35]

What, we may ask, is the quality in literature that forms an order in it? Frye's answer is that the archetype is the unifying force and it is the task of the literary critic to explain the structure of literature, its origin and development, and the reason for the recurrent return of creative writers to certain figures and themes. In order that one can best analyse the structure of a form one has to go back to its archetype, the primordial image, which is best expressed through a myth, legend, ritual, or folk-tale.

The archetypes of literature can be traced by studying the archetypes of the collective unconscious. As Jung has pointed out, man saw in the beginning years a correspondence between the cycles of four ages of man, the four seasons of the year, and the four periods of the day. The Sphinx's question to Oedipus testifies this fact of correspondences. Adopting Jung's interpretation of the correspondences, Frye says:

> "In the solar cycle of the day, the seasonal cycle of the year, and the organic cycle of human life, there is a single pattern of significance, out of which myth constructs a central narrative around a figure who is partly the sun, partly vegetative fertility, and partly a god or archetypal human being."[36]

The hero of a myth may be a demi-god, or man with extraordinary strength, intelligence, and skill in warfare who represents the aspirations of the entire community, and in his triumph or defeat lies the comic or tragic vision of the people. The central theme of the myth is quest of something indispensable and invaluable without which the community would be almost lifeless. The other myths have arisen from epiphany and the oracle.

---

35. Northrop Frye, "Archetypes of Literature", *Twentieth Century Criticism*, p. 237.
36. *Ibid.*, p. 240.

The forms of literature have their origin in the myths, which have been created on the basis of the phases of man's life, the seasons of the year, and the four periods of the solar day. Frye enumerates the following table to explain the reason for the formation of the genres of poetry and drama in the beginning of literary creation.

"1. **Phase One: The dawn, spring, and birth phase:** Myths of the birth of the hero, of revival and resurrection, of creation (because the four phases are a cycle) of the defeat of the powers of darkness, winter, and death. Subordinate characters: the father and the mother. The archetype of romance and most dithyrambic and rhapsodic poetry.

2. **The zenith, summer, and marriage or triumph phase:** Myths of apotheosis, of sacred marriage, and of entering into paradise. Subordinate characters: the companion and the bride. The archetype of comedy, pastoral and idyll.

3. **The sunset, autumn, and death phase:** Myths of fall, of the dying god, of violent death and sacrifice, and of the isolation of the hero. Subordinate characters: the traitor and the river. The archetype of tragedy and elegy.

4. **The darkness, winter, and dissolution phase:** Myths of the triumph of these powers; myths of floods and the return of chaos, of the defeat of the hero, and gottera-mmerung myths. Subordinate characters: the orge and the witch. The archetype of satire."[37]

Frye is critical of the New Critics who analyse a literary text isolating it from its social and cultural context. According to him, literature is essentially a social product and in order we can fully comprehend its form, meaning, and function, we should go back to its archetypes as expressed in myths, legends, and folk-tales. He concludes his arguments:

37. Northrop Frye, "Archetypes of Literature", *Twentieth Century Criticism: Major Statements*, p. 240.

> "The social function of the arts seems to be closely connected with visualizing the goal of work in human life. So, in terms of significance, the central myth of art must be the end of social effort, the innocent world of fulfilled desires, the free human society. Once this is understood, the integral place of criticism among the other social sciences, in interpreting and systematizing the vision of the artist, will be easier to see."[38]

To summarize the points, myth criticism takes help of both anthropology and psychology, and interprets a literary text in social-historical context. It tries to connect modern man with the ancient people and establish the fact that inspite of the progress of civilization there is no basic difference in them in emotional responses to natural events and challenges of life. A work of art, although a creation of an individual, is a social product. The creative writer is a member of her/his society and a part of its culture. Again, the given society cannot be isolated from its history. Man's history is not only social, political and economic; it is psychological also. A deep study of man's consciousness and psyche (both conscious and unconscious) is necessary to understand the meaning of a work of art. A great writer is a part of tradition, both literary and socio-cultural. Her/his collective unconscious is not solely her/his; it is almost like that of other members of her/his race. A great work of art moves us deeply not because the artist has presented her/his ideas in a novel way, but because the employed figures and symbols are concrete expressions of the archetypes of the collective unconscious. A text is great because it contains the wisdom of mankind stored in the collective unconscious, a wisdom that can regenerate men from spiritual breakdown.

(D) RUSSIAN FORMALISM

Russian Formalism began in the second decade of the twentieth century. Roman Jakobson founded the Moscow Linguistic Circle in 1915, and Viktor Shklovsky, the Society for the Study of Poetic Language (OPOYAZ) in 1916. Although,

---

38. Northrop Frye, "Archetypes of Literature", *Twentieth Century Criticism: Major Statements*, p. 242.

these two groups did not collaborate, yet they shared a common ground for the study of literature. They all agreed to establish a centre of study of literature on scientific grounds, and make formal and linguistic analysis to determine what makes a speech act literary and distinguishes it from other modes of discourse. Since, they—Roman Jakobson, Jurij Tynyanov, Viktor Shklovsky, and Boris Eichenbaum[39]—aimed at specifying the formal and linguistic properties of literature, they called themselves specifiers.[40]

As they developed their poetics on the basis of linguistics, it is necessary to know Ferdinand de Saussure's concepts of (a) signifier and signified, (b) phone and phoneme, (c) langue and parole, and (d) diachromic and synchromic studies of language, and correlate them with the Formalist concept of literature, literary text, literary criticism, and literary history.

The relation between the *signifier* (word) and the *signified* (meaning/concept) is arbitrary, that is, there is no logical relationship between a sign and the concept it refers to.

The signifier *cat*, for example, refers to the concept of the animal cat, not the object, and the relationship between the two is based upon convention. Closely related to it is the concept of phoneme, the smallest unit in the sound system of a language. A speech sound (*phone*) becomes a phoneme in a language in its contrastive relationship with the other speech sounds in that language. For example, the speech sound is a phoneme in English, because it is in contrast with other phonemes in the language. From this follows that all the phonemes derive their meaning from their mutual relationship, and so do words in the system of a language. The Russian formalists, on this basis of the arbitrary relationship of the signifier and the signified, and interdependence of sentences for their meaning, challenged the mimetic theory that poetry is an imitation of reality. They argued if words are signifiers of concepts and we come to know concepts through words, a literary text, which is basically a linguistic structure, is a signifier of reality. There is, of course, the world of reality outside the text, but the author encodes it in

39. "Eichenbaum" is spelt "Eikhenbaum" in some books.

40. In this respect, they are very near to Dandin and Bhamaha.

words, which form the created work. Readers know the author's perception of reality through the text. The reality readers perceive is embedded in the text. In other words, literature is a semiotic mediation of reality.

Following the concept of phoneme that it exists because of its difference from other phonemes, they concluded that a text exists in contrast with other texts in the literary system and derives its meaning from its mutual relationship with them.

The formalists followed the concept of *langue* and *parole* in defining the nature and function of literary criticism. De Saussure defined *langue* as the system of language, and *parole* as individual speech acts. Tynyanov and Jakobson accepted the great linguist's emphasis on *langue* as it is limited and is the key factor of language and, on that pattern, argued that the primary concern of criticism is to concentrate on the text, not biography, history of ideas, sociology, or religion. According to them, the basic function of literary criticism is to trace or describe the principles that work in the composition of a poem, novel, or drama as a particular kind of discourse.

Finally, they maintained, following Saussure's division of diachronic and synchronic study of language, that it is beyond the jurisdiction of literary criticism to study the historical development, and so, it should concentrate on the text itself and leave the historical and biographical reasons aside for its structural analysis. As such literary criticism is essentially a-historical and it is the task of literary history to study the chronological development of literature. Eichenbaum said:

> "The study of literary genetics can classify only the origin of a device noting more; poetics must serve different functions in different literary texts."[41]

Roman Jakobson as late as in 1958 repeated his contemporary in the "closing statement" in a seminar organized by Indiana University:

41. Quoted by Tony Bennet, *Formalism and Marxism*, (London and New York: Methuen, 1979), p. 52.

> "Literary studies, with poetics as their focal portion, consist like linguistics of two sets of problems: synchrony and diachrony. The synchromic description envisages not only the literary production of any given stage but also that part of the literary tradition which for the stage in question has remained vital or has been revived .... A thoroughly comprehensive historical poetics or history of language is a super structure to be built on a series of successive description."[42]

This quotation needs explanation. Diachrony is the study of the development of language from the time of its beginning to the present, and it is also called Historical Linguistics. Synchrony is the study of language at a given time. The other name of synchrony is Descriptive Linguistics. Historical Linguistics or diachronic study depends on the findings of synchronic study. In the same way, literary history depends on poetics or literary criticism for its method and technique.

After making a distinction between literary history and literary criticism, the formalists contended that the study of literature should become an autonomous science having its own principles and techniques. In the words of Tony Bennet:

> "Such a science would need first to specify the nature of the object to which it would address itself, to state clearly what it was to be a science of, and to map out clearly the conceptual space it would occupy."[43]

The formalists first concentrated on the language of a text and then contrasted it with other modes of discourse. They followed Saussurian principle of contrast. Since a literary work stands in contrast with other works in the system of literature, the task of criticism is to determine the inter-relationship between texts, and trace the principle of their composition. The main problem, they said, is to make distinction between the literary and non-literary, and so, to quote Jakobson:

---

42. Printed under the title: "Linguistics and Poetics", *Modern Literary Criticism and Theory*, ed. David Lodge, (London: Longman, 1988), p. 34.

43. Tony Bennet, *Formalism and Marxism*, p. 48.

> "The real field of literary science is not literature but literariness; in other words, that which makes a work literary."[44]

Enumerating the six functions of language—referential, emotive, poetic, conative, phatic, and metalingual—he made this oft-quoted statement:

> "The poetic function projects the principle of equivalance from the axis of selection into the axis of combination."[45]

David Lodge has explained this cryptic statement lucidly in the footnote to Jakobson's essay "The Metaphoric and Metonymic poles".[46] "The axis of selection" means the selection of words from the appropriate set of words in a language. Combination means the organization of the selected words according to the grammar of language. If Milton wrote the first line of "On His Blindness":

When I consider how I become blind,

We would have made a referential use of language. The words "light" and "spent" in the poem are selected from the set of words in English language, but their use is not referential; it is metaphorical, and hence, poetic. Secondly, equivalence plays the pivotal role at the sound level, word level, and phrase level. Jakobson refers to Hopkins and Sanskrit *Kavya* and the famous sentence of Julius Caesar "*Veni*, *vidi*, *vici*" (I came, I saw, I conquered) to illustrate his point. In short, Jakobson considers the writer's special way of selecting words and combining them into words for poetic and emotive use of language on the basic quality of literariness in both prose and verse.

Shklovsky posited the concept of *defamiliarization.* In the famous essay "Art as Technique", he wrote:

> "The purpose of art is to impart the sensation of things as they are perceived, and not as they are known. The technique of art is to make objects "unfamiliar", to make

44. Quoted by Tony Bennet, *Formalism and Marxism*, p. 55.
45. Roman Jakobson, "Linguistics and Poetics", *Modern Literary Criticism and Theory,* p. 39.
46. David Lodge, "Footnote", *Modern Criticism and Theory*, p. 57.

> forms difficult, to increase the difficulty and length of perception because the process of perception is aesthetic end in itself and must be prolonged. Art is a way of experiencing the artfulness of an object; the object is not important."[47]

In his brilliant anlaysis of Tolstoy's technique in the same essay he used the term *defamiliarization*, as the basic feature of literariness/art.

"Tolstoy makes the familiar seem strange by not meaning the familiar object. He describes an object as if he were seeing it for the first time, an event as if it were happening for the first time. In describing something he avoids the accepted names of its parts and instead names corresponding parts of other objects. For example, in "Shame" Tolstoy *defamiliarises* the idea of flogging in this way:

> 'to strip people who have broken the law, to hurl them to the floor, and to rap their bottoms with switches' and after a few lines, 'to lash about on the naked buttocks.'

Then he remarks:

> 'Just why precisely this stupid, savage means of causing pain and not any other.... Why not prick the shoulders or any part of the body with needles, squeeze the hands or the feet in a vise, or anything like that?'

I apologise for this harsh example, but it is typical of Tolstoy's way of pricking the conscience. The familiar act of flogging is made unfamiliar both by the description and by the proposal to change its form without changing its nature. Tolstoy uses this technique of *defamiliarization* constantly."[48]

Boris Eichenbaum used the term *bestrangement* while analysing *Sevastopol Sketches*, the first collection of short stories of Tolstoy. The word *bestrangement* is derived from the root word "strange" to which the prefix be- and suffix—ment are added, and it means the condition of being strange or unfamiliar. Eichenbaum's and Shklovsky's concepts are very much similar to Bhamaha's and

---

47. Viktor Shklovsky, "Art as Technique", *Modern Criticism and Theory,* p. 20.

48. *Ibid.*, p. 21.

Kuntaka's. The Sanskrit critics used the term *vaichitrya* (strangeness) and *strikingness* as the basic feature of literariness.[49]

Shklovsky and Eichenbaum made distinction between *fabula* (the raw material) and *sjuzet* (the plot) and stated that a literary text is a transformation of the reality perceived by the writer into a code, and the main device for transcreation is the technique of defamiliarization or bestrangement masterly perfected by Leo Tolstoy.

The great contribution of the formalists was that they made literary criticism as objective and methodical as science, and opened a new path to the study of literature. They were the first to employ the findings of linguistics for the analysis and evaluation of literary works as art and make literary criticism autonomous. Their work did not stop with them. Roman Jakobson, after-leaving the USSR, collaborated with the French anthropologist Claude Levi-Strauss and laid the foundation stone of French structuralism, and Mikhail Bakhtin added the "social element" after some time in the erstwhile USSR. His view that language in use is "dialogic", that is, every speech act springs from previous utterance and structured in expectation of previous response, and that there is "polyphony of voices" in a novel has gained momentum in our time.

(E) STRUCTURALISM AND POST-STRUCTURALISM

Structuralism and post-structuralism reached the English speaking world almost at the same time. The late arrival of structuralism was due to the second world war. The famous article "Problems in the Study of Literature" by Jurij Tynyanov and Roman Jakobson is widely accepted as the foundation stone of structuralism in general. The limitations of Russian Formalism were first pointed out by Leon Trotsky that it did not take the social purpose of literature in account and the authors of "Problems in the Study of Literature", too felt so. As mentioned in the previous chapter Mikhail Bakhtin laid stress on the social aspect of literature and placed the novel in the centre, it will be an injustice to the Russian formalists if we accuse them of being too narrow and myopic. The fact is that they were deeply

49. See the chapters on Bhamaha and Kuntaka.

engrossed in developing their aesthetic principles and found little time to pay attention to the relation between art and social structure.

After October Revolution in 1917, Jakobson emigrated from the USSR and founded the Prague School of Linguistics. He came in contact with Claude Levi-Strauss, a great French anthropologist, highly interested in literature. Both in collaboration analysed Baudelaire's "Les Chats" and from here began the French Structuralism. Levi-Strauss propounded the theory that all human activities are structured like language, and that language is a part of culture and should be studied in relation to its other components. Applying Saussure's concept of *langue* and *parole* in his anthropological studies he analysed ancient myths, numbering more than eight hundred, and concluded that all myths are related and are formal transformation of one another.

While interpreting myths and analysing mythical thought Levi-Strauss used two terms: bricolage and bricolour. According to him, a bricolour is an artisan who reconstructs a new structure out of the existing materials of a dismantled old structure. For reconstruction, he uses the existing tools and does not invent a new one. His art is called bricolage. The myth-maker is a bricolour who reconstructs the myth he has access to, and mythical thought is a kind of intellectual bricolage.[50]

Gerard Gennette, one of the leading French structuralists, in his lucid essay "Structuralism and Literary Criticism" (1964) refers to Levi-Strauss' concept of engineer and *bricoleur*, and quotes the following sentence where the distinction is made.

> "[The engineer] questions the universe, while the bricoleur addresses himself to a collection of oddments left over from human endeavours, that is, only a subset of culture."[51]

50. Claude Levi Strauss, "The Science of the Concrete", *Twentieth Century Criticism: Major Statements*, p. 442.
51. Gerard Gennette, "Structuralism and Literary Criticism", *Modern Criticism and Theory*, p. 64.

Then he comments that the creative writer can be substituted for engineer and the critic for bricoleur to define the status of literary criticism. He writes:

> "The creative writer while questioning the universe builds a structure. The bricoleur or the critic breaks down the structure into its elements...one element per card...and next he builds up a new structure."[52]

In other words, the critic's task is to break the text into structural units and restructure them into a new structure after her/his own reading. One must not add anything from one's own side; on the other hand one

> "must make it possible to uncover the connection that exists between a system of forms and a system of meanings, by replacing the search for term-by-term analysis with one for overall homologues."[53]

It is not enough for the critic to study the structure of poetic language and the forms of literary expression, he/she has also to analyse the relation between code and message. The limitation of Russian formalism was that it narrowed it to the confines of textual study. Gerard Gennette comments that structuralism released literary criticism from the blind alley of formalism, which considered literature as a mere dialect. These are his words:

> "Literature being primarily a work of language, and structuralism for its part, being pre-eminently a linguistic method, the most probable encounter should obviously take place on the terrain of linguistic material; sounds, forms, words, and sentences constitute the common object of the linguist and the philologist to such an extent that it was possible in the early enthusiasm of the Russian formalist movement, to define literature as a mere dialect, and to envisage its study as an annex of general dialectology."[54]

---

52. *Ibid.*, p. 66.
53. *Ibid.*, p. 67.
54. *Ibid.*, p. 65.

It is difficult to agree with this estimate of Gerard Gennette that the Russian Formalists made literary criticism a mere extension of dialectology. As said earlier, Tynyanov and Jakobson laid the foundation of structuralism and later on, the latter collaborated with Levi-Strauss in forming French structuralism.

Post Structuralism

Roland Barthes is the greatest post-structuralist critic. Structuralism began before the second world war. Soon after the war, the world scenario changed and existentialism came to the fore in literature and also Albert Camus' philosophy of the absurd. Ideology that was a kind of anathema earlier gained prominence. The fall of the empires changed the political scene. Naturally, criticism had to take note of the relation between code and message, and say that the message is embedded in the text and the critic's task is to make textual anlaysis.

Barthes found that structuralism gave socio-cultural base to literary criticism, but not history, nor ideology. Basically a Saussurian, he combined philosophy, history, and sociology together for the study of literature. His essay "Criticism as Language" published in *The Times Literary Supplement* (1963), which created a stir in the British and American literary circle may be said to be the first text of post-structuralism.

He begins the essay by mentioning the main critical trends in France, namely Existentialism, Marxism, Psycho-analysis, and Structuralism. Being a great admirer of Jean Paul Sartre, who had tried to combine Marxism and Existentialism, he finds ideology as one of the most important elements of criticism. He writes in a satirical vein:

> "Criticism is something other than making correct statements in the light of 'true' principles. It follows that the major in criticism is not to have an ideology but to keep quiet about it."[55]

A little later he throws light on a new aspect of the function of criticism:

55. Roland Barthes, "Criticism as Language", *20th Century Criticism*, ed. David Lodge, p. 648.

> "Criticism is not in any sense a table of results of a body of judgements; it is essentially an activity, that is to say a series of intellectual acts inextricably involved with the historical and subjective (the two terms are synonymous) existence of the person who carries them out and has to assume responsibility for them."[56]

Barthes adopts the postulates of structuralism and says that literature is a linguistic structure, a semiotic organization of signification, which deals with the universe, and criticism is a comment on the linguistic structure. He names the language of the text "object language", as it codes the author's perception of reality, and the language of criticism "meta-language", which explains the object language. Criticism takes two kinds of relationship into account:

> The first is "...the relationship between the critical language and the language of the author under consideration", and the second is "the relationship between the latter (language-as-object) and the world."[57]

It is this dual relationship that defines criticism and brings it near to logic which is "entirely founded on the distinction between language-as-object and meta-language." As logic is concerned with validity, criticism, too, is concerned with validity, not truth. Therefore, Barthes says:

> "We might say that the task of criticism (and this is the only guarantee of its universality) is purely formal; it does not consist in "discovering" something "hidden" or "profound" or "secret", which has so far escaped notice (through what "miracle"? Are we more perceptive than our predecessors?) but only in fitting together...the language of the day (existentialism, Marxism, or psycho-analysis) and the language of the author...."[58]

What Barthes emphasises here is the importance of the language of the text, which is before him as it is. It is something like a chessboard on which all chessmen are clearly present and move

56. *Ibid.*, p. 649.

57. *Ibid.*

58. *Ibid.*, p. 650.

according to the rule. There is nothing hidden from the eyes of the players nor of the spectators. As players read the moves of the other, the critic or reader, too, reads the meaning of the text by textual analysis.

Coming to the relationship between literature and criticism, Barthes says that criticism is a formal activity in the logical sense of the term, not in the aesthetic sense. Literature is

> "neither ever quite meaningless (mysterious or inspired) nor ever quite clear; it is, so to speak suspended meaning; it offers itself to the reader as a declared system of significance, but as a signified object it eludes his grasp."[59]

It is because of it being "a very special semantic system", literature is elusive. Its aim is to put meaning into the word but not a meaning.

It is this typical nature of literature that invites literary criticism to be formal like logic and to have base in linguistics. The function of criticism is to reconstitute the system and determine the formal structure. He concludes the essay:

> "Literature, since it consists at one and the same time of the insistent offering of a meaning and the persistent elusiveness of that meaning, is definitely no more than a language, that is, a system of signs; its being lies in the system, not in the message. This being so, the critic is not called upon to reconstitute the message of the work, but only its system just as the business of the linguist is not to decipher the meaning of a sentence but to determine the formal structure, which permits the transmission of meaning."[60]

Barthes's analysis of texts such as Balzac's "Sarrasine" and Poe's "Valdemar" and the stories of *Decameron* is the practical application of his critical theory propounded in "Criticism as Language", *S/Z* and *Image-Music-Text.* He accepts Claude Levi-Strauss' notion of structure and structural analysis, but

59. *Ibid.*, p. 650.

60. *Ibid.*, p. 651.

makes the modification that structural analysis is applied to above all, oral narrative (i.e., myth) and textual analysis exclusively to written narrative. Textual analysis does not try to describe the structure of a work, although it follows the structural principles. Barthes writes in "Poe's Valdemar":

> "[Its main task is to produce] a mobile structuration of the text (a structuration which is displaced from reader to reader throughout history), of staying in the signifying volume of the work, in its 'significance'. Textual analysis does not try to find out what it is that determines the text (gathers it together as the end-term of a casual sequence) but rather how the text explodes and disperses."[61]

The procedure of textual analysis is first to divide the text into *Lexie*, very short linguistic units, which can be a sentence, part of a sentence, or at most a group of three or four sentences. The next step is to observe the meanings to which the *lexie* give rise. Here the aim is not to find the meaning or even a meaning but to manage to perceive the plurality of the text, the opening of its significance. The reading is like a slow-film or unfolding the pages slowly to follow the structure. In the quoted passage Barthes echoes Hopkins who too had said that a good poem explodes at the end in meaning. The meaning comes at the end with a plosion, sphota was first propounded by Dhvanikara and Anandavardhana in their *Dhvani* theory.

Finally, in textual analysis, the reader has to consider departures of meanings, not arrivals. Barthes writes:

> "what founds the text is not an internal, closed, recountable structure but the outlet of the text on to other texts, other signs; what makes the text intertextual."[62]

Barthes means to say that while reading some meanings are forgotten. This forgetting is not a bad thing; it shows that some things are more significant as they are available in other texts. A text has its meaning in relation to other texts. The departures of meaning can be best deciphered in the cultural code of which all

61. *Modern Criticism and Theory*, p. 172.

62. *Ibid.*, p. 651.

other codes are subspecies. Barthe's aim is high. He wants the principles of literary criticism universally applicable not confined to a region or even a continent. The greatness of Barthes is that he fuses linguistics, sociology, psychology, and anthropology together in his critical theory. Besides, his view that ideology plays a very important role in the structure of a text is of immense value. Terry Eagleton has accepted it and called ideology "the non-said" in a writer's work.

Jonathan Culler and Richard Ohmann, besides the French structuralists, need mention. Both Americans have applied Noam Chomsky's T.G. Grammar in the analysis of literary texts and tried to trace the contents of its deep structure Jonathan Culler is more theoretical in his approach and the analyses he has made of Blake's "London" and the poems of William Carlos Williams in the article "Structuralism and Literature" are not very different from those of F.R. Leavis, Cleanth Brooks and Elder Olson except the terms used such as "the symbolic code", "the artificiality of literature", "strangeness" (Eichenbaum's term bestrangement) and "signs". He himself admits in the same essay that the interpretation of a poem may not be significantly different from what is revealed by a more conventional kind of analysis. What is significant, he affirms, is that it makes explicit the process we take for granted.

Richard Ohmann employs Chomsky's transformational rules[63] as given in *Syntactic Structures* and *Aspects of the Theory of Syntax*. In his anlaysis of the victorian prose he shows how the thought process takes place at the deep level and finds its expression at the surface level through a set of transformational rules. The same kernel sentence can generate different kinds of sentences—negative, passive, imperative, and interrogative—at the surface level and a writer chooses the transformational rules to form sentences for the desired expression. "The stylistic choices" to quote his own words:

63. In T.G. Grammar transformational rules are those rules which change the form of the Kernel sentence, which is simple, active, positive/affirmative and declarative, into different kinds of sentences according to the meaning the speaker desires to express. For example, the Kernel sentence "He went home" can generate "Did he go home", "He didn't go home", "Didn't he go home", which differ in meaning from one another.

> "operating among alternate formulations of propositional content form a pattern that implies a characteristic way of conceiving, relating, and presenting content."[64]

Towards the end of the essay "A Linguistic Appraisal of the Victorian Style" he, like the structuralists, gives due importance to culture in shaping a writer's mind and like Barthes accepts the importance of history.

> "A man who occupies a given spot in history and culture is urged by his intellectual world to think and feel in certain ways, but the forming power of intellectual culture operates on a mind already formed, deeply and intricately, by a thousand sub-cultures, from the nursery on up. Style is responsive to the cut of a writer's mind, and that is only trimmed and decorated by intellectual culture, not created by it."[65]

He fully agrees with the Russian Formalists and French Structuralist that literary criticism is synchromic study of literature and concludes the essay with the following remark.

> "Those of us interested in Victorian prose style will do will to study individual writers intensively, and with the best linguistic theory available to discover the unique and intriguing shapes that mind and language take among the Victorians.... Reliable judgements about the history of style will come after on understanding of styles, and may be quite other than what the text books say."[66]

Ohmann's approach is in the line of post-structuralists who consider a text a part of the writer's culture. He is different from the Brish stylisticians like Turner, Leech, Criper, and Widdowson who are solely interested in the linguistic signals and deviations at morphological and syntactic levels in lines like "A grief ago"

---

64. Richard Ohmann, "A Linguistic Appraisal of Victorian Style," *The Art of Victorian Prose*, ed. George Levin and William Madden, (New York: OUP, 1968), p. 294.

65. *Ibid.*, p. 308.

66. *Ibid.*, p. 309.

of Dylan Thomas and "The unchilding, unfathering, widow-making deep" of Hopkins.

Ohmann is of the view that it is the intended meaning formed in the mind of the author that forces upon him to make choices of selection and combination in his writing.

The method of textual analysis

The post-structuralist critics, led by Roland Barthes, make distinction between "structural anlaysis" and "textual analysis". The structural anlaysis is applied to oral narratives, especially myths, and textual analysis which is very much like "close reading" of New Critics is applied exclusively to written texts. Since, for every reader, certain linguistic signals are more significant than the others in a given text, textual analysis aims at "producing a mobile structuration of the text (a structuration which is displaced from reader to reader throughout history) of staying in the signifying volume of the work, in its significance."[67]

As already discussed textual analysis begins from the title of the novel/short story/poem under study and moves from the first line to the last line till the entire sequence gathered causally explodes and disperses in meaning. The view that the meaning comes with a plosion is very much like that of Hopkins who in his letter to Robert Bridges on 8 Oct, 1879 wrote:

> "One of two kinds of clearness one should have either as fast as one reads or else, if dark at first reading, when once made out to explode."

Let us remember that Barthes was a great admirer of Hopkins. With these basics, the structural critic follows the following points in textual analysis.

i. As every text offers plurality of meaning, the aim of the critic/reader is not to find *the meaning*, but to locate and classify the form and code according to which meanings are possible.

ii. As every text is a kind of narration, and the authorial voice is continually discermible, the technique of narratology is applied to establish the relationship

67. Roland Barthes, "Poe's Valdemar," *Modern Criticism and Theory*, p. 172.

between functions and their actants, and trace the dialectical progression of the text. The functions are initiating action, the counter action, the catalyzing action, and the terminating action.

iii. Distinction is made between the *fabula* (the raw material) and the *sjuzet* (text) to trace the deviation and stylistic choices made by the author in composing the surface structure of the text.

iv. The technique of rhetorical analysis is applied to find out how the linguistic mediation of a story determines its meaning and effect.

v. The text is divided into *lexie* (lexias), units of reading (textual signifiers), which may a be a sentence, half of a sentence and, at most, a group of two or three sentences.

vi. Finally, the reading shall begin with the title, which always has a double function; enunciating and deictic[68], and end at the closing lines. While interpreting the text, not only the signifiers and syntactic structures in the text but also the author's biography, his writings relevant to the text, comments of other writers, social and intellectual background and ideology should be given due consideration. Apart from Roland Barthes, Jonathan Culler, and Richard Ohmann, David Lodge is one of the best structuralist critics and his *Working With Structuralism* is one of the classics of practical application of the structuralist theory.

A. Deconstruction

The leading theoretician and practitioner who has deconstructed the classical western concept of binary opposition and Saussurian concept of superiority of speech over writing and the one to one relation of *signifier* and *signified* is Jacques Derrida, a French philosopher and linguist.

Derrida propounded his philosophy and concept of language in *Of Grammatology*, a treatise written originally in French and translated by Gayatri Chakravorty Spivak with an elaborate

68. Deictic = a word whose meaning is dependent on the context.

introduction in about one hundred pages. Deconstruction should not be thought of as a negative term. No doubt, it deconstructs the past philosophical constructs[69] in the West, it posits an entirely new theory of interpreting literary and non-literary texts.

In the western philosophy there is the basic assumption that there is an order of meaning—truth, logic, logos—which serves as foundation. On the basis of this assumption the Western philosophers have mooted the idea that there is a centre and conceived meaning, essence, serious, transcendental and positive as prior or fundamental; form, accident, non-serious and negative as complication, derivation or manifestation of the first.[70] After examining the texts of philosophers, Derrida has successfully demonstrated how these hierarchical structures are subverted by the very texts and arguments they rely on them. Helen Cixous has followed his theory and practice in her famous article "Sorties" where she has challenged the construct that woman is subordinate of man. Derrida's main tool of the anlaysis of philosophical and literary texts is modern grammar/linguistics. He rejects the primacy of speech and concentrates on writing as it can be analysed many a time critically and discussed too. Derrida's deconstmetion has influenced literary criticism greatly. Following are the salient features of deconstruction as a theory of literature.

There is no centre

In his historic paper titled "Structure, Sign and Play in the Discourse of Human Sciences", contributed to a conference held at Johns Hopkins University in 1966, Derrida wrote:

> "The centre is not the centre.... The concept of centred structure ,.... is contradictorily coherent. And as always, coherence in contradiction expresses the force of desire.

---

69. Construct = theory consisting of a series of concepts.

70. Derrida writes: "Its matrix ... is the determination of being as presence in all senses of this word. It could be shown that all the names related to fundamentals, to principles, or to the centre have always designated an inevitable presence—*eidos, arche, telos, energia, ousia* (essence, existence, substance, subject) alethiea, transcendentality, consciousness, God, man and so forth.

> The concept of centred structure is in fact the concept of a play based on a fundamental ground, a play, constituted on the basis of a fundamental immobility and a reassuring certitude, which itself is beyond the reach of play."[71]

A little later, he writes in the same paper

> "And again on the basis of what we call the centre (..... because it can be either inside or outside, can also indifferently be called the origin or end, *arche* or *telos*).... [its] origin may always be reawakened or whose end may always be anticipated in the form of presence."[72]

After refuting Claude Levi-Strauss' concept of structure in particular and the traditional concept of *centre*, Derrida makes his deconstructive statement.

> "If this is so, the entire history of the concept of structure, before the rupture of which we are speaking, must be thought of as a series of substitutions of centre for centre, as a linked chain of the determination of the centre."[73]

Derrida's conclusion is that it is the play of the signs that determines everything in the human discourse.

It follows then that no text, literary or non-literary, has a centre. It is a discourse where signs play and there is no existence of a central essence in a text round which the whole story/narration revolves.

There is no ultimate or final meaning of a text; it is always undecided

Aporia or undecidability is the chief characteristic of every *ecriture*.[74] While writing, every author has choices at morphological and syntactic levels. He or she may choose one and drop the rest. Meaning suspends between the chosen and

---

71. Jacques Derrida, "Structure, Sign, and Play in the Discourse of Human Sciences," *Modern Criticism and Theory*, ed. David Lodge, p. 109.
72. *Ibid.*
73. *Idem.*
74. Ecriture =mode of writing.

not chosen. Derrida writes in the concluding paragraph of "Structure, Sign and Play in the Discourse of Human Sciences":

> "I do not believe that today there is any question of *choosing*...in the first place because we must first try to conceive of the common ground, and the *difference* of this irreducible difference."[75]

The reason for *difference* or *aporia* is that the author while writing a text passes through the stages of conception, formation, gestation, and labour. The entire process is like child-bearing. As a text is not written with a centre which is fixed, there is always the element of difference/aporia or undecidability—'differ' and 'defer'. The element of contradictoriness is easily discernible as it has been ably traced by Derrida in the analyses of the writings of Claude Levi-Strauss and Karl Marx's *The Eighteenth Brumaire of Louis Bonaparte*. There is contradiction in these texts because of the constructed nature of words and their metaphorical and metonymic meanings.

Every text contains two meanings: surface and hidden

All languages are metaphorical because they are all evolved from metaphors in their primary stage. A word was coined to signify a concept. The meaning of the word was extended to those concepts that were related to the first concept. For example, the signifier "burn" referred to the concept of the burning of fire. As fire is associated with heat and destruction, its extended meaning was realized in uses like "He was burning with desire", "I have a burning sensation in my heart", "She was burning with anger". Similar is the case with the word "red", which is used metaphorically frequently.

Later on, what was a metaphorical use became a common use, and thus the sediment of metaphor covered the vocabulary. When a writer writes now, he or she uses a language which is metaphorical. The fact is that language speaks through him. In order that the intended meaning be discovered, the reader should

75. *Modern Criticism and Theory*, p. 122. David Lodge comments on the word difference: Derrida's term punningly writes the senses of "to differ" and "to defer".

remove the sediment of metaphor. In the analysis of *The Eighteenth Brumaire of Louis Bonaparte*, Derrida has shown the role played by metaphors in this powerful essay of Karl Marx.

The meaning of a text is always suspended and hence plurality of meaning

In the words of David Lodge, "deconstructive criticism aims to show that any text inevitably undermines its own claim to have a determinate meaning, and licences the reader to produce his own meanings out of it by an activity of semantic 'free play'."[76]

The reason for the semantic free play is that every text poses structural problems before its reader. These problems are the relations between speech and writing, presence and absence, simple word and metaphor, ecriture and trace, signifier and signified, and sign and free play. Deconstruction exposes the peculiar uncanny relations within signifiers and the signified, within texts and between texts. It repudiates the New Critics assumption that the conflicting emotions in a poem are resolved into a higher unity. On the other hand, the meaning is always suspended and never reaches its finality.

Deconstruction has made a great impact on new trends in criticism, especially feminist criticism and psycho-analytic criticism of today. Helen Cixous' "Sorties" is a brilliant example of the impact of deconstruction on feminist criticism. Cixous begins the essay with the binary opposition of the constructs:

Where is she?

Activity/passivity
Sun/moon
Culture/nature
Day/night
Father/mother
Head/heart
Intelligible/sensitive
Logos/pathos

76. *Modern Criticism and Theory*, p. 108.

Form, convex, step, advance, seed, progress, matter, concave, ground—which supports the step, receptacle.

Man/Woman

Following Derrida, she challenges the superiority of man over woman. She deconstructs the age old construct and these famous lines of the Bible.

> "And Lord God caused a deep sleep to fall on Adam, and he slept; and he took one of his ribs, and closed up the flesh in its place.
>
> Then, the rib which the Lord God had taken from man, he made into a woman, and he brought her to the man.
>
> And Adam said: This is now bone of my bones and flesh of my flesh; she shall be called woman, because she was taken out of man."

At the end of her essay she pleads for the transformation of all forms and systems to put man and woman on the same footing.

The leading critics are Paul de Man, J. Hillis Miller, Harold Bloom, Gayatri Chakravorty Spivak, and Geoffrey Hartman.

Rezeption-Aesthetic and Reader-Response Theories

Both the theories, the first German and the second American, maintain that the meaning of a text is the realization of aesthetic pleasure by the reader or the reading process. The proponents of Rezeption-Aesthetic are Robert Jaus and Wolfgang Iser, and of Reader-Response is Stanley Fish. As the German theory is the original and the American is its extension, we shall first discuss Rezeption-Aesthetic.

(F) REZEPTION-AESTHETIC

Rezeption-Aesthetic, to quote David Lodge:

> "developed in Germany concurrently with, but more or less independently of, a shift in French and Anglo-American criticism from a structuralist focus on the literary text as a realization of underlying systems to a post-structuralist view of the text as a site for the production and proliferation of meaning."

Reception theory (Rezeption-Aesthetic) is the successor of the Geneva school of phenomenological criticism and the hermeneutic criticism of the German philosopher Hans-Georg Gadamar. David Lodge points out:

> "It owes much to the philosophical tradition of phenomenology that began with Husserl, especially the aesthetics of the Polish scholar Roman Ingarden and the humeneutics of the German philosopher Hans-Georg Gadamar, a tradition which stresses the centrality of consciousness in all investigations of meaning."[77]

The other great phenomenologist to influence this theory is Georges Poulet. Reception theory stresses the importance of the reader and a thorough-going reading process, as rigorous as hermeneutics. What follows here is a summary of Wolfgang Iser's seminal essay "The Reading-process: A Phenomenological Approach", which gives a lucid account of the basics of the theory.

A literary work has two poles: the artistic and the aesthetic. The artistic is the author's creation and the aesthetic is the realization accomplished by the reader or the reading process. Iser makes distinction between the literary work and the literary text. The literary text is the author's creation and the work is the "convergence of the text and the reader", and "this convergence can never be precisely pinpointed but must always remain virtual, as it is not to be identified either with the reality of the text or the invidual disposition of the reader."

The truth is that the text arouses the reader from passivity to activity or what I.A. Richards has said in "Preface" to *Principles of Literary Criticism:* "A book is a machine to think with."

He/she uses the various perspectives offered by the text in order to relate the patterns and the "schematised views to one another and sets the work in motion." This very process results ultimately in the awakening of responses within him/her.

The reading process has three important aspects that form the basis of the relationship between the reader and the text. They are:

---

77. David Lodge, *Modern Criticism and Theory*, p. 211.

(a) the process of anticipation and retrospection;

(b) the consequent unfolding of the text as a living event; and

(c) the resultant impression of lifelikeness.

(a) The process of anticipation and retrospection

The reading process is the formation of *gestalt*.[78] How do we form gestalt while reading a text? Iser refers to Roman Ingarden's concept of *intentionale satzkorrelate* (intentional sentence correlatives). He writes:

> "As a starting point for a phenomenological analysis we might examine the way in which sequent sentences act upon one another. This is of special importance in literary texts in view of the fact that they do not correspond to any objective reality outside themselves. The world presented by literary texts is constructed out of what Ingarden has called *intentionale satzkorrelate*."[79]

Ingarden explains the term "intentional sentence correlatives" thus:

> "Sentences link up in different ways to form more complex units of meaning than reveal a very varied structure giving rise to such entities as a short story, a novel, a dialogue, a drama, a scientific theory.... In the final anlaysis, there arises a particular world, with component parts determined this way or that, and with all the variations that may occur within these parts...all this as a purely intentional correlative of a complex of sentences. If this complex finally forms a literary work,

78. Gestalt means a compact whole which is meaningful. When we look around in a strange place or situation our tendency is to order the things which are apparently random or disordered. We order them by filling the gaps by comparing the situation with our previous experience(s) by means of retrospection. For example, our ancestors made the signs of zodiac by filling in the gaps between the bright stars. A text does not show us its centre nor tells us its meaning. We form a *gestalt* by means of retrospection. For getting a good idea of the term *gestalt* students are advised to read R.S. Woodworth, *Contemporary Schools of Psychology*.

79. Wolfgang Iser, "The Reading Process: A Phenomenological Approach", *Modern Criticism and Theory*, pp. 213-14.

> I call the whole sum of sequent intentional sentence correlatives the "world presented" in the world."[80]

This view of Roman Ingarden is not different from that of structuralism that a text is a linguistic structure and reality is embedded in it.

While reading a text, the reader conceives the connection between the correlatives by anticipation and retrospection. He/she has the prior knowledge and experience of the reality embedded in the text and anticipates that his/her expectation would come true. But it does not happen in many cases, especially when the viewpoint is strikingly new. Then he/she retrospects. It is certain that a good text is seldom hackneyed. Iser concludes the elaboration of the point:

> "As we have seen, the activity of reading can be characterized as a sort of kaleidoscope of perspectives, recollections. Every sentence contains a preview of the next and forms a kind of view-finder for what is to come, and in this turn changes the preview and so becomes a view-finder for what has been read."[81]

(b) Unfolding of the text

Literary texts are full of unexpected twists and turns. A reader's expectation is frequently frustrated. There is always some kind of blockage. This blockage, says Ingarden, must be overcome if the reading is to flow once more. The reader's task is to fill in the gaps, as a literary text does not describe everthing straightforwardly. Gaps are left and they provide the reader the opportunity to bring into play his/her own faculty for establishing connections. In addition they have a different effect of the process of anticipation and retrospection, and thus, on the "gestalt of virtual dimension, for they may be filled in different ways."[82] It is upto the reader to decide how the gaps are to be filled.

Thus, reading is a dynamic process. The reader unfolds the text by employing his/her imagination, with its base on past

---

80. Quoted by Wolfgang Iser, *Ibid.*, p. 214.

81. *Modern Criticism and Theory*, p. 219.

82. *Ibid.*, p. 223.

experience; while filling the gaps left between sentences he/she forms a gestalt that enriches his/her knowledge or experience.

(c) The resultant impression of likeness

This is the third feature of reading process. After forming the gestalt, the reader compares the author's experience with his/her own. The world of the text is a kind of illusion and so is the reader's. Iser expands this idea:

> "The picturing that is done by our imagination is only one of the activities through which we form the "gestalt" of a literary text.... This "gestalt" must inevitably be coloured by our own characteristic selection process.
>
> For it is not given by the text itself; it arises from the meeting between the written text and the individual mind of the reader with its own particular history of experience, its own consciousness, its own outlook."[83]

While forming the gestalt of a literary text we are influenced by alien associations of our experiences of life. We oscillate between the illusion of the text created by us and the reality of the world we have experienced. Thus, the act of recreation or formation of gestalt is not a smooth or continuous process. In the words of Iser:

> "We look forward, we look back, we decide, we change our decisions, we form expectations, we are shocked by their non-fulfilment, we question, we muse, we accept, we reject, this is the dynamic process of recreation."[84]

Finally, while reading, we react against and think with the author. Thus, in reading there are two levels..."the alien me and the real virtual me which are never completely cut off from each other."[85]

While reading we are always active in the process of formulating a gestalt by filling in the gaps in the sentences, paragraphs, and chapters.

83. *Ibid.*, p. 227.

84. *Ibid.*, p. 215.

85. *Ibid.*, p. 216.

This gestalt is not entirely our own; it is of the author whose experience and outlook become a part of our experience and outlook with a changing effect.

Rezeption-Aesthetic (Reception theory) is now a well-established approach to literature. Although, basically a German theory, it has taken the best of the British, the American, the French, and the Russian approaches to literature. Rooted in the gestalt theory of Werheimer, Koehler, and Koffka, it follows their concepts of anticipation, introspection, and retrospection, the basic steps in the process of learning. Any kind of reading is a step towards learning. A literary text is a kind of problem and its reading is a kind of problem solving which is done by the reader's effort in the formation of gestalt. Iser calls the newly formed gestalt "recreation", which is almost equivalent to the structuralist's "structuration". Criticism, right from its beginning, is the perceptive reader's response to literature. Critics have formulated principles of studying it. The great contribution of Reception theory is that it enlightens us with a scientific description of the reading process and how a reader benefits by a good literary work.

B. Reader-Response Theory

Although claimed by a few that Stanley Fish is a theoretician like Richards, Ransom or Crane, he is not so. At best, he is a brilliant analyst and interpreter of literary texts. David Lodge puts him between Wolfgand Iser and Jacques Derrida, and praises him for his questioning the efficacy of "The New Critics effort to locate meaning in the formal features of the text rather than in the author's intention or the reader's response." In our opinion, Stanley Fish has largely followed the theory and practice of Roman Ingarden, the great phenomenologist of Poland and Georges Poulet of Geneva school. Following are the basic principles of Reader-Response Theory.

A Literary text has no fixed meaning

Fish explains this point and defines his position while criticizing the practices of the editors of variorum editions,[86] who give a fixed meaning to a poem or a passage:

86. A variorum edition includes variant readings from manuscripts or earlier editions.

> "Editorial practices like these [of fixing meanings] are only the most obvious manifestations of the assumptions to which I stand opposed: the assumption that there is a sense, that it is embedded or encoded in the text, and that it can be taken in at a single glance. These assumptions are, in order, positivist, holistic, and spatial, and to have them is to be committed both to a goal and to a procedure. The goal is to settle on a meaning, and the procedure involves first stepping back from the text, and then putting together or otherwise calculating the discrete units of significance it contains. My quarrel with this procedure (and with the assumptions that generate it) is that in the course of following it through the reader's activities are at once ignored and devalued."[87]

Fish illustrates his viewpoint in the detailed analysis of Milton's three sonnets: "Lawrence of virtuous father virtuous son", "Avenge O' Lord thy slaughtered saints", and "On His Blindness". He discusses the problematic words and explains how they evoke different responses.

The word "spare" in the thirteenth line of "Lawrence of virtuous father virtuous son" may mean either "leave time for" or "refrain from". If one reader follows the first meaning, there will be one interpretation of the poem, and if the second meaning is followed, there will be another interpretation. Fish comments:

> "Obviously the point is crucial if one is to resolve the sense of the lines. In one reading "those delights" are being recommended...he who can leave time for them is not unwise; in the other, they are the subject of a warning.... He who knows when to refrain from them is not unwise."[88]

87. Stanley Fish, "Interpreting the *Variorum*", *Modern Criticism and Theory*, p. 319. The last sentence is wrongly constructed. Perhaps, there is printing error in the text.

88. *Ibid*., p. 313.

Similarly, in the second sonnet beginning with the line "Avenge O' Lord thy slaughtered saints" the phrase "thy way" invokes two contrasting interpretations: one optimistic, the other grim. Fish comments:

> "These two readings are answerable to the pulls exerted by the beginning and ending of the poem."[89]

The third sonnet "On His Blindness", too, invites different readings. Fish writes:

> "The interpretive crux again concurs the final line: They also serve who only stand and wait. For some this is an unqualified acceptance of God's will, while for others the note of affirmation is muted or even forced."[90]

The reader introspects and retrospects while reading a text

While reading a poem, play or novel, the reader is between his previous knowledge which, in fact, is the background knowledge of literature, and the knowledge s/he is gaining through the text in hand. There is occasional encounter between the two. S/he asks: why is this expression or use of the word? Is it justified or out of place? Are the two ideas expressed by means of words compatible or contradictory? The total strategy of the reader is to trace the author's intention as expressed in the literary text. Fish says:

> "This then is my thesis: that the form of the reader's experience, formal units, and the structure of intention are one, that they come into view simultaneously, and that, therefore the questions of priority and independence do not arise."[91]

Finally, there is no fixed reading

The same reader will perform differently when reading two different texts and different readers will perform similarly when

89. *Ibid.*, p. 316.

90. *Ibid.*, p. 317.

91. *Ibid.*, p. 323.

reading the same text. This is because every reader employs her/his own strategy in reading a text under the influence of certain pre-conception related to the genre and the author of the text. For example, *Lycidas* is a pastoral monody[92] and its author is John Milton. A reader has a certain notion about the pastoral monody and John Milton. The other reader has a different notion about *Lycidas* and its author. Then there are readers who want to write texts. Their strategy will be different from other readers. Fish calls such readers "interpretive communities". The members of one interpretive community may accuse the other community of being reductive while the other will call their accusers superficial.

Wolfgang Iser approaches the differences in reading process in another way. He very rightly points out that there is a potential time sequence as it is impossible to absorb even a short text in a single moment. While reading, there are pauses and use of introspect and retrospect. When we read the same text the second time, the whole perspective has changed. In the words of Iser himself:

> ".... When we have finished the text, and read it again, clearly our extra knowledge will result in a different time-sequence; we shall tend to establish connections by referring to our awareness of what is to come, and so certain aspects of the text will assume a significance we did not attach to them on a first reading, while others will recede into the background."[93]

Iser is quite explicit and factual. Our response to a literary text is not the same in subsequent readings. It follows then that there is difference between the first reading and the second reading of a text by the same reader. Fish and Iser do not contradict but complement each other on this aspect of reading-process.

---

92. Monody, a Greek word, now replaced by the more common term "elegy".
93. Wolfgang Iser, "The Reading Process: A Phenomenological Approach", *Modern Criticism and Theory,* p. 217.

Reception Theory (Rezeption-Aesthetic) and Reader-Response Theory are not very much different. However, Iser's and Jauss' Rezeption-Aesthetic is more comprehensive as it has its base in humeneutics of Gadamar and phenomenology of Poulet and Ingarden. Fish's contribution to literary criticism is that he has made a practical application of the continental Reception Theory and added a new dimension to it.

(G) FEMINIST CRITICISM

Feminist criticism analyses literary texts and evaluates creative writers from the woman point of view. Feminist criticism has its roots in feminism, a movement that exposed the ulterior motives of some men in power in making laws for the subjugation of women. With the rise of the middle class in the thirteenth century, the well meaning men and a few self-educated women raised voice against the unjust treatment to women. Among the creative writers was Aphra Behn (1640-89) who pleaded for a mature relationship between man and woman in her novels, plays, and prose romances. Later on, Mary Wollstonecraft wrote the famous book *A Vindication for the Rights of Woman* (1772), which was badly criticised by the male chauvinists but J.S. Mill's *The Subjugation of Women* (1869) silenced them and people began to think about women in a new way. France led the feminist movement and it soon spread all over Europe. The real thrust came with the publication of Frederick Engel's *The Origin of the Family* (1884), which gave a theoretical base to a movement for equality between man and woman. Virginia Woolf in her *A Room of One's Own* (1929) discussed in detail the unequal treatment given to women who were deprived of admission to prestigious universities like Oxford and Cambridge. After Engel's *The Origin of the Family*, the book which accentuated the growth of feminist movement was Simon de Beauvoir's *The Second Sex* (1949).

Feminist criticism right from the beginning has been continental and trans-Atlantic. It was a toddler during the period 1950-60, but soon came to its own in nineteen-sixties. Basing its theory in the writings of the above mentioned writers, it attacked the partisan view of male critics and strove hard to bring to light the forgotten women writers of the seventeenth and eighteenth centuries. The result was the revival of Aphra Behn and Maria Edgeworth.

At present, feminist criticism has got a theoretical base. However, we should not assume that feminist criticism has only one theory as its base. The French critics are more influenced by Freud, Marx, post-structuralism, and deconstruction, the Americans by the liberal humanist approach to literature, and the British by Marx, Engels, Raymond Williams, and Arnold Kettle.

The leading Indian critics like Gayatri Chakravorty Spivak are influenced by French deconstruction, Marxism and Post-colonial theory of literature. As enumerated by Elaine Showalter, there are four major trends in feminist criticism: biological, linguistic, psycho-analytic, and cultural. She uses the term Gynocritics for feminist criticism.

Gynocritics

Showlter pleads for "a feminist criticism that is genuinely women centred, independent, and intellectually coherent". The basic need, she writes:

> "[is to] ask much more searchingly what we want to know and how we can find answers to the questions that come from our experience."[94]

She is of the view that criticism has remained androcentric right from the beginning to the present day[95] and this kind of criticism cannot do justice to women writers and their creative works. Quoting the famous lines of Virginia Woolf and Helen Cixous, she stresses the point that the term *feminine* is yet to be defined. She explains why Woolf and Cixous wrote that the term feminine was yet to be defined.

> "In the past decade I believe, this process of defining the feminine has started to take place. Feminist criticism has

94. Elaine Showalter, "Feminist Criticism in the Wilderness", *Modern Criticism and Theory*, p. 334.

95. "Feminist Criticism in the Wilderness" was published in *Critical Inquiry* in 1981.

> gradually shifted its centre from revisionary readings to a sustained investigation of literature by women. The second mode of feminist criticism engendered by this process is the study of women as writers, and its subjects are the history, styles, themes, genres, and structures of writing by women; the psychodynamics of female creativity; the trajectory of the individual or collective female career; and the evolution and laws of a female literary tradition."[96]

What Showalter aims at is a theoretical base and scientific method of analysing the texts written by women. Since there is no English term for this kind of criticism and the term "feminist criticism" is inadequate, she coins the term *Gynocritics*. The shift here is from the erstwhile dominant androcriticism (male-centric criticism) to gynocentric criticism, which aims at solving these main problems:

(a) How to constitute women as a distinct literary group?

(b) What is the "difference" of women's writing?

Patricia Mayer is the first critic who has demonstrated in her book *The Female Imagination* (1975) how women writing has a *different* expression, that is, a voice of its own. The leading French critic Helen Cixous has laid emphasis on *ecriture* feminine in *The Laugh of the Medusa*. She writes:

> "It is impossible to define a feminine practice of writing, and this impossibility that will remain, for this practice will never be theorized, enclosed, encoded-which does not mean that it does not exist."

Inspite of Showalter's efforts, the term "gynocritics" has not gained popularity and the old term has remained intact. Now all leading feminist critics are of the view that *ecriture* feminine exists, but it is not very different though distinct from the other *ecriture* (mode of writing) and there is the need of assimilation as male and female are complementary to each other. Helen Cixous ends her powerful "Sorties" thus:

96. *Ibid.*, p. 335.

> "Let us imagine simultaneously a *general* change in all of the structure of formation, education, framework, hence of reproduction, of ideological effects, and let us imagine a real liberation of sexuality.... Then "feminity", "masculanity" would inscribe their effects of difference, their economy, their relationships to expenditure, to deficit, to giving, quite differently. That which appears as "feminine" or "masculine" today would no longer amount to the same thing."[97]

It is clear that the theory and practice of contemporary feminist criticism is to establish a distinct position of *ecriture* feminine in the centre and raise the position of women to the level of men through the process of assimilation.

With the aim of reviving the neglected but gifted women writers, tracing of the basic elements of women's problems as expressed through women characters, exposing the chauvinism of men in the past and the present, and bringing women to the level of men, feminist critics examined texts from four distinct points of view: biological, psychological, linguistic, and sociological in the late seventies. Elaine Showalter has named these four viewpoints *models* in her article "Feminist Criticism in the Wilderness".

The four models (according to Showalter) are:

i. Biological: women's writing and woman's body

Showalter is critical of this model. She comments:

> "Biological criticism is also one of the most sybilline and perplexing theoretical formulations of feminist criticism. Simply to invoke anatomy risks, a return to the crude essentialism, the phallic and the ovarian theories of art, that oppressed women in the past."[98]

In fact, this model is outdated and has had undesired effects as had Freud's Oedipus complex on creative writers, especially in India. Writers like Shobha De, Kamala Das, Kamala

---

97. Helen Cixous, "Sorties", *Modern Criticism and Theory*, p. 292.

98. Elaine Showalter, "Feminist Criticism in the Wilderness", *Modern Criticism and Theory*, p. 337.

Markandaya, and Manju Kapoor have gone to the extreme in sexual revolution against men. It is certain that there are biological differences between men and women, but on intellectual plane they are not different. Therefore, it is a wrong assumption that women's writing always originates from the woman's body.

There are two aspects of this kind of criticism. The first is that it can be rewarding when it investigates the tender feelings and care for a child by a mother or a woman's emotional response to her people around her. Bodily, father and mother, brother and sister are different and, therefore, their emotional responses to the other will be different. Showalter accepts this positive aspect of biological model but, she rejects, the negative aspect, description of the nakedness of body, which will make women vulnerable. Nowadays, the negative aspect of biological model is fully rejected and only the emotional responses of women are considered valid.

ii. Linguistic model

It is concerned with women's writing and women's language. Kate Miller, while criticizing the biological model, has commented that the difference of women's literary practice must be sought in "the body of her writing and not the writing of her body." This comment leads us to study *ecriture* feminine (women's writing). The focus of the linguistic model is to know how far women's writing truly represents the feelings, attitude and thought process of women creative writers. The French feminist criticism is largely devoted to the linguistic analysis of literary texts, tracing the gender bias which has been created by the man-made world. Showalter quotes Carolyn Burke:

> "The central issue in much recent women's writing in France is to find and use an appropriate female language. Language is the place to begin, capture of consciousness must be followed by a capture of speech.... In this view, the very forms of the dominant mode of discourse shows the mark of the dominant masculine ideology. Hence, when a woman writes or speaks herself into existence, she is forced to speak in something like a

> foreign tongue, a language with which she may be uncomfortable."[99]

Burke's estimate of French feminist criticism is partly true. The French critics are highly influenced by Claude Levi-Strauss and Jacques Derrida. Helen Cixous, for example, adopting the philosophy of Jacques Derrida deconstructs the age-old binary dependency of concepts such as virtue-vice, day-night, light-darkness, active-passive, and man-woman. She stresses the need for a change in the language created by men as this language is logocentric and phallocentric. Once the age-old logocentrism and phallocentrism is demolished, there will be a new kind of language equally just for both men and women. And this process of change has begun and the old structure will collapse soon.

Julia Kristeva, Helen Cixous, and Gayatri Chakravorty Spivak[100] have made use of linguistics, post-structuralism, deconstruction and post-colonial theory to reach a higher goal than interpreted by Showalter and Carolyne Burke. The French feminist criticism is really deep and wide in scope.

iii. Psycho-analytic model

This model accepts Freud's psychology largely but, at certain vital points, revises it. The concepts that are attacked are "the lack", "the castration complex" and "the Oedipal phase". The French psychoanalyst and literary critic Jacques Lacan, who has put Freud in the structuralist frame, has extended castration into a total metaphor for female literary and linguistic disadvantage. Helen Cixous very rightly revises Freud's concept of man-woman difference:

> "That the difference between the sexes may have psychic consequences is undeniable. But, they are surely not reducible to those designated by a Freudian analysis."[101]

---

99. Elaine Showalter, "Feminist Criticism in the Wilderness", *Modern Criticism and Theory*, p. 339.

100. Gayatri Chakravorty Spivak, an Indian in origin, belongs essentially to French feminist criticism. She has made use of post-colonial theory in her long article *Can the Subaltern Speak?*

101. Helen Cixous, "Sorties", *Modern Criticism and Theory*, p. 291.

She pleas for equality between men and women in their productive and social activities and abolition of Freud's and Lacan's phallocentrism.

iv. Cultural model: women's writing and women's culture

Elaine Showalter considers the cultural model the fittest model of Gynocritics. She is of the view that biological, linguistic, and psycho-analytic models function within a cultural context. She writes:

> "Indeed, a theory of culture incorporates ideas about women's body, language, and psyche, but interprets them in relation to the social contexts in which they occur. The ways in which women conceptualize their bodies, and their sexual and reproductive functions are intricately linked to their cultural environments.[102]

She considers that all women, despite their differences in race, nation, and colour belong to one cultural environment. The cultural model acknowledges this truth and also that there are:

> "important differences between women as writers: class, race, nationality, and history are literary determinants as significant as gender. Nonetheless, women's culture forms a collective experience that binds women writers to each other over time and space."[103]

To prove that women's culture is distinct and it can be differentiated from men's, she quotes Gerda Lerner:

> "Women have been left out of history not because of the evil conspiracies of men in general or male history only in male-centred terms. We have missed women and their activities because we have asked questions of history which are inappropriate to women. To rectify this, and to light up areas of historical darkness we must, for a time, focus on a woman-centred inquiry, considering

102. Elaine Showalter, "Feminist Criticism in the Wilderness", *Modern Criticism and Theory,* p. 345.

103. Idem.

> the possibility of the existence of a female culture within the general culture shared by men and women."[104]

To the question what female culture is, Gerda Lerner answers that it is an assertion of equality and awareness of sisterhood, the communality of women. She declares:

> "It is important to understand that woman's culture is not and should not be seen as a sub-culture.... Women live their social existence within the general culture and, whenever, they are confined by patriarchal restraint or segregation into separateness (which always has subordination as its purpose), they transform this restraint into complementarity (asserting the importance of woman's function, even its "superiority") and redefine it. Thus, women live a duality as members of the general culture and as partakers of women's culture."[105]

Towards the end of her article, Showalter reaches the wilderness where she finds that all the feminist critics have failed to see the reality, the reality embedded in women's writing. In other words, the main task is to study the works of women writers and discover the true self of "woman".

II

The leading women critics of the twenty first century have crossed the wilderness. They do not follow one model. They focus on women's writing and analyse texts from linguistic, sociological, psychological, and historical points of view, all combined meticulously like an alloy. They know that there can be no writing or criticism totally outside the social structure constituting both man and woman. No publication can be fully independent of the economic and political pressures of the male-centred society. Thus, women writing is not inside or outside of the male tradition; it is in Ellen Moers's metaphor, an undercurrent in the mainstream.

Julia Kristeva, Catherine Belsey, Juliet Mitchell, and Gayatri Chakravorty Spivak have widened the horizons of feminist

104. Quoted by Elaine Showalter, *Modern Criticism and Theory*, p. 345.

105. *Ibid.*, p. 346.

criticism. They have rejected Showalter's cultural model and combined the sociology of Marx, Engels, Durkheim, and Althusser, the psycho-analysis of Freud and Lacan, structuralism of Barthes, and deconstruction of Derrida. Gayatri Spivak added the post-colonial theory in *Can the Subaltern Speak*?

Catherine Belsey in her short but highly original paper "Literature, History, Politics" demolishes the theory and practice of F.R. Leavis, E.M.W. Tilliyard and the question pattern in Oxford and Cambridge universities, and pleads for a close analysis of texts as storage of knowledge. If we want to read literature as a value and category, as Tony Bennet has argued, we need to replace the quest for value by an analysis of the social contestation of value. Women's writing should be studied in the light of the sociology of Marx, psycho-analysis of Lacan, structuralism of Barthes, and deconstruction of Derrida, Belsey emphasises.

Juliet Mitchell has applied Belsey's literary theory in the paper "Feminity, Narrative and Psycho-analysis" (1972), later on, printed in her book *Women: The Longest Revolution*; *Essays on Feminism, Literature and Psychoanalysis* (1984). She has focused on English literature, politics, psychoanalysis, and feminism, the four areas her contemporary Catherine Belsey lays emphasis on. Here she accepts Lacan's idea that castration, "the lack" and pre-Oedipal and Oedipal phases are symbolic. They symbolise the defiance of law set up by the authority, fascist and patriarchal. Mitchell says that "politically speaking, it is only the symbolic, a new symbolism [of the carnavalesque, the disruptive], a new law, that can challenge the dominant law."

It is on Lacanian theory of literature, she bases her arguments in the analysis of Emily Bronte's *Wuthering Heights* and arrives at the conclusion that it is "a story of bisexuality".

> "Each is the bisexual possibility of the other one [Catherine and Heathcliff], evoking a notion of oneness, which is the reverse side of the coin of diverse heterogeneity. This type of "Oneness" can only come with death. Catherine dies; .... Heathcliff himself waits the whole stretch of the

> novel to have his own dream, which is to get back to Catherine. He dies getting back to her. "Oneness" is the symbolic notion of what happens before the symbolic; it is death and has to be death."[106]

Mitchell's emphasis is on the oppressive patriarchal law, which forbids both men and women in the process of becoming what they should naturally be. She is critical of the present bourgeois capitalism, which has made women writers "hysteric", the word used by Julia Kristeva and ends the paper with a reference to Jacques Derrida's deconstruction.

> "I would like to end with asking a question: *in the process of becoming what*? I do not think that we can live as human subjects without in some sense taking on a history; for us, it is mainly the history of being men or women under bourgeois capitalism. In deconstructing that history, we can only construct other histories."[107]

Gayatri Chakravorty Spivak combines deconstruction and post-colonial theory in her critical theory—the long essay *Can the Subaltern Speak?* In the beginning of the essay she refers, first, to a conversation between Michel Foucault and Gilles Deleuze, and criticises the concept of Subject in Western philosophy. She takes the help of Marx's philosophy and discusses in detail the concept of "desire". There is a conflict between "power" of the subject and desire of the other (the workers). Then she comes to Edward W. Said's critique of power in Foucault as a captivating and mystifying category. Her conclusion on the issue is:

> "This subject, curiously sewn together into a transparency by denegations, belongs to the exploiter's side of the international division of labour. It is impossible for contemporary French intellectuals to imagine the kind of Power and Desire that would inhabit the unnamed subject of the Other of Europe."[108]

106. Juliet Mitchell, "Feminity, Narrative and Psychoanalysis", *Modern Criticism and Theory,* p. 429.

107. *Ibid.*, p. 430.

108. Gayatri Chakravorty Spivak, *Can the Subaltern Speak?*, p. 10.

The main reason for their myopic view is that they have not included the economic factor and, so, failed to notice the epistemic violence that constitutes the colonial subject as other.

If Said is satisfied with the "We" of the West and "They" of the East (especially the Semitic people), Chakravorty Spivak broadens the concept to all levels. She refers to the Hindu law and the hegemony of the Brahmans of India (specifically Bengal) and the praise of Sanskrit to language and literature by the British colonisers. Then she comes to Gramsci's term "subaltern classes" and applies it to the woman class in general and the women of Bengal as illustration. She is at pains that the intellectuals who study this phenomenon have remained silent. She says:

> "The first part of my proposition—that the phased development of the subaltern is complicated by the imperialist project—is confronted by a collective of intellectuals who may be called the "Subaltern Studies' group. They must ask, Can the subaltern speak?"[109]

At present, she continues, there is a clean division of labour between the elite world of the West and the erstwhile colonised countries. But, there is every possibility of resistance. She exposes the design of the USA:

> "This benevolent first-world appropriation and reinscription of the Third World as an other is the founding characteristic of much third-worldism in the U.S. human sciences today."[110]

Supporting Derrida's exposure and deconstruction of Europe's ethnocentrism, she criticises Foucault for his partisan attitude to capitalist imperialism of Europe.

The Britishers made the propaganda that by abolishing the *sati* system they saved the brown women from the brown men. The fact is that the scriptures never advised a widow to burn herself on a funeral pyre. It is clearly written in the *shastras* that a widow is entitled to possess the entire property of her diceased husband.

---

109. *Ibid.*, p. 13.

110. *Ibid.*, p. 19.

Gayatri Chakravorty Spivak's arguments can be summarised thus:

She as a post-colonial intellectual finds the differences created by the West (the *subject*). The colonised people are the *Other* and in Gramscian term the subaltern class. At present, there is a divide between the labour of the West and the labour of the East, the latter being subaltern. Women are subaltern at the global level, but they are in a worse position in the third world. History tells how women have been subjugated in the past. *Sati* has been opposed but *johar* (collective self immolation) glorified. Queen Padmini and her maids burned themselves for the fear that Allauddin Khalji's soldiers would defile them or make them slaves. But, what happened in India in the twelfth century has happened recurrently all over the world. Women have been made slaves and defiled most shamefully. Women immolated themselves in groups to save their honour and permanent protection from physical violence.

The last paragraph, three lines only, exhorts the women intellectuals to speak for the women, the subaltern class.

> "The subaltern cannot speak. There is no virtue in global laundry lists with "woman" as a pious item. Representation has not withered away. The female intellectual as intellectual has a circumscribed task, which she must not disown with a flourish."

Feminist ciritcism is now a dominant theory of literature. It has gleaned the best of the recent theories of literature and armed itself with the most progressive contemporary schools of psychology. In addition, the tone is sober and approach to life positive.

(H) POST-COLONIAL THEORY OF LITERATURE

Post-colonial theory of literature emerged in the late eighties. Peter Barry has named it Post-colonial criticism, Bill Ashcroft Post-colonial studies of literature, Leela Gandhi Post-colonial theory, and F. Barker and P. Hulme colonial discourse/post-colonial theory. Before discussing post-colonial theory of literature it is important to know the meaning of colonialism.

According to *Concise Oxford English Dictionary* (1999), the word colony means:

> "a country or area under the political control of another country, and occupied by settlers of that country."

It defines colonialism that it is:

> "the policy or practice of acquiring political control over another country, occupying it with settlers, and exploiting it economically."

According to *Britannica Ready Reference Encyclopedia* (2006), colonialism is "control by one power over a dependent area or people. The purposes of colonialism include economic exploitation of the colony's natural resources, creation of new markets for the colonizer and extension of the colonizer's way of life beyond its national borders. The most active practitioners were European countries; in the years 1500-1900, Europe colonized all of North and South America and Australia, most of Africa, and much of Asia by sending settlers to populate the land or by taking control of governments."

Colonialism is the highest form of capitalism. Capitalism is a form of control of private hands over the means, mode, and distribution of industrial and agricultural products. Imperialism is the next stage. A capitalist nation, not satisfied with the profits and the scale of business attacks the weaker country and subjugates it. Colonialism is the highest stage of capitalism. Here, the imperialist nation or state settles its own people in the controlled country, makes the native people their slaves economically and politically. In order to consolidate its position it convinces the colonized people of the superiority of its race, culture, and civilization, and constantly reminds of their backwardness, lack of education, and inferiority of their race. Europeans recurrently told the people of Africa, Asia and Latin America that they were of inferior kind and only the rule of the white could make their life happy. For example, the English people imposed their language, literature, and culture on the Indian people with a view to making young Indians, Indian in appearance but English at heart.

Edward Said is the propounder of Post-colonial Theory of literature. Inspired by Anwar Abdel Malek's article "Orientalism in Crisis" (1963) he analysed the cultural imperialism of the European colonizers in his famous book, now a classic, *Orientalism* (1978). It is not that these two persons were the first to realize the tactics of the colonizers. Dr Douglas Hyde, one of the greatest men of letters of Ireland in the nineteenth century, in his famous speech "De-Anglicizing of Ireland" exhorted the Irish people to get rid of the cultural rule of England and revive their own glorious past. Yeats read the speech in the journal *Ireland* and wrote to the editor:

> "I agree with every word you said last week about Dr Hyde's lecture and like many others, am deeply grateful to you for your reprint of it in the current number.... It seems to me the best possible augury for the success of the movement we are trying to create."

What the creative writers were doing in Ireland was also being done in India to revive her glorious past and arouse the spirit of nationalism. But, it was all done at a local level. Frantz Fanon, a psychiatrist from Martinique, raised a strong voice in *The Wretched of the Earth* (1961) against the French cultural empire. In the words of Peter Barry, he

> "argued that the first step for colonized people in finding a voice and an identity is to reclaim their own past."

The second step was to erode the colonialist ideology by which that past (the pre-colonial period) had been devalued.

The great contribution of Said as a propounder of post-colonial theory is that he gave a scientific explanation of the kind of literature that was being written in European countries during the colonial period. As said earlier, his *Orientalism* is based on the findings of Anwar Abdel Malek's article "Orientalism in Crisis." Said acknowledges his indebtedness and quotes a large passage from the article as a base of his starting point.

The important parts of the passage are quoted here.

(a) On the level of the position of the problem, and the problematic...the Orient and the Orientals [are considered by Orientalism] as an "object" of study, stamped with an otherness.

(b) On the level of the thematic [the Orientalists] adopt an essentialist conception of the countries, nations, peoples of the Orient under study, a conception which expresses itself through a characterized ethnist typology...and will soon proceed with it towards racism.[111]

(c) This essentialist conception is both historical and a-historical. It is historical in the sense that Orientalists go back to the dawn of civilization and ahistorical because the object (people of the Orient) are transfixed and non-evolutive. The normal man is the European man of the historical period. It is easy to see:

"how much from the eighteenth century to the twentieth century, the hegemonism of possessing minorities, unveiled by Marx and Engels, and the anthropocentrism dismantled by Freud are accompanied by the europocentrism in the area of human and social sciences, and more particularly in those in direct relationship with non-European peoples."[112]

After quoting the passage from Malek's, Said exposes the hypocrisy of the Orientalists. Great philologists like Daniel Jones, Franz Bopp, Jakob Grimm Sacy, and Burnouf made their philological discoveries after studying books brought from the East and stored in the libraries of London and Paris, but their students, the Orientalists, adopted a scornful attitude to the people of the Orient. He comments on the two traits of Orientalism:

> "From the outset, then Orientalism carried forward two traits: (1) a newly found scientific self-consciousness based on the linguistic importance of the Orient to Europe and (2) a proclivity to divide, sub-divide, and redivide its subject matter without ever changing its mind about the Orient as being always the same unchanging, uniform, and radically peculiar object."[113]

---

111. Quoted by Edward Said, "Crisis in Orientalism", *Modern Criticism and Theory*, p. 298.

112. *Ibid.*, p. 299. The sentences not within inverted commas are ours and they summarise the argument of Malek preceding the words quoted.

113. Edward Said, "Crisis in Orientalism", *Modern Criticism and Theory*, p. 299.

Said makes a clear distinction between the coloniser and the conolised, the subject and the object, the "we" and the "other", the western concepts, which are deconstructed in Gayatri Chakravorty's long article *Can the Subaltern Speak*?

After making the distinction and defining the European attitude to Asian, African, and Latin American countries, he says that India was spared partly because Sanskrit belongs to the Indo-European family and so is the Old Iranian. He quotes a remark of Schlegel's "It is the Orient that we must search for the highest Romanticism" and then comments: "He meant the Orient of the *Shakuntala*, the *Zend Avesta*, and the *Upanishads*".

Here, Edward Said is slightly prejudiced and erroneously general in his assessment of the Sanskrit and Old Iranian scholars of Europe. The fact is that the real scholars whose end was research and discovery of the real past were quite objective and there was a healthy collaboration between them and Asian scholars, and it was their joint endeavour that the people of the region saw the past glory hidden by the clouds of ignorance. Excepting this point, Edward's post-colonial theory is valid. Following are the main points of his theory.

(i) There has been the European hegemony since the eighteenth century. It is the hegemony of a minority.

(ii) A distinction has been observed by the Europeans between "we" (Europeans) and "other" (the colonised people).

(iii) The Orientalists (the European scholars of Oriental studies) view the Orient as something whose existence is not only displayed but has remained fixed in time and space in the West.

(iv) The West is the actor, the Orient a passive reactor; it is the spectator, the judge and jury, of every facet of Oriental behaviour.

(v) The present crisis in Orientalism (the studied attitude of the West toward the Orient) dramatises the disparity between text and reality.

Said's *Orientalism* has opened a new vista for the literary critics to analyse and evaluate texts written during the colonial period from a new angle. Earlier the values set by European critics were supposed to be universal but now we have come to realize that they are partisan and not of much use for the people of the Orient. His analysis of Jane Austen's *Mansfield Park* is an authoritative piece of post-colonial criticism. Here,[114] he points out that the peace and cosiness of *Mansfield Park* is based upon Sir Thomas Bertram's estate in Antigua, West Indies, where the native people are exploited like bonded labourers. The central irony is that the estate in England, which represents an ideal order and civilization, is sustained by another estate, a world where there are the planter class and working slaves who grow sugar-cane for the Europeans.

Post-colonial theory has had many ramifications in the hands of Homi K. Bhabha, Aijaz Ahmed, E. Boehmer, and Gayatri Chakravorty Spivak. However, it is limited in scope and is basically an offshoot of Marxist criticism which aims at universal brotherhood.

The main points of Post-colonial theory of literature at present time are as follows.

(a) European colonialism began in the sixteenth century. The leaders were Spain, Portugal, France and, a little later, England. It reached its height towards the end of the seventeenth century. In order to consolidate their position in the colonised countries of Asia, Africa, and Latin America, these countries established schools of Oriental studies. The Orientalists, that is European scholars of oriental studies, made distinction between "we" (subject) and "other" (object). The actor, subject, was the colonialist and the passive reactor was the colonised. The literature written during the period 1701-1950 reflects the colonial mind of European writers such as Joseph Conrad, Rudyard Kipling, Arthur Rider Haggard, R.M. Ballantyne and the writer of the Tarzan series.

(b) The European critics praised such books as glorified the adventures of the heroes in the mysterious and dark

114. Edward Said, *Culture and Imperialism* (1993).

lands of Asia, Africa, and Latin America. They did not care to notice the distinction between "we" and "other", which is quite obviously seen in the post-colonial era. It follows then that the liberal humanist critic's notion of a universal standard of literature is false. Culture, region, and colour are to be taken in account.

(c) After the fall of the colonial powers, the literature of the colonised people is in search of its roots. The African literature of which Chinua Achebe, Wole Soyinka, and Thiongo Wa Ngugi are the celebrated writers has found its roots. There is a note of assertion and aspiration for waking a new edifice out of the ruins.

(d) There is a revision of canon. Now there is emphasis on world literature in India and the syllabus of English has included Indian writers in translation and Indian poetics.

Stylistics

Although stylistics is not a literary theory, it is useful for students of literature in the analysis of literary texts. It is very much like Richards's practical criticism and New Critics' close reading. The difference is that it has its base in modern linguistics.

Definition and Theoretical Background

G. Turner defines stylistics:

> "Linguistics is the science of describing language and showing how it works; stylistics is that part of linguistics which concentrates on variation in the use of language often, but not exclusively with special attention to most conscious and complex uses of language in literature."[115]

A linguist is concerned with the structure of language, which consists of phoneme, morphene, word, phrase, clause, and sentence, and its function as a means of communication in society; the stylistician studies the choices of the author from the level of phoneme to the level of sentence. The stylistician to quote Turner again:

---

115. G. Turner, *Stylistics*, (London: Penguin, 1970), p. 7.

> "needs to begin with a theory of the linguistic scheme and relate it to particular speeches and writings, even if he is ultimately justified as the linguist not of our abstract competence in language but of our particular performance."[116]

Language operates at two levels: the deep level and the surface level. At deep level there are concepts and the writer chooses words for them and constructs simple sentences and then makes use of transformational rules to arrive at the surface level. For arriving at the surface level he chooses structures for the expression of the desired meaning and sound effect.

Language has the property of creativity and, so, there is infinite scope of choices at both word level and sentence level. A writer while choosing words and structure has the liberty to deviate from tradition.

He/she deviates at phonological, morphological, syntactic, and semantic levels. He/she also deviates (of course, within the norms of convention) from the scheme, and uses variations. He/she does so to produce novelty by creative jump. A scheme of language is never complete and static. People go on experimenting with words, phrases, and syntax. Poets coin new words when they find that the existing words do not express their feeling or idea. Making new phrases is a common practice. Most of the figures of speech are the result of experiments in language. Besides old words are given new meaning in new contexts.

Literary language is different from other kinds of discourse. It establishes relationship with the scheme of core language by using linguistic elements to build new schemes of its own. In all genres of literature—literary essay, drama, poetry, and novel—the writer devises his/her own way of structuring sentences, choosing words and phrases, and making sound effects. Hopkins was fond of alliteration and blend words. Lewis Caroll's experiments with language in *Alice in Wonderland* and *Through the Looking Glass* are well-known. Shakespeare accumulated a cluster of metaphors in the highly emotional speeches of

116. *Ibid.*, p. 14.

Hamlet, Othello, Macbeth, and Lear. Browning's syntax demands speculation and syntactic ambiguity is common in poetry.

The creative writer's choice of vocabulary, word collocation, phrase, and structure of sentences defies occasionally the already existing scheme of language and gives a novelty to his/her style. In the words of Turner:

> "The superimposition of literary schemes on the scheme of ordinary language creates a very interesting stylistic study because the two schemes are consciously played off one against the other, but the existence of multiple schemes is not in itself special to literary language."[117]

Method and Technique of Analysis

Every creative writer follows the literary tradition and makes innovation. When he/she follows tradition he/she retains the old paraphernalia of the literary tradition of which he/she is a part and conforms with the scheme of language use in the past. Minor writers and versifiers follow tradition without making any kind of innovation. Good writers depart from tradition and make creative use of language. Wordsworth departed from the eighteenth century tradition of the use of heroic couplet and wrote poetry in different metres.

Stylistics studies and analyses the creative use of language; it is in the creative use of language that a writer's originality and individuality is clearly manifest. For creativity the writer makes the original use of the established possibilities of language and, in other cases, goes beyond them, that is, he/she creates new communicative possibilities, which are not already in the language. If we compare the essays of Bacon and Lamb, we will find that Lamb has deviated significantly from his predecessor. Similarly, Shakespeare and Milton departed from the Italian tradition of the sonnet and Hopkins wrote the *curtal sonnet* "Pied Beauty". T.S. Eliot's experiments are well-known.

There are three main levels of language: realization (sound) form (structure), and semantics (meaning). This three level model is applicable to both productive and receptive processes of language, and the four possibilities. The four possibilities are:

117. *Ibid.*, p. 37.

i. Homophony: same pronunciation but different forms (spelling (right) site; incite-insight; hair-hare).

Here is the famous line of Shakespeare "When I eyed your eyes".

ii. Differentiation: same form (spelling) but different pronunciations (bow; minute; wind).

iii. Synonymy: same meaning but different forms (blue-azure; feeble-weak; sky-firmament).

iv. Polysemy: same form, different meanings (light; grave, fire).

Creative writers operating at the three levels sound, form, and meaning, and four possibilities of language deviate from the tradition in the areas of lexis, grammar, graphology, and history.

(a) Lexical deviation

There are three kinds of lexical deviation:

i. *Neologism or coining a new word*

The new words are called nonce-formations. Here an existing rule of word formation is applied with greater generality than customary. Shakespeare used the word *unsex* in Lady Macbeth's speech on the pattern of unleash, unhorse. Similarly, Hopkins made use of the prefix *un*—in the words *child* and *father* and the word *make* with the noun *widow* in the line.

"The unchilding, unfathering, widow-weaking deep."

Similarly T.S. Eliot has coined the word *foresuffer* on the pattern of foresee, foreknow and foretell.

ii. *Blend or portmanteau words*

Blends are compounds of two words that at the time of blending lose some segments. After listening to "Jabberwocky" Alice asks its meaning because she does not understand the meaning of words like "brillig" and "mimsy". She is given the explanation that they are *portmantean* words *Brillig* is made of two words *broil* + thing, that is, four o'clock in the afternoon, the time for broiling things for dinner. Similarly, *mimsy* is a combination of *miserable* and *flimsy*. Many words have been coined by blending and now they are a part of the dictionary.

iii. *Word-collocation*

Poets make unusual word collocation by deviating from the normal one. Dylan Thomas's poem "A Grief Ago" has an unusual word collocation. The word ago is an adverb of time and it is not collocated with an abstract noun. But, Thomas has collocated it with the abstract noun *grief* and similar is the case with the word *moonlong*. *Farmyards away* is another deviation. Yeats' "translunar paradise" and Eliot's "April...the cruellest month" are other examples of deviation from normal word-collocation.

(b) Grammatical Variation

It is better to call it syntactic variation. For poetic effect, for emphasis or for sound effect writers deviate from the normal sentence structure. Miltonic inversion is quite famous. The first line of *Paradise Lost*, Book I begins with the adjunct "Of man's first disobedience" and the long stanza ends with the main verb "sing". The main reason for the syntactic deviation is to lay emphasis on man's first disobedience by foregrounding it. Similarly, in Section II of *The Waste Land*, Line 97 begins with the preposition *above* and the entire sentence is a syntactic deviation.

> "Above the antique mantel was displayed
> As though a window gave upon the sylvan scene
> The change of Philomel, by the barbarous King
> So rudely forced;...." (97-100)

(c) Graphological Deviation

There is a system of printing poetry; capitalization (each line begins with a capital letter), length of lines and metrical pattern are all regular. But, poets have deviated from time to time. Browning is fond of using dashes in the middle of lines. Hopkins's sprung rhythm, Whitman's uneven length of lines and free verse in our time are some of the examples of graphological deviation. George Herbert's poem "Altar" is printed as an altar (the length of the lines make it so) and "Easter Wings" in the form of a pair of wings. Some modern poets have given up the convention of beginning a line with capital letters. E.E. Cummings never begins a line with a capital letter nor does he write his name with a capital letter, and William Carlos Williams does it occasionally.

(d) Historical Deviation

A poet does not always restrict himself or herself to the current vocabulary of his/her time. For the expression of the desired meaning he/she explores the vocabulary of the past and sometimes borrows words and phrases from other languages. Milton used English words in their original Latin meaning. Hopkins used words of Celtic origin. Eliot used a number of expressions from foreign languages including Sanskrit. In other words, poets use archaic words, phrases, and structures for richness of meaning and novelty of expression.

Apart from these four possibilities of deviation, stylistics takes note of tropes like foregrounding, parallelism, repetition, metaphor, symbolism, imagery, metonymy, metre, rhythm, and the irrational in poetry.

Stylistics, though limited in scope, has opened a new door for the analysis of literary writing. It has made it possible to make distinction between different kinds of discourse by tracing the linguistic signals specific to them.

7

PRACTICAL CRITICISM AND SCANSION

Practical criticism is a method of objective analysis and interpretation of poetry. While teaching literature at Cambridge University, I.A. Richards found that his undergraduate students made stock responses to the poems they were asked to interpret. As an experiment, he gave them ten poems, called "protocals", without disclosing their titles and names of poets. On reading the answers, he discovered that most of the interpretations were subjective, and the students did not read what was written in the poems but what they wanted to read.

Richards, then, prepared a guideline for reading poerty, which he called practical criticism and the book in which he discussed the experiment and the principles of reading poetry, he titled *Practical Criticism.* He pointed out that there are four kinds of meaning: sense, feeling, tone, and intention. A poem or literary piece can be fully understood when all these four meanings are taken in account.

i. Sense

A poet says something in a poem. It may be a thought, an experience, or expression of some emotion. While reading it we make a progression and reach the end with a sense of finality. Sense is grasped by the literal meaning of the lines and their logical relationship. It is also important to know the meaning of the words used and their relation with other words in the structure of the poem.

ii. Feeling

Poetry is never dull and dry like physics and mathematics. The poet is more sensitive than an ordinary human being. He/

she wants to evoke in the listener/reader the same kind of emotion that he/she had at the time of some unusual experience. Naturally, he/she writes with the kind of feeling that he/she has in heart. The language of poetry is emotive as the poet presents an experience with some feeling. The feeling may be of pain, pleasure, sorrow, happiness, loss, joy, desire, anger, disillusionment, or anger. Feeling is always related to the poet's attitude to the subject-matter.

iii. Tone

Tone is the poet's attitude to the reader. It is the emotional colouring of the writer or speaker. In conversation people seldom speak in a flat or monotonous tone; there is always a continual up and down of the pitch of their voice and variation in stress. It is also to be noted that feeling and tone are often intermixed. Let us take the opening stanza of Yeats's "Easter 1916".

"I have met them at close of day
Coming with vivid faces
From counter or desk among grey
Eighteenth century houses.
I have passed with a nod of the head
Or polite meaningless words
Or have lingered a while and said
Polite meaningless words,
And thought before I had done
Of a mocking tale or a gibe
To please a companion
Around the fire at the club,
Being certain that they and I
But lived where motley is worn:
All changed, changed utterly
A terrible beauty is born."

The poet narrates his past experience of meeting with the heroes of the Easter Rising in 1916. The meeting, he says, was casual and insignificant, and the exchange of words between him and them was of phatic communion, limited only to formal greeting, or nodding of heads. Besides, they were all common Irish people rather comic figures. The poet humorously says that they belonged to the country "where motley is worn". The word "motley" refers to the dress worn by a joker in a circus or on a stage. The tone is casual and humorous as the poet laughs at himself that he, too, is a member of the nation where motley is worn. Then the tone changes suddenly. Their martyrdom transforms them from the laughable comic figures to tragic heroes, terribly beautiful.

As said earlier, feeling and tone are complementary to each other. Feeling is a part of the human psyche, and tone is its concrete realization by modulation of voice.

iv. Intention

There is always a purpose behind every writing. Why does a poet write a poem, a play, or a novel? It may be his/her desire that other people will share his/her joy, sorrow, or the knowledge gained by the experience. The intention may be overt or covert in the text. Inferior writers are usually overt. Great writers convey their intention covertly and artistically. Eliot's intention in *The Waste Land* is covert, and it is only after a close reading of the text we are in a position to realize his intention. In "All Day I Hear" James Joyce's intention is covert.

"All day I hear the noise of waters
Making moon
Sad as the sea-bird is, when going
Forth alone,
He hears the winds cry to the waters'
Monotone
The grey winds, the cold winds are blowing
Where I go,
I hear the noise of many waters
Far below
All day, all night, I hear them flowing
To and fro."

In this poem the narrator hears the sad moaning of the sea, the sea-bird, and the wind. Nowhere does he say about his own sadness. But he hears their sad cry day and night. Why? If we answer this question, we shall understand his intention. The underlying reality is that the sea, the bird, and the wind, all represent the poet's sadness. In other words, the poet's intention is to tell the readers of sadness through a set of images or to create the mood of sadness by means of objective correlative.

Practical Criticism and Close Reading

I.A. Richards and William Empson made a great impact on the New Critics of America. John Crowe Ransom added the concepts of *logical structure* and *irrelevant local texture*. He and Cleanth Brooks used the term *Close Reading* at the place of *Practical Criticism*, and Brooks in collaboration with Robert Penn Warren wrote *Understanding Poetry* and *Understanding Fiction* and with Robert Heilman *Understanding Drama*, which are the classics of *Close Reading.*

Logical Structure and Irrelevant Local Texture

According to Ransom, logical structure is the argument of a poem. A poet has something to say about his/her feeling, idea or experience. He or she orders it in a special way so that the entire narration will be logical. Thus, a text is logically structured. But, a poet does not think in abstract terms; he/she thinks metaphorically. Naturally, his/her statements are expressed through tropes.

Writing poetry is just like weaving a piece of cloth. There is the structure made of plain threads. The shuttle moves up and down and fills in the gaps. If the piece of cloth is to be made artistically beautiful, threads of different colours make a picture or a pattern. This is the texture made by the shuttle. Tropes like image, symbol, simile, metaphor, and metonymy constitute the texture, which enhances the artistic perfection of a literary text.

The main idea of the following poem by Cummings is that if the objects of nature, animate and inanimate, go against their own nature, it will be incredible indeed, and so will be the case with man if he is rid of animality. This is the logical structure. But, the poet does not convey this idea plainly; he presents it through a set of images and a diction strikingly novel.

> "When serpents bargain for the right to squirm
> and the sun strikes to gain a living wave

when thorns regard their roses with alarm
and rainbows are insured against old age
when every thrush may sing no new moon in
if all screech-owls have not okayed his voice
and many have signs on the dotted line
or else an ocean is compelled to close
when the oak begs permission of the birch
to make an acorn—valleys accuse their
mountains of having attitude—and much
denounces april as a saboteur
Then will believe in that incredible
un animal mankind (and not until)."

The beauty of the poem lies in the images, all taken from nature except one "rainbows are insured against old age". It is the freshness of the images that enhances the richness of meaning.

Tropes and Poetic Devices

(i) Imagery

Imagery is a set of images in a poem, play, or fiction. The term image gained prominence in England and America with the Imagist Movement led by T.E. Hulme. By image is meant picturisation of an object in concrete words. For example, the opening lines of A.E. Housman's "The Cherry Tree":

Lovelist of trees, the cherry now
Is hung with bloom along the bough,
And stands about the woodland ride
Wearing white for Eastertide.

In these lines the cherry tree is presented in concrete words like "hung", "bloom", "bough", "stands", and "woodland side". The phrase "wearing white" gives it the human form and also its purity which is accentuated by "Eastertide".

(ii) Metaphor

The general definition of metaphor is that it is compressed simile. "He was like an anchor of our hope" can be compressed to "He was an anchor of our hope" to make the former sentence an example of metaphor, by omitting the word "like". The other definition is that when there is a shift from the general meaning of a word it becomes a metaphor. For example, in the line "Life is a walking shadow", there is the metaphorical use of the word "walk". Similarly, in Philip Larkin's "Aubade", there is the use of metaphor in the phrases "telephones crouch" and "intricate rented world". The lines are:

"Meanwhile *telephones crouch*, getting ready to ring
In locked-up offices, and all the uncaring
Intricate rented world begins to rouse."

There is a shift from the general meaning in "telephones crouch" and "intricate rented world".

(iii) Metonymy and Synecdoche

Metonymy is a figure of speech in which the adjective of a word stands for the noun:

"The best lack all conviction."
"The deep moans."

The adjective "best" stands for the best people and "the deep" for the sea.

Synecdoche is a figure of speech in which a part stands for its whole:

"Five hands are working in my office."

After Roman Jakobson's brilliant analysis of *aphasia*[1] and the slip of the tongue, scholars have begun to consider synecdoche as a part of metonymy.

(iv) Symbol

A symbol is a concrete object that stands for an abstract idea. The difference between metaphor and symbol is that a metaphor does not grow whereas a symbol grows richer in meaning with recurrent occurrence in a text or different texts of an author. In Yeats's "Lapis Lazuli" the *long-logged bird* is a symbol of longevity, and the *blessed isles* in *Mourning Becomes Electra* is a place in the beginning, but after subsequent references it becomes the symbol of purity and innocence, a kind of Eden Garden where there is no inkling of guilt. We realize towards the end of the play

1. aphasia = language disorder.

that it stands in contrast with the sinister Mannon House, which is a symbol of hatred, pride, and guilt.

(v) Irony

It is a literary device, which conveys the meaning opposite to the literal meaning of a word, phrase, or sentence. The eighteenth century writers were perfectly skilled in the use of irony for humour and mild criticism. Irony is of two kinds: the irony of speech and the irony of situation. In the irony of speech the speaker himself may be the victim of irony or the listener. The speaker is usually the victim in the irony of situation. When he/she says that it is the best time for him/her, he/she is hardly aware of the coming disaster. In modern times, irony is used very subtly. There is a very subtle irony in the opening lines of *The Waste Land.*

> "April is the cruellst month, breeding
> Lilacs out of the dead land, mixing
> Memory and desire, stirring
> Dull roots with spring rain."

The speaker is unhappy with the month of April, the month when the spring season begins. He does not like the blossoming of lilacs. He wants to remain dull and dry. The irony is that the speaker is so much spiritually dry that he has no desire for regeneration. If we compare these lines with the opening lines of *The Canterbury Tales*, we soon realize the contrast.

Cleanth Brooks has defined irony in a new way. For him irony is the meaning of a speech act warped by its context. He has discussed his idea of irony in the essay "Irony as a Principle of Structure".

(vi) Paradox

Paradox is an apparently false statement, but actually true. It is a very effective figure of speech to arrest the attention of the reader or listener as it shocks him/her. Bernard Shaw revelled in paradoxical statement. The following line of *Julius Caesar* is a famous example of paradox:

"Cowards die many times before their death."

Similarly, there is paradox in this line of Emily Dickinson:

> "My life closes twice before its close."

There is a difference between paradox and oxymoron. In oxymoron two words or phrases opposite in meaning or contradicting each other are juxtaposed.

"Oh none, unless this miracle have night—
That in black ink my love may still shine bright"
(Sonnet 65)

Here "black ink" and "shine bright" are opposite in meaning, but at deep level they support each other. It is not necessary that words opposite in meaning be placed together in paradox.

(vii) Foregrounding

It is a device to enlarge the importance of an idea or significance of an object by bringing it to the front. Usually, the idea or object is brought forward to begin a line in poetry. The reason for doing so is that an object in front arrests our attention. Milton's *Paradise Lost Book I* begins with the phrase "Of man's first disobedience" as it is the main theme of the epic. Keats has placed the word "forlorn" at the beginning of the concluding stanza of "Ode To A Nightingale" for the sake of emphasising its significance.

"Forlorn! The very word is like a ball
To toll me back from thee to my self!"

Similarly, Eliot has foregrounded the words *The Hanged Man* in the following lines of *The Waste Land*:

"..., and this card
Which is blank, is something he carries on his back,
Which I am forbidden to see, I do not find
The Hanged Man, Fear death by water."

The foregrounding of "The Hanged Man" is significant.

(viii) Backgrounding

Backgrounding is comparatively a new literary devices. It first began in France in painting. An artist painted a picture in which an elderly man was standing in the background and watching children playing in the foreground. The elderly man was painted in detail and he drew more attention of the viewers than the children's play. That picture inspired poets to employ the device of backgrounding in poetry. The following passage illustrates how effectively Eliot has made use of backgrounding.

"A current under sea
Picked his bones in whispers. As he rose and fell
He passed the stages of his age and youth
Entering the whirlpool."
(*The Waste Land*: IV, Death by Water)

In this passage the accent falls on the last word in each line. The words in the foreground are much less important than the ending words, and both the sentences end with word beginning with whi- for half-rhyme and complete the meaning. Finally, there is emphasis on the word whirlpool where the current falls and deposits the bones.

(ix) Parallelism

In this figure of speech two lines of the same length and pattern are placed together with a few differences at the level of sound or word for contrast. In *The Waste Land*, the line "O keep the Dog far hence, that's friend to man" runs parallel to the line "O keep the Wolf far hence, that's enemy to man" in the Dirge in *The White Devil* of John Webster. Eliot has used parallelism in "Marina" where the last stanza runs parallel to the first stanza.

The first stanza

"What sea what shores what grey rocks and what islands
What water lapping the bow
And scent of pine and the wood thrush singing through the fog
What images return
O my daughter."

The last stanza

"What seas what shores what granite islands towards my timbers
And wood thrush calling through the fog
My daughter."

Pericles speaks when the island is at a distance and his daughter is not clearly visible, in the first stanza. In the second stanza he is nearer. The "grey rocks" are now "granite islands" and "o" is deleted as his daughter Marina is nearer and clearly visible.

Dylan Thomas's use of parallelism in "Fern Hill" is equally effective.

The first stanza

"Now as I was young and easy under the apple boughs
About the lilting house and happy as the grass was green,
The night above the dingle starvy,
Time let me hail and climb
Golden in the hey days of his eyes."

The last stanza

"Oh as I was young and easy in the mercy of his means,
Time held me green and dying
Though I sang in my chains like the sea."

The contrast is quite sharp between the two periods of time.

(x) Repetition

Repetition of words and phrases is considered a disqualification in writing, but poets repeat them for richness in meaning. The fact is that repetition becomes a trope when it is used deftly for sound effect and wider connotation. In *The Waste Land* the repetition of the phrase "so many" enhances the beauty of sound effect and richness of meaning.

"A crowd flowed over London, so many
I had not thought death had undone so many."

Similarly, the word "yesterday" occurs at the beginning of the first line of the first six stanzas, "tomorrow" in stanzas 18-20, and "To-day" in stanzas 21 and 22 in Auden's "Spain 1937".

The repetition of these three words is not only for emphasis but also for contrast. The big achievements of the past and the bright hope of the future are contrasted with the present, which is bitter and sad.

Robert Frost has repeated the same line in "Stopping By Woods On A Snowy Evening".

"And miles to go before I sleep,
And miles to go before I sleep."

The second line has a wider meaning. The second "sleep" means man's final sleep.

(xi) Juxtaposition and Contrast

Juxtaposition is placing of two words opposite in meaning or sound generally. The common use of juxtaposition is for contrast but sometimes, if both the words are similar in meaning, for emphasis. Hopkins is the master of juxtaposition. These lines from "Pied Beauty" are a good specimen of his art.

> "All things counter, original, spare, strange;
> Whatever is fickle, freckled (who knows how?)
> With swift, slow, sweet, sour; adazzle, dim
> He fathers forth whose beauty is past change;
> Praise him."

(xii) Alliteration

Alliteration is the recurrence of the same sound(s) in a line of a poem. If the recurrence is of a consonant or more than one consonant it is called consonance and if it is a vowel or more than one vowel it is assonance. The Celtic poetry was highly alliterative. William Langland's poetry is famous for alliteration. Hopkins, a Victorian poet, but considered a modern, is the greatest master of alliteration. His alliteration is not only for sound effect, it adds meaning to the word by juxtaposition and contrast. These are the opening lines of the sonnet "God's Grandeur":

> "The world is charged with the grandeur of God,
> It will flame out, like shining from shook foil;
> It gathers to a greatness, like the ooze of oil
> Crushed. Why do men then now not reck his rod?"

W.B. Yeats's "The Lake Isle of Innisfree" is famous for its assonance.

METRE AND STANZA FORMS OF ENGLISH POETRY

Comments on the metre pattern and stanza form are an important part of practical criticism. It is expected that a student is able to read a poem rhythmically and know why the poet has chosen a particular stanza form and, also, what kind of deviation he/she has made from the traditional form if any.

A. Metre

In the past, when the printing machine was not invented, poets recited their poems before the public. Even today, the reading of a poem by the poet is highly welcomed by the lovers of poetry. The main reason for this is that the modulation of voice cannot be printed on a piece of paper. When a person speaks, he/she never maintains the same pitch of voice. There is always modulation of voice according to the poet's feelings and attitude to the subject and the audience. The rise and fall in the pitch of voice, pause, lengthening of a vowel, and changes in tone determine the speech rhythm of a speaker. The rhythm of speech is like the movement of a wave, up and down, fast and slow, and always changing the direction, never straight and flat.

There is a difference between the rhythm of prose and of poetry. Conventions have made the rhythm of poetry different from that of prose. Stress plays the most important role in determining the rhythm of speech in English. In poetry, it determines the length of a line and the metrical pattern. The knowledge of the following terms will help a student of poetry understand the metre of a poem.

(a) *Stress*

Stress is the result of extra muscular effort in the articulation of a speech sound. While articulating the word "dentist" we make extra muscular effort in pronouncing the first syllable "den" and relax when we reach the next syllable "-tist". Thus, the first syllable receives stress or is stressed. In English language, nouns, adjectives, verbs, and adverbs receive stress and articles, pronouns, prepositions, and conjunctions remain unstressed generally.

(b) *Syllable*

Consonants are articulated with some obstruction in the mouth. Vowels are produced without complete obstruction and the pulmonic[2] air passes through the oral passage[3] freely. Thus, vowels release the air accumulated in the oral passage during the articulation of one or more consonants. Once the air is released a syllable is produced. It means that the number of syllables in a word are determined by the number of vowels it

2. pulmonic = of the lungs.
3. oral passage = mouth.

contains. The English writing system is not scientific like the writing systems of Indian languages. The number of vowels is counted by pronunciation in English. For example, there is only *one* vowel in the following words:

gain, site, tooth, tour, train, waste, year.

(c) *Foot*

The length of a line in poetry is measured by the number of *foot*. A *foot* consists of one stressed syllable and one or two unstressed syllables. However, it is not necessary that there should always be an unstressed syllable in a foot. It is the stressed syllable, which is the nucleus of a foot, and the unstressed syllables are marginal, though important, elements. A line may consist of one foot and can go upto ten feet or more. Generally, the length of a line in English poetry is limited to six feet and rarely more than seven feet. Following are the names given to lines according to their length. A stressed syllable is marked (ˊ) and an unstressed syllable (˘ or ×).

i.	Monometre: A line consisting of *one* foot	ăwáy; bĕcóme
ii.	Dimetre: A line consisting of two feet	ŭnréal cĭ́ty
iii.	Trimetre: A line consisting of three feet	Ĭ hắd n̆o hú̆man feárs
iv.	Tetrametre: A line consisting of four feet	Ă slúmbĕr dĭ́d m̆y spír̆it seal
v.	Pentametre: A line consisting of five feet	Th̆e cúrfĕw tólls th̆e knéll ŏf párting dáy
vi.	Hexametre: A line consisting of six feet (Alexandrine)	Th̆at líke ă wóundĕd sńake drăgs itś slow leńgth ălóng

(d) *Stress variation/Stress pattern*

There are six standard stress variations in English poetry.

i.	Iamb	∪ /	unstressed stressed syllabic pattern
ii.	Trochee	/ ∪	stressed unstressed syllabic pattern
iii.	Anapaest	∪ ∪ /	two unstressed syllables followed by a stressed syllable
iv.	Dactyl	/ ∪ ∪	a stressed syllable followed by two unstressed syllables
v.	Spondee	//	a foot of two stressed syllables
vi.	Pyrrhus	∪ ∪	a foot of two unstressed syllables

The last two metres exist only in books of rhetoric and prosody, but are not seen in actual writing.

While naming the metre pattern of a poem, we write both the number of feet and the stress pattern. The division of a line into feet is shown by a slash (/) generally. Some people underline the feet. For example,

Ĭ wán / derĕd lovely ás / ă ćloud	Iambic tetrametre
Ĭ ḿade / m̆y sóng / ă coát	Iambic trimetre
Téll m̆e / nót ĭn / móurnfŭl / númbĕrs	Trochaic tetrametre

(e) *Scansion*

Scansion is the method of analysing the metre pattern of a poem and naming the stanza form. It answers the question why the poet has chosen a particular metre and made certain variations, that is, mixed iamb with anapaest and trochee with dactyl and varied the length of lines. For example, Wordsworth has written the poem "A Slumber Did My Spirit Seal" in iambic tetrametre and trimetre alternately. Why has he done so? Is he successful in his experiment? Spenser wrote *The Fairy Queen* in a stanza form which consists of nine lines, the first eight in iambic pentametre and the last in iambic hexametre or alexandrine. His innovation was novel and bold. Readers admired it. Now this new stanza form is named after him, Spenserian stanza. This leads us to the main stanza forms.

B. Stanza Forms

(a) *Couplet*

It is a stanza of two lines of equal length, which rhyme together. Thom Gunn, in the poem "Flying Above California", describes the Pacific coastline in couplets. Of course, he has deviated from the tradition of capitalizing the first letters of the lines.

> "On fogless days by the Pacific,
> there is a cold hard light without break
>
> that reveals merely what is—no more
> and no less. That limiting candour,
>
> that accuracy of the beaches,
> is part of the ultimate richness."

(b) *Heroic Couplet*

One of the oldest stanza forms, highly popular in the eighteenth century, the *Heroic Couplet* consists of two lines of iambic pentametre rhyming together. Since most of the classical heroic poetry was written in this stanza form, it got the name heroic couplet. All the eighteenth century poets wrote their poems in this stanza form so much that the romantics abandoned it completely. Here are six lines from Dryden's *Mac Flecknoe*:

> "All human things are subject to decay,
> And, when Fate summons, monarchs must obey;
> This Flecknoe found, who, like Augustus young,
> Was called to empire and had governed long;
> In prose and verse was owned, without dispute,
> Through all the realms of nonsense, absolute."

(c) *Quatrain*

It is a stanza of four lines. Donne's poem "A Valediction Forbidding Mourning" is one of the early examples of poems written in quatrain.

> "As virtuous men pass mildly away,
> And whisper to their souls to go,
> Whilst some of their sad friends do say,
> The breath goes now, and some say, no."

(d) *Terza Rima*

It is a stanza of three lines, the first and third lines rhyme together. The first line of the next stanza rhymes with the second line of the first stanza and this scheme continues throughout. All lines are in iambic pentametre. First written in a sustained way by Dante in *Divine Comedy*, it was perfectly handled by P.B. Shelley, one of the greatest masters of poetic craft. His "Ode To The West Wind" and "The Triumph Of Life" are the superb examples of Terza Rima. Here are the first three stanzas from "Ode To The West Wind":

> "O wild West Wind, Thou breath of Autumn's being, a
> Thou, from whose unseen presence the leaves dead b
> Are driven, like ghosts from an enchanter fleeing, a

Yellow, and black and pale, and hectic red, b
Pestilence-stricken multitudes: O thou, c
Who chariotest to their dark wintry bed b

The wingéd seeds, where they lie cold and low, c
Each like a corpse within its grave, until d
Thine azure sister of the Spring shall blow" c

(e) *Rhyme Royal*

Chaucer is the first established poet who wrote *Troilus and Criseyde* in rhyme royal. Rhyme royal is a stanza of seven lines in iambic pentametre. The rhyme scheme is ab ab b cc.

W.B. Yeats's "A Bronze Head" is written in rhyme royal with a superb artistic touch.

"Here at right of the entrance this bronze head,
Human, superhuman, a bird's round eye,
Everything else withered and mummy-dead.
What great tomb-haunter sweeps the distant sky
(Something may linger there through all else die;)
And finds there nothing to make its terror less
Hyterica passio of its own emptiness?"

(f) *Ottava Rima*

A favourite of W.B. Yeats, this stanza form is most suitable for serious poetry. It is an eight line stanza in iambic metre, slow and majestic, with the rhyme scheme ab ab ab cc.

"That is no country for old men. The young
In one another's arms, birds in the trees
—Those dying generations—at their song,
The salmon-falls, the mackerel-crowded seas,
Fish, flesh or fowl, commend all summer long
Whatever is begotten, born and dies.
Caught in that sensual music all neglect
Monuments of unageing intellect."

(g) *Spenserian Stanza*

A nine line stanza in iambic metre was first introduced successfully by Edmund Spenser in *The Fairy Queen*. The special quality of this stanza is that the first eight lines are in iambic pentametre and the last line is hexametre, also called alexandrine.

(h) *Blank Verse*

Blank verse has remained the most popular and effective form of writing narrative poetry. The lines are in iambic pentametre, but they do not rhyme. The plays of Shakespeare, Milton's *Paradise Lost*, and Wordsworth's long poems are all written in blank verse.

"Five years have past; five summers, with the length
Of five long winters! and again I hear
These waters, rolling from their mountain-springs
With a soft inland murmur.—Once again
Do I behold these steep and lofty cliffs,
That on a wild secluded scene in press
Thoughts of more deep seclusion: and connect
The landscape with the quiet of the sky."

("Tintern Abbey")

(i) *Free Verse*

Free verse is different from blank verse. In free verse the lines are of uneven length and the stress pattern varies. It is the English version of the French verse-libre. Among the great poets, Eliot was the first to use it.

"I grow old... I grow old....
I shall wear the bottoms of my trousers rolled.
Shall I part my hair behind? Do I dare to eat a peach?
I shall wear white flannel trousers, and walk upon the beach
I have heard the mermaids singing each to each.
I do not think that they will sing to me."

("Love Song of J. Alfred Prufrock")

Free verse has come to stay; yet most of the poets like to write in the time-hallowed stanza forms and blank verse. Of course, they make deviations from the convention and vary the rhyme-scheme for a proper correlation between sound and sense. Shelley ended each stanza of "Ode To The West Wind" with a couplet, though the entire poem is written in terza rima.

APPRECIATION OF POETRY AND PROSE (LITERARY)

Poetry and prose are distinctly different. Poetry can be recited but not prose. Poetry follows certain conventions, such as metre, stanza form, rhyme, and beginning of every line with a capital letter, which are not followed by prose. Yet, there are certain elements that are common to both poetry and literary prose. The essays of Lamb, Virginia Woolf, and Hazlitt have the elements of poetry in them. The main reason for their being poetic is that these writers have made use of emotive language. They carry us to a novel and charming land by their art of bestrangement or defamiliarization. They make use of tropes and occasionally rhyme. While appreciating a prose passage, we have to take note of the literary devices employed by the author, but let us take poetry first.

A. Appreciation of Poetry

The first step in the appreciation of a poem is to read it aloud at least twice. As poetry is the best words in the best order; the reader must pay full attention to every word and its relationship with other words at both sound and sense levels. The great advantage of loud reading is that it helps us realize the rhythm of the poem and forces us to pay attention to each and every word. The next step is to consider the following points:

(a) What the poem is about (subject-matter or theme).
(b) The kind of tone of the poem (feeling and attitude of the poet).
(c) The tropes and literary devices.
(d) The intention of the poem (the poet's purpose as realized in the text).
(e) The metre and stanza form, and stylistic deviations.
(f) The poem's success as a work of art.

Let us take Sylvia Plath's "Mirror".

Mirror

I am silver and exact. I have no preconceptions.
Whatever I see I swallow immediately
Just as it is, unmisted by love or dislike.

I am not cruel, only faithful—
The eye of a little god, four-cornered.
Most of the time I meditate on the opposite wall.
It is pink, with speckles. I have looked at it so long
I think it is a part of my heart. But it flickers.
Faces and darkness separate us over and over.

Now I am a lake. A woman bends over me,
Searching my reaches for what she really is.
Then she turns to those liars, the candles or the moon.
I see her back, and reflect it faithfully.
She rewards me with tears and an agitation of hands.
I am important to her. She comes and goes.
Each morning it is her face that replaces the darkness.
In me she has drowned a young girl, and in me an old woman
Rises toward her day after day, like a terrible fish.

We can understand this poem by answering the following questions.

i. What does the poem describe and what is its subject-matter?

Ans. This poem is about a mirror hanging on a wall. Its subject matter is the change of a young girl into an old woman—"a young girl drowned" and "an old woman rises toward her".

ii. What is the tone of the poem?

Ans. The tone is neutral. There is no question or exclamation mark. The words "silver", "exact", "no preconceptions", "unmisted by or dislike", "not cruel", and "faithfuly" make the speaker's tone neutral.

iii. What are the figures of speech?

Ans. Metaphors: "the eye of a little god", "I am a lake"

Images: "unmisted by love or dislike", "in me she has drowned a young girl", "in me an old woman rises", and "a terrible fish".

iv. What is the poet's intention in this poem?

Ans. The intention is to express the anguish that comes over to people when they become old and see the changes in their face, and experience the painful loss of youth and beauty.

v. What is the metre of the poem and what are the stylistic deviations?

Ans. The poem does not follow the traditional stanza form nor is it written in the standard metre of English poetry. It is written in free verse. The sentences are short and simple, all the words used are modern and restricted to the core vocabulary of English.

The deviation from the convention is that a line sometimes consists of two sentences (lines 1, 7, 8 and 15). After this basic understanding of the poem, we are in a position to appreciate it in terms of theme, tone, imagery, and diction.

Appreciation of "Mirror"

This short poem of seventeen lines is a narration by a mirror that hangs between two walls painted pink long ago as the reflection of the opposite wall on the mirror shows speckles. The narrator is objective and exact, not blurred by the emotions of love and hatred. It reflects everything truthfully just like the neutral eye of a goddess with the only difference in shape as it is square with four corners. There is a passage between the walls and its view is obliterated by the people passing by and darkness, too.

In the second stanza, there is a change. The mirror is no more an ordinary mirror, a reflector of objects; it is a lake, the archetype of the collective unconscious. According to Jung, the collective unconscious, which is the storehouse of ancient wisdom, appears as a lake to the troubled soul who, either in a dream or vision, sees his/her real self in his reflected image there. Jung calls the image reflected in the lake "shadow", which terrifies the dreamer or visionary. The troubled soul must dive deep into the lake to know the meaning of life. The woman is terrified. She weeps to see the change in her face, perhaps shrunken and wrinkled. She sees her true self but is unable to accept the reality. She searches her by gone days, which will never come back; what she faces is the coming of old age in the form of a terrible fish to swallow her.

Poems for Exercise[4]

1. Read the following poems and answer the questions asked at the end.

(a) **Hyla Brook**

By June our brooks *run out of song and speed.*
Sought for much after that, it will be found
Either to have gone groping underground
(And taken with it *all the Hyla tree-toad breed*
That shouted in the mist a month ago,
Like Ghost of sleigh bells in a ghost of snow)—
Or flourished and come up in jewelweed,
Weak foliage that is flown upon and bent
Even against the way its water went.
Its bed is left *a faded paper sheet*
Of dead leaves struck together by the heat—
A brook to none but who remember long.
This as it will be seen is other far
Than with brooks taken otherwhere in song
We love the things we love for what they are.

i. What was the activity of the toads when there was water in the brook?
ii. What images strike you most?
iii. Explain the expressions in italics in the poem.
iv. Find out two stylistic deviations.

(b) **Futility**

Move him into the sun—
Gently it awoke him once,
At home, whispering of fields unsown.
Always it woke him, even in France,
Until this morning and this snow.
If any thing might rouse him now
The kind old sun will know.

4. In the past, poems were given without title for "close reading" or practical criticism. Now in the light of post-structuralism titles are being given as they are a key to the structure of a poem.

Think how it wakes the seeds—
Woke, once, *the clays of a cold star*,
Are limbs, so dear-achieved, are sides
Full-nerved—still warm—too hard to stir?
Was it for this *the clay* grew tall?
—O what made *fatuous sunbeams toil*
To break earth's sleep at all?

i. Of what kind is this poem?
ii. Why does the poet ask "him" to be moved into the sun?
iii. Explain the italicised expressions in the poem.
iv. Comment on the metre and stanza form and tone.

(c) **Triple Time**

This empty street, this sky to blandness scoured
This air, a little indistinct with autumn
Like a reflection, constitute the present—
A time traditionally soured.
A time unrecommended by event.

But equally they make up something else:
This is the future furthest childhood saw
Between long houses, under travelling skies,
Heard in contending bells—
An air lambent with adult enterprise

And on another day will be the past
A valley cropped by fat neglected chances
That we insensately forbore to fleece
On this we blame our last
Threadbare perspectives, seasonal decrease.

i. What "times" are presented in this poem?
ii. Comment on the mood and tone of the poem?
iii. Explain these expressions:

"to blandness scoured", "unrecommended by event", "an air lambent with adult enterprise", "a valley cropped up by fat neglected chances", "threadbare perspectives", and "seasonal dicrease".

iv. Scan the first stanza and name the metre. Why is it that the second line in each stanza does not rhyme with any other line? What is the poet's intention in doing so?

(d) **Tamer and Hawk**

I thought I was so tough
But gentled at your hands
Cannot be quick enough
To fly for you and show
Than when I go I go
At your commands.

Even in flight above
I am no longer free:
You sealed me with your love,
I am blind to other birds—
The habit of your words
Has hooded me.

As formerly I wheel
I hover and I twist
But only want the feel
In my possessive thought
Of catcher and of caught
Upon your wrist.

You but half-civilize,
Taming me in this way.
Through having only eyes
For you I fear to lose,
I lose to keep, and choose
Tamer as prey.

i. What clues do you find to name the bird?
ii. Comment on the imagery and tone of the poem?
iii. Rhyme plays an important part in poetry. Why is it that the second line rhymes with the last line in each stanza?
iv. Explain the last stanza.

(e) **Considering The Snail**

The snail pushes through a green
night, for the grass in heavy

with water and meets over
the bright path he makes, where rain
has darkened the earth's dark. He
moves in a wood of desire,

pale antlers barely stirring
as he hunts. I cannot tell
what power is at work, drenched there
with purpose, knowing nothing.
What is a snail's fury? All
I think is that if later

I parted the blades above
the tunnel and saw the thin
trail of broken white across
litter, I would never have
imagined the slow passion
to the deliberate progress.

i. Why has the poet chosen a snail as his subject-matter?
ii. Explain the following expressions: the bright path, what power is at work, drenched there with purpose, a snail's fury, the slow passion, that deliberate progress.
iii. What does the poet intend to convey through this poem?
iv. Can the snail be compared to man?
v. Why does line number five in stanza 2 begin with a capital letter set?
vi. Scan the poem and name its metre.

B. Appreciation of Prose

In literary prose, writers use the same devices and figures of speech that poets use in poetry. Juxtaposition, contrast, antithesis, parallelism, irony, alliteration are commonly seen in novels, short-stories, and personal essays. The difference is that prose-writers do not take liberty with syntax and avoid archaic words. If they do so, there will be utter confusion. In prose, clauses are closely related and words are placed in their normal structural position. The following passage from William Golding's *Lord of the Flies* will explain the point.

"Ralph looked at him dumbly. For a moment he had a fleeting picture of the strange glamour that had once invested the beaches. But the island was scorched up like dead wood. Simon was dead and Jack had.... The tears began to flow and sobs shook him; he gave himself up to them now for the first time on the island; great, shuddering spasms of grief seemed to wrench his whole body. His voice rose under the black smoke before the burning wreckage of the island; and infected by that emotion, the other little boys began to shake and sob too. And in the middle of them with filthy body, hair and unwiped nose, Ralph wept for the end of innocence, the darkness of man's heart, and the fall through the air of the true, wise friend called Piggy."

Let us look at the structure of the sentences. Many of them are short and the long ones are neatly divided into short clauses by using semi-colon.

(a) "The tears began...shook him; he gave...the island; great...whole body."

(b) His voice...the island; and infected...and sob too.

The last sentence begins unusually with the conjunction "And" to give finality to the paragraph.

The images are fresh and original: "fleeting picture of the strange glamour", "scorched up like dead wood", "shuddering spasms of grief", "the end of innocence", "the darkness of man's heart", and "the fall through the air".

Alliteration occurs naturally in "dead wood", "shuddering spasms", and the "end of innocence".

The passage builds emotion slowly. The feeling of loss overpowers the reader gradually and finally the strong emotion, the untidy physical appearance, and the realization of truth amidst the grim tragedy—the fall through the air of the true, wise friend Piggy—arouses the emotions of pity and fear in our heart.

EXERCISES

1. Read the following passages slowly and answer the questions given at the end.

(a) In the slave plantations of the Caribbean Africans existed two worlds. There was the world of the day; that was the white world. There was the world of night; that was the African world of spirits and magic and the true gods. And in that world ragged men, humiliated by day, were transformed—in their own eyes, and the eyes of their fellows—into kings, sorcerers, herbalists, men in touch with the true forces of the earth and possessed of complete power. A king of the night, a slave by day, might be required at night never to exert himself; he would be taken about his fellows in a litter. To the outsider, to the slave-owner, the African night world might appear a mimic world, a child's world, a carnival. But to the African, it was the true world; it turned white men to phantoms and plantation life to an illusion.

i. Explain how the device of antithesis is employed in the passage.

ii. Find out the emotive words used in the passage and explain the kind of emotion they arouse.

iii. Explain the following expressions.

"it turned white men to phantoms"; "the true forces of the earth"; "a king of the night, a slave by day"; "a mimic world".

(b) But the pupils—the young noblemen! How the last faint traces of hope, the remotest glimmering of any good to be derived from his effort in this den faded from the mind of Nicholas as he looked in dismay around! Pale and haggard faces, lank and bony figures, children with the countenance of old men, deformities with iron upon their limbs, boys of stunted growth, and others whose long meagre legs would hardly bear their stooping bodies, all crowded on the view together. There were little faces, which should have been handsome, darkened with the scowl of sullen, dogged suffering; there was childhood with the light of its eye quenched, its beauty gone, and its helpless alone remaining; there were vicious-faced boys, brooding with leaden eyes like malefactors in a jail.

i. Show how overstatement or exaggeration is employed for an emotional appeal.

ii. Some of the sentences can be written in the form of free verse. Do one of them. Remember Thom Gunn's poem "Considering The Snail".

iii. Explain the meaning of:

"stunted growth"; "dogged suffering"; "leaden eyes"; "malefactors in a jail".

SELECT BIBLIOGRAPHY

Indian Poetics (Chapter 1)

1. Bharata, *Natyashastram,* Chowkhamba Sanskrit Sansthan, Varanasi.
2. Dandin, *Kavyadarshah*, Chowkhamba Sanskrit Sansthan, Varanasi.
3. Bhamaha, *Kavyalankarah,* Chowkhamba Sanskrit Sansthan, Varanasi.
4. Vamana, *Kavyalankarasutrani,* Chowkhamba Sanskrit Sansthan, Varanasi.
5. Anandavardhana, *Dhvanyalokah,* Chowkhamba Sanskrit Sansthan, Varanasi.
6. Abhinavagupta, *Abhinavabharati*, Chowkhamba Sanskrit Sansthan, Varanasi.
7. Kuntaka, *Vakroktijeevitan*, Chowkhamba Sanskrit Sansthan, Varanasi.
8. Kane, P.V. *History of Sanskrit Poetics.*
9. De, S.K. *History of Sanskrit Poetics.* Firma K.L. Mukhopadhyay, Kolkata.
10. Deshpande, G.T. *Abhinavagupta,* Sahitya Academy, New Delhi.
11. Vatsayan, Kapita *Natyashashtra*, Sahitya Academy, New Delhi.
12. Dwivedi, R.C. ed. *Principles of Literary Criticism in Sanskrit*, Motilal Banarasidas, Varanasi.

Western Criticism (Chapters 2-5)

13. Abrams, M.H. *The Mirror and the Lamp*, New York, OUP, 1953.
14. Atkins, J.W.H. *Literary Criticism in Antiquity*, Vol. I&II, Cambridge, CUP, 1934.
15. Atkins, J.W.H. *Literary Criticism*, Vol. I–IV, London, Methuen, 1951.
16. *The Cambridge History of Literary Criticism*, Cambridge, CUP, 2002.
17. Wellek, Rene. *A History of Modern Criticism*, Vol. I–VI.
18. Wimsatt, W.K. and Cleanth Brooks, *Literary Criticism, A Short History,* Delhi, Oxford and IBH, 1960.
19. Daiches, David. *Critical Approaches to Literature*, London, Longman, 1958.

Contemporary Criticism Anthologies (Chapter 6)

20. Coyle, Martin et al. ed. *Encyclopaedia of Literature and Criticism*, London, Routledge & Kegan Paul, 1990.
21. Handy, W.J. and Max Westbrook, ed. *Twentieth Century Criticism: Major Statements*, Delhi, Light & Life Publishers, 1976.
22. Lodge, David ed. *20th Century Criticism: A Reader,* London, Longman, 1972.
23. *Modern Criticism and Theory*, London, Longman, 1988
24. Niall, Lucy ed. *Post Modern Literary Theory: An Anthology,* Indian reprint, Delhi, Atlantic Publishers and Distributors, 2002.
25. Rivkin, Julie and Michael Ryan, ed. *Literary Theory: An Anthology*, rev. edn. Indian rpt., Delhi, Atlantic Publishers and Distributors, 2002.
26. Sedden, Raman ed. *The Theory of Criticism*, London, Longman, 1988.

Introductions to Modern Critical Theories

27. Barry, Peter, *Beginning Theory*, 2nd edn., Manchester, Manchester University Press, 2002.
28. Bertens, Hans *Literary Theory*: The Basics, London, Routledge, 1995.
29. Chandra, N.D.R. ed. *Modern Literary Criticism: Theory and Practice*, Delhi, Authors Press, 2003.
30. Krishnaswamy, N. John Verghese, and Sunita Mishra, *Contemporary Literary Theory*, Delhi, Macmillan India, 2001.
31. Nayar, Pramod K. *Literary Theory Today*, Delhi, Asia Book Club, 2002.
32. Roy, Mohit K. ed. *Perspectives on Criticism*, Delhi, Atlantic Publishers and Distributors, 2002.
33. Ryan, Michael *Literary Theory: A Practical Introduction*, Indian reprint, Delhi, Atlantic Publishers and Distributors, 2002.
34. Webster, Roger *Studying Literary Theory: An Introduction*, 2nd edition, London, Arnold, 1990.